FENG SHUI

HARMONY BY DESIGN

FENG SHUI

HARMONY BY DESIGN

NANCY SANTOPIETRO

With a Foreword by Professor Lin Yun

A PERIGEE BOOK

The poem that appears on page vii is
used by permission of Evi Seidman, Poet.

A Perigee Book
Published by The Berkley Publishing Group
200 Madison Avenue
New York, NY 10016

First edition: December 1996

Published simultaneously in Canada.

The Putnam Berkley World Wide Web site address is
http://www.berkley.com/berkley

Library of Congress Cataloging-in-Publication Data

SantoPietro, Nancy.
    Feng shui : harmony by design / Nancy SantoPietro ; foreword by
professor Lin Yun.
          p.   cm.
    "A Perigee book."
    ISBN 0-399-52239-5
    1. Feng-shui.   I. Title.
BF1779.F4S36   1996
133.3′33—dc20   96-22780
                                                          CIP

Printed in the United States of America

10   9   8   7   6   5   4   3   2   1

This book is dedicated, with love, to my mother, Matilda Amendolare,
my niece, Jovan Novellino,
and to my teacher and mentor, Professor Thomas Lin Yun.
Each has touched my life, deeply and profoundly. Thank you.

It's a Good Thing I'm not in Charge Here

I could never have thought of a pinecone
or a porcupine or a pomegranate
and even if I'd thought of one
how on earth would I have engineered a comet?
or organized life in a pond?

Where would I have found the energy
to make each and every snowflake different?
(It's more like me to make one or two
passable models, build a mold
and crank 'em out)

And it's not like me at all to finish up
an entire mountain range, then go
back and carefully touch up with tiny
forests of moss on the north side of
every stone

I've got a pretty good head for details
but it does seem likely that I'd have
left off the dots on a lady bug's back

And I'd have neglected to tie in
each and every strand of silk
to every kernel of every ear of corn

(Why, I lived in a house for two years
before I hung curtains in the bedroom
—I'd probably never get around
to making a waterfall)

And I can't keep my mind on one thing
long enough to be a river
nor concentrate deeply enough
to become a deep cool spring

And even if I had little boxes
of just the right atoms and molecules
how long would it take me to assemble them
into even one drop of water?

And the shine that sparkles from that drop?
Why, I imagine I will spend the rest of forever
seeking the beginning of that Light

You see, it's a good thing I'm not in charge here

—Evi Seidman

CONTENTS

	Acknowledgments	xi
	Foreword by Professor Lin Yun	xiii
	Introduction: What Is Feng Shui?	xxi
ONE	Tools for Beginning the Process	1
TWO	How to Assess Your Space and Make Adjustments	33
THREE	Health, Wealth, and Relationships	59
FOUR	Designing with Consciousness: Low-Cost–High-Gain Tips	79
FIVE	Using Color to Enhance Your Life and Create Happiness	99
SIX	Solutions for Dealing with Life's Obstacles	129
SEVEN	Creating a Sacred Space	155
EIGHT	Changing Your Life: One Room at a Time	187
	Conclusion: Making the Changes That Will Change Your Life	217

ACKNOWLEDGMENTS

From the inception of this project, there were many caring and pivotal people whose contributions to my life and my work helped direct my path and transform this book into a reality. Some did this knowingly, while others, unknowingly—nonetheless, I thank them all for the gifts they contributed: Lisa Weiner, Gibbs Smith, Mary Placek, Harriet Miller, Jane Allison, Dr. Howard Bezoza, Suzanne Alleyne, Melissa Hoffman, Jed Devine, Josephine Vizzari, Donna Palmer, Sharon Lovich, Paul Leavin, Evi Seidman, Crystal Chu, Diana Leong, Nancy Wang, my Black Hat Sect Family and Colleagues, all my clients and students who, in trying to better their lives, singlehandedly made the world a much nicer place to be.

I would like to thank all the "little munchkins" in my family—Gina Harrison, Jessica Harrison, Vincent Failla III, and Jovan Novellino—for their patience during my absence throughout the last year, and my family, especially my mother and stepfather, Dominick Amendolare, for their encouragement and support.

I would also like to offer a special thanks to: my brilliant editor, Irene Prokop; my wonderful agent, Doveen Schecter, for believing in me and always honoring my work; Cynthia Chomos, my senior consultant in Seattle; Dr. Lien Nguyen for always being a "helpful person" and pointing me in the right direction; Sarah Rossbach, whose books on Feng Shui changed the course of my life; Nancy Rosanoff—my first mentor—whose teachings on intuition, the chakras, and spirituality are still with me today; Pamela Laurence for her home in the country and Pinocchio; my dear friend and colleague R. D. Chin for his continual love and support; and Donna Caliri, who always encouraged me never to settle for less.

I have had the good karma throughout my life to be blessed with nurturing and supportive friends who have stood by me during difficult times and cheered me on through all my successes. They are my "chosen family" and without their encouragement, support, and love I would not be here today and this book would never have been written. So with deep gratitude and love I especially want to thank: Robin Spiegel for seventeen years of undying friendship, love, and wise counsel. Greer Jonas, my dear friend and muse, who always knew I should write; her unwavering support has provided me with the inspiration for all my work. My cousin and lifelong friend, Susan Olsen, for contributing nine selfless months of typing, editing, humor, and unflagging support; she truly was the "wind beneath my wings." And Pat Dawkins, for her beautiful artwork and photography, who taught me about unconditional love and provided me with the enormous gift of helping me heal my life, and to whom I am forever grateful. And finally, my sincerest thanks to my spiritual mentor and teacher, Master Thomas Lin Yun, the "Living Buddha," whose teachings and compassion for all people deeply touched my soul, redirected my path, and gave me the wings to fly.

FOREWORD

BY PROFESSOR LIN YUN

"Feng Shui" is a concept originated by ancient Chinese for constructing residences, tombs, stores, government offices, temples, and palaces. It includes garden design, interior decorating, placement of objects in our environment, and the spread, layout, framework, color, and shape of building structures. Feng Shui allows one to make the most ideal arrangements at the most ideal time and place from the perspective of folklore, artistry, and religious belief. Therefore, those directly involved firmly believe that from Feng Shui one can expel negativity and admit auspiciousness, as well as attain a state of longevity, happiness, wealth, and prosperity.

However, since China has vast land and rich natural resources, each location has a drastically different ecological environment. In the universe, climates, as well as the force and direction of the winds caused by the atmosphere, are not necessarily the same. The depth, length, and width of the rivers also run differently. All this has a great impact on the living and working patterns of the people inhabiting the land. Therefore, the so-called intellectuals of the time would wrack their brains to come up with methods for overcoming these difficulties based on folklore and local beliefs. These methods included how to choose land, how to construct buildings, how to take into consideration the direction of the water and the wind, and even how to use spells, incantations, and other mystical ways to solve all problems. As a result, Feng Shui experts from all locations rose because of these opportunities, and each conducted Feng Shui in various ways he thought was correct. Over time, geomancy naturally became a phenomenon where all schools of thought contended for the spotlight. The various schools of Feng Shui, such as the Three Harmony School, Three Yuan School, Nine Star School, Cantonese School, Taoist School, Eclectic School, Yin-Yang School, and the Buddhist School, all made the study of Feng Shui more mysterious and profound than ever. Because there are no versions that are easily learned and understood, and because its definitions often take on "spiritual ominousness," it is quite difficult to logically explain Feng Shui to those who do not understand its subtle theory. This causes most people to mistake Feng Shui as a "superstition."

Realistically, whether Feng Shui is indeed a "superstition" depends on the perspective from which it is seen. Everyone has different views; everyone presents a different version. When I teach my students, I tell them not to force anyone to believe, and not to coerce anyone to disbelieve. Everything is karma, so we should allow all things to take their natural course. Therefore, I often advise and admonish my students not to criticize other schools, and to respect the views of all other Feng Shui experts. We should try our best to understand the views of others, but at the same time retain what we gained from our own unique study. We should never "dwarf others to elevate ourselves." We should know that we need to work hard and study diligently, whether it be learning theories or investigating actual sites, in order to cultivate accordingly. Therefore I established the "Theory of Multiple Cause and Effect," as well as the "Theory of Ling Particles and Ch'i," with an emphasis on relative position. This is different from the traditional theory in which Feng Shui is characterized by the combination of "astrological sign" and "absolute direction." I find that the author of this book, Ms. Nancy SantoPietro, places a special emphasis on my theory and concept of Ch'i. This made me deeply realize that she is no longer confined by the boundaries set by traditional theories, and has stepped solidly into the sanctuary of Feng Shui from the Perspective of Black Sect Tantric Buddhism.

My ancestral home is at Taichung, Taiwan, but since both my parents were deeply involved in the Sino-Japanese War and joined the Taiwan Cultural Association, they moved our entire family to Beijing and regained Chinese nationality. At the time our family lived close to the renowned lamasery Yong-He Palace, and I was fortunate to be able to study under the Learned Monk Ta-Teh. Then I became the pupil of the revered scholar Master Hui Chieh-Fu from

Shantung Province. After that I became a disciple of the Black Sect Tantric Buddhism Master, Cheng Kuei-Ying. Besides teaching the I-Ching, Chinese poetry, and calligraphy, I also advocate the promotion of the so-called "Religious Reform" of Buddhism, which favors the modernization of Buddhism and the study of Buddhism using modern methods. This allows Buddhist concepts, whether it be meditation or spiritual cultivation, to measure up to standards of modern science. Therefore I have established a new school in the study of Feng Shui, and that is "Feng Shui from the Perspective of Black Sect Tantric Buddhism." Even though this new school sets itself apart from other traditional schools of Feng Shui, it adheres to this consistent point of emphasis, which is to combine the merits of the various other schools with perspectives from modern psychology, physiology, geographical ecology, ecology, architecture, medical science, aesthetics, artistry, and folklore to exalt the unique and matchless art that is called Feng Shui. We replaced the old with the new by using modern knowledge, techniques, and theories to establish a brand-new school of Feng Shui.

In geomancy, our new school, "Feng Shui from the Perspective of Black Sect Tantric Buddhism," advocates superimposing the eight trigrams from the I-Ching over the floor plan, lot or room of a person's home or office. By superimposing we mean to memorize the eight trigrams by heart. That way when we are reading the Feng Shui of a particular site, we need not bring a compass. It is not that we oppose other people using compasses. It is just that we do not often use a traditional compass. We take the main divination signs from our Black Hat compass—the eight trigrams—and memorize them and assign to each area a "relative position." This method is actually also known as the "Ever-changing Eight trigrams," and the using of the Bagua Map. So what is the main content of Feng Shui from the Perspective of Black Sect Tantric Buddhism? Generally speaking, it includes areas that are "Visible," of which we can actually see shape, and areas that are "Invisible," of which there is only a consciousness.

From the "visible" aspect, when we are investigating the Feng Shui of a site, we should pay attention to the ch'i of the land, the shape of the land, the shape of the house, the floor plan of the house, and other factors. We should pay extra attention to these "other factors," which include "interior factors" and "exterior factors."

"Interior factors" refers to the placement and decoration within the house, such as how the bed is placed, how the stove is designed, what the relationship is between the doors and windows, whether there are any beams and columns, where the staircase is located, what the colors and light intensity of the rooms are, and so on.

As for "exterior factors," they refer to the situation outside of the house, such as whether the front door faces the road, whether there are any bridges nearby, whether there are any rivers or oceans nearby, whether the site is surrounded by green fields, whether the site is "in front of a shrine or behind a temple," whether there are any large trees nearby, whether the ridges and corners of the neighbor's roof face your house, whether there are any transformers or power lines nearby, and so on. Of course, one should also pay close attention to the "color" of the surrounding environment.

From the perspective of the "invisible," one needs to know the "Three Secret Reinforcements," the "Ever-changing Eight Trigrams," the "Interior Ch'i Adjustments," the "Exterior Ch'i Adjustments," the "Eight Door Wheel," the "Tracing of the Nine Stars Path," the "Constant Turning Dharma Wheel," the "Predecessor Law," and others. These are all invisible to the human naked eye. The consideration for these all rely on one's consciousness and intuition. This is what we mean when we read Feng Shui from the "invisible" perspective.

In Feng Shui from the Perspective of Black Sect Tantric Buddhism, we gave "Feng Shui" a definition: mankind using various existing knowledge to choose, construct, or create the most suitable living and working environment. Of course, this also takes into consideration geological problems, such as the richness of the soil or the fertility of the land. It also includes geological and ecological studies ranging from the influence of abundant sunshine, clear flowing water, the rising and ebbing of the tides, the direction of the winds, as well as the components of time and space. The comprisal of all these factors is the study of Feng Shui. Its goal is to explain by using modern knowledge, and to create by using modern technology. The combination of this along with personal aesthetics and an artful eye will assist one in finding the most suitable living and working environment that is perfect for them.

Among scholars who can truly exalt the orthodox Black Sect Tantric Buddhism Feng Shui Perspective in Europe and the United States, the most renowned would probably be the author Sarah Rossbach. Ms. Rossbach has already published three books related to the study of Feng Shui based upon Black Sect Tantric Buddhism. Her books have been cited as exemplary by

European and American Feng Shui experts. In fact, many of these Feng Shui experts of different nationalities have gone as far as describing Ms. Rossbach's works as the "Bible" of geomancy. Although these may just be words of praise, it is a fact that these three books of hers have already been translated into German, French, Italian, Thai, and Chinese. It is like a whirlwind that is sweeping across the European and American geomancy fields. Some geomancers have formed Feng Shui centers and are regularly holding classes and performing on-site Feng Shui consultations for home and businesses as well. This is all possible due to the pioneering vision of Ms. Rossbach, who publicizes and exalts Feng Shui from the Black Sect Tantric Buddhism Perspective. At the same time she has also paved the way for me to travel the world and to present my theory of Feng Shui.

The author of this book, Ms. Nancy SantoPietro, is also an excellent scholar, whom I met in 1990 when teaching in New York. I find Nancy to be extremely gifted, sincere, intelligent, and diligent. She is a hard worker who places strong emphasis on the actual investigation of a site. She is spiritually cultivated, and she deeply respects her teachers and their teachings. In addition to the contents being clear and easy to read, this book also provides chapter summaries and meditation techniques. What is more, there are outlines and charts based on extensive research in multiple areas, including working with crystals and aromatherapy oils. These features all enable the complex theory of Feng Shui and its adjustment methods to be simplified, rationalized, and clarified. I find that the most precious part of Nancy's book is her emphasis on case studies. She maintains that besides locating the best possible natural site and what adjustments can be performed to better the site, it is absolutely crucial to ensure the sanctity of the site. This can be achieved by conducting blessing ceremonies to expel negativity and attract prosperity.

For those beginners who are studying Feng Shui for the first time, this is the perfect textbook. For those who have studied Feng Shui, this book provides a clear overall review. The Chinese have a saying: "One learns new things by reviewing old things." A careful reading of this book will let those who previously did not understand Feng Shui acquire a good sense of what Feng Shui is about. It will then lead to the understanding of how Feng Shui affects lives, followed by how to read Feng Shui, how to adjust Feng Shui to make life more blissful, families more happy, careers more thriving, and wealth more flourishing. I am absolutely delighted to compose this foreword for Nancy's new book, and I take this opportunity to let the readers know that the Feng Shui according to Black Sect Tantric Buddhism is unique. It is a school of thought that was established by me. Its approach creates a new Feng Shui perspective which combines the merits of the various traditional Feng Shui schools with the advancement of various modern knowledge and technologies. Using clear and concise theories, we in Black Hat Sect Feng Shui aim to exalt this great Chinese school of thought.

The publication of Nancy's teachings raises Feng Shui scholars up to a higher plateau. This book emphasizes the relationship of ch'i and life. Using meditation, spiritual cultivation, and Feng Shui adjustment to adjust one's ch'i will significantly influence one's life, which will in turn influence one's relationships, increase one's wisdom and spiritual instincts. This would enable the relationships between man and man, man and object, as well as man and environment to achieve a harmonious balance. Furthermore, this practical book tells us that the proper usage of color and furniture placement would harmonize man's ch'i and his living environment. This book also provides thorough insights regarding time, space, money, and energy. The author even includes theories and methods regarding the mundane and the transcendental solutions, in order to teach readers to use existing knowledge and explore unknown knowledge to solve everyday problems. Most important of all, Nancy is not so self-satisfied by her studies that she forgets where her knowledge has come from; that is why she has asked me to write this foreword. Nancy is one who respects her teachers, and I am very pleased that she possesses that spirit. I am even more pleased at the rare fact that she still remembers to acknowledge Sarah Rossbach and the influence of her works, because many other authors have benefited from Sarah's books but have forgotten to mention it.

Among my non-Asian students, Ms. Sarah Rossbach has studied with me for nearly twenty years, in which time she published the three previously mentioned books. Now, Ms. SantoPietro joins the select few who are able to lift their pens to describe my theory and school of thought on the practical application of Feng Shui combined with psychology and spirituality. This is also something that I am very pleased with. Nancy, like Sarah, brings the merits of the ancient Eastern culture into the West, and along the way terminates the conflicts that may have surfaced. At the same time, they let society become aware that modern facilities such as subways, high-rise buildings, and airports could have problems with Feng Shui and its effect on our environment. These were unheard of in traditional Feng Shui studies. Sarah Rossbach's three books made great contributions as they interested and influenced the whole European and American societies and their ways of perceiving and practicing Feng Shui. Now I see Nancy's book, *Feng Shui: Harmony by Design,* and I believe that it, too, in the near future, will let friends in the Feng Shui field, or even those who have never studied Feng Shui, experience tremendous results from reading this book.

Most notably, Nancy is the chairperson of the Feng Shui Studies Department at the Metropolitan Institute of Interior Design in Plainview, New York. This institute is the first school in the United States to recognize credits in the study of Feng Shui. This is very comforting. Furthermore, in her book she has introduced four or five different Black Sect Tantric Buddhism methods to adjust ch'i, alter luck, meditate, and cultivate spirituality. This serves to enhance the book's honor. It truly deserves a careful reading. Its contribution to society is going to be great beyond imagination. Black Sect Tantric Buddhism has always emphasized the importance of allowing karma to take its course. To be able to respect all the different religions and their teachings, and to be able to read this book all serve as good karma and good cause. To the readers: if you could make the most of this good karma, you will naturally receive good effects. This is the inevitable phenomenon of studying Feng Shui and the methods of ch'i adjustment.

—Lin Yun, April 1996

TRANSLATED BY MARY HSU

INTRODUCTION

WHAT IS FENG SHUI?

Feng Shui has been around for over four thousand years. Although recently rediscovered, its original objective has always remained the same—to assist individuals in creating environments that support and nurture their needs, desires, and overall well-being. In many ways, Feng Shui (pronounced Fung Shway) began before the onset of human existence, when the earth was formed thousands of years ago. There were no fancy designers or architects on hand; instead Mother Nature unfolded and created some of the most incredible and breathtaking art that was ever made. With absolutely no input from us, mountains were sculpted, trees were planted, and magnificent rivers were formed. The sun had its daily "dusk to dawn" assignment, the moon knew when to appear, and the stars held their own position in the sky. The earth and the galaxy that it lived within were perfectly created to work in tandem with the universe. It was a system that was designed to work in harmony and support all living creatures who eventually would reside on it. These natural forces of nature were built in to the makings of the world, and all that was needed to survive on the planet would derive from these primary elements.

Ever since life began to form around these elements, humankind has been preoccupied with creating ideal places in which to live and work. As individuals scrambled to find the best locations to set up their homes, certain conditions became more desirable to live among than others. Factors such as clean water, warm sun, and lush vegetation tended to attract settlement. As they moved onto the land, people eventually created families, businesses, and communities around these nourishing elements of nature.

Initially these elements were accepted without a second thought. As these prime areas of land became in demand, people started questioning what caused calmer waters on one shore versus choppy waters on another? What created protective mountains on one horizon, while on another, rocky and dangerous terrain? Why certain places had better living conditions than others.

Thousands of years ago in China, people believed that an invisible energy force from the earth's center called ch'i was responsible for the way certain locations thrived more than others and thus were more sought after and inhabitable. They believed that ch'i was the powerful life force that existed within all things and that ch'i was the single most important factor that influences our lives for better or for worse. They also believed that our bodies possessed ch'i and that whether or not our ch'i is flowing well would determine if we would enjoy good health and, subsequently, good fortune. Similarly, if the ch'i of the land was not obstructed and flowing well, that environment would also attract good energy and subsequently good things.

The farmers believed that land that possessed good *Feng Shui* (which, translated, means "wind and water") had tall mountains behind it to shield the crops from the wind and water in front of it to nourish the land and its crops. With these supportive elements in place, a family could look forward to a good rice crop, and a good rice crop led to a well-fed family, which equaled a healthy family. An abundant rice crop also led to surplus rice, which was sold and contributed to a prosperous and happy family life.

The Feng Shui of our surroundings creates a set of opportunities, for better or for worse, which ultimately determines and shapes the quality and the direction of our lives. As you begin to work with Feng Shui you may be surprised to find that you have already been working with this energy force for most of your life. The energy force (ch'i) that exists around us in our environment also exists within us. It permeates and surrounds all living things. The same ch'i that determines a potentially good crop also influences many personal factors in our lives. The strength of our health, our level of motivation, our ability to express ourselves, be creative, open our hearts, stimulate our intellect, generate money, attract relationships are all influenced by the inexplicable power of ch'i. The ch'i is the invisible force that flows through us and determines the difference between being alive or being dead. It takes otherwise nonfunctioning organs such as the heart, brain, lungs, liver, and arteries and pumps a life force through them that turns them into a living being. Without it, there is no life in the body—just a body with organs, bones, and skin; ch'i is the magical spark that turns an egg and sperm into an alive embryo and a wish into a miracle. Understanding and working with the principles of Feng Shui is the key to harnessing the power of ch'i in a way that will support you and benefit your life. The Feng Shui of your surroundings acts as a mirror image to your life and its various circumstances. It emphasizes the concept that everything in life is interrelated and strung together by a series of events that all lead up to a certain outcome or situation. This theory is also known as the theory of karma, and it is the backbone of all Black Hat Sect Feng Shui principles taught and developed by the honorable Professor Thomas Lin Yun.

Professor Lin Yun, spiritual leader of the Black Hat Sect of Tibetan Tantric Buddhism School of Feng Shui, popularized Feng Shui with his charm, wit, and uncanny ability to understand and have compassion for the human struggle. His life's work as a scholar, calligraphy artist, and world-renowned Feng Shui Master took him from his homeland, China, on a journey West to Berkeley, California. Back in the mid-eighties he opened The Yun Lin Temple and began his teachings on Black Hat Sect Tibetan Tantric Buddhism and Feng Shui. As the popularity of his teachings grew, specialists like myself have had the honor of studying under his tutelage and becoming disciples of his and his teachings. I have been graced with the opportunity to be instructed by him in the principles, rituals, solutions, and transcendental cures of this age-old practice. My work, in turn, is to translate this knowledge into simple, practical, and understandable information that Westerners, professionals and novices alike, can easily grasp and apply to better the circumstances of their lives. Being able to work with this information serves to bridge the gap between the wisdom of venerable sages and the conflicts of modern man we face today. It's a growing eco-art that changes and adapts itself to the changes and needs of a modern civilization. The original concerns about the positioning of high mountains or the location of underground streams have directly transcended to our concerns about a towering skyscraper or the impact that an underground subway system might have on the quality of the Feng Shui in our homes, and thus our lives.

The majority of us do not have the means or the luxury of building our living spaces from scratch on lots of land that are open and fertile like those that existed back in China. The land that now exists in China and throughout the world is heavily populated and becoming scarcer and scarcer. Within the USA there are more than 260 million people alone! As our population rapidly grows, we continue to build more and more places to house all these people. By erecting these dwellings without consciousness or awareness of how the interior and exterior design affects the energy balance of the land, we inadvertently throw off the natural Feng Shui of the land.

Subsequently, that imbalance affects our ability to maintain our own internal balance of ch'i. And from a Black Hat Sect Feng Shui perspective, the strength, the quality, and the balance of the ch'i that exists within us is the most important factor that determines the quality of our life and the opportunities that we draw to us.

The Chinese believed that the formula for success is a combination of preparation and opportunity (S=P+O). Feng Shui is the karmic element that helps you with the opportunity. To harmoniously rebalance the Feng Shui in our lives, we first have to work on restoring the Feng Shui in our homes, workplaces, and communities. As the natural flow of energy in our personal environments is rebalanced, it inadvertently creates a rippling effect throughout the rest of the world because everything in life is interrelated, especially energy flow. Thus, by just working on our personal spaces we not only make a major contribution to our own lives, but to the bigger picture of everyone's life as well.

Feng Shui uses our homes and offices as the mediums to help us get our lives back on track and flowing in a balanced order, supported by the natural forces of nature. The "adjustments" or "solutions" of Feng Shui design are the tools we use to implement the changes we are attempting to set forth. And by learning how to rearrange your furniture, work with color, and locate energy blocks, you can restore the natural flow of energy to your home and your life.

As you learn to identify how the ch'i flows through your home, you will be able to locate the various compartments and pockets of energy that specifically oversee different areas of your life. For example, aspects of your life regarding finances, relationships, career, family, and health can all be directly traced back to corresponding areas of your home and workplace.

Ch'i is the energy force that permeates all space around you. It moves similarly to the way air circulates; and its flow is directed and shaped by all the objects in its path that it needs to navigate around. If the object that it is navigating around happens to be an awkwardly placed bed or a narrow entranceway, then that particular design layout would contribute to distorting the natural flow of the ch'i or the Feng Shui of your home. The specific area in your home that is being altered by the positioning of these objects, on an energetic level, has a life force that directly supports the energy connected to different areas of your life. If the flow of ch'i that is being altered happens to oversee the area of your home that relates to your career or intimate relationships, then that area of your life may be affected. By learning to use Feng Shui as a form of interior design, you are actually giving your home an "acupuncture treatment," opening up the blocked areas and enhancing the circulation of the ch'i in your environment. The results from aligning your own energy with the natural flow of energy in your environment can be overwhelmingly profound. In many ways it's similar to having your car's steering and tires realigned. Prior to having the alignment work done, your car might have run okay and was able to get you to your destination, but it took more of your energy and focus to keep that car moving straight ahead and on the road. All the pulling to the left or right is wearing to the car and draining on your energy. But after the car has been repaired and the wheels aligned, it is able to go straight down the road; as the driver you feel more secure and in control, and exerting less effort and concentration to direct the vehicle. Feng Shui works quite often in the same way. Feng Shui is a process of alignment which lifts the extra burden and obstacles that prevent you from getting to your personal wishes and desires. It attempts to remove that sense of "swimming against the current," as you pursue your goals of relationships, happiness, health, and prosperity.

Feng Shui does not claim to cause miracles, but I have personally witnessed many wonderful and empowering changes in the lives of many individuals. We are just beginning to explore the way that energy works and many levels that it exists on, even though we don't fully understand all of it yet. But what you will experience when you place yourself and your environment in a conducive order with nature is that things which once appeared out of reach become clearer and more accessible. **Relationships and creativity flourish. Businesses, careers, finances thrive. Health stabilizes. Opportunities manifest themselves.** For each individual, what unfolds in his or her life will take a different form and outcome. For example, adjusting your Wealth corner doesn't mean that you will necessarily hit the lottery that week.

If you do, it would be because you were karmicly meant to hit the lottery and that it was part of your destiny to do so. The Feng Shui adjustments would have served to remove the blocks that may have been related to you not winning. Someone else making the same adjustment in his or her Wealth corner may experience something completely different. It's hard to predict how Feng Shui will fully manifest itself or why some receive results in a week while others have to wait several months. It is not meant to be a "magic bullet cure" but a catalyst that sets off a series of events on an energy level that has profound effects on the quality of one's life. Feng Shui is another tool given to us by the universe to help us overcome our difficulties, support our challenges, and smooth over life's conflicts.

We continue to experience and research the results of working and designing with energy. The whole topic is a vast, wide-open field that is still in the beginning stages of understanding.

With all that in mind, this book has been written as a "how-to" guide for those of you who want to get started and participate in your own process of working with the energy principles of Feng Shui. By taking these principles of a thousand years ago and making them applicable to modern-day life, I endeavored to put otherwise-esoteric concepts into simpler, uncomplicated, and user-friendly terms—concepts and design approaches that anyone, regardless of their level of skill or creativity, can confidently apply to what's problematic in their lives. Many of the suggestions in this book will seem easily accessible and you will find yourself acting on them immediately. Other changes will take you longer to implement, while still others might take you months to complete. Don't be thrown off or feel overwhelmed by the process, for it can be fun, inspiring, and very much life changing. Most attempts to change situations in our lives often take time. In addition, when we use Feng Shui, we are attempting to make these changes by working with energy. Sometimes shifts in life's circumstances happen immediately, but other times they take longer. Often Feng Shui affects our life in such subtle ways that it isn't until we review our life in retrospect that we can identify the changes that have occurred. Energy itself is a very powerful tool, and as much as we try to direct it, it really has a life force all its own that requires our respect and patience as it takes hold and unfolds.

As you begin your Feng Shui process, you will feel like an armchair detective looking for clues, searching for areas in your home that may be blocking the energy flow or are in need of change. You will be contemplating situations and making connections to the Feng Shui design in your home, and how those factors affect and reflect your life's circumstances.

This doesn't have to be a complex project; actually it can be rather simple if you choose to follow the sequencing of the steps offered in this guide. I will walk you through every phase of the process starting with step-by-step instructions on how to draw a simple floor plan. After that you'll learn how to locate all the power spots in your home that oversee everything in your life ranging from your finances to your relationships, and you'll discover different cost-effective ways to enrich those various areas. You learn the best positions in which to lay out your furniture, how to use "conscious intentions" to obtain what you desire, and which paint colors to choose to enhance your energy. You'll explore inexpensive ways to design your space by working with the ch'i force, transcendental ways of problem solving, and how to work with crystals and aromatherapy oils to enhance your health. In addition, you will be taught how to create a sacred space in your home, set up altars, and do your own personal blessing ceremony.

If you have been attracted to this book, you are probably going through a major transformation, even if you are not aware of it yet. When I started to write, I knew that this would be a powerful book that would change lives. I was very aware of my "conscious intentions" and responsibility when I began the manuscript because I strongly believe in the concept of karma. I trusted that the right people who would benefit from these teachings would synchronisticly find their way to this book, just as I did six years ago when I stumbled across Sarah Rossbach's books on Feng Shui. Those books changed the course of my life and my life's work. They enabled me to pursue my destiny by connecting me not only to Feng Shui but also to my teacher and mentor, Master Thomas Lin Yun. It's through Master Lin Yun's teachings, blessings, and guidance that my life has changed, my health has been transformed, and my work has taken me on another magical journey. I am proud and honored to bring these teachings to you to help you transform your life and guide you to a better place.

When I am studying in Master Lin Yun's class and someone in the class asks a Feng Shui question, Master Lin Yun answers and then turns to the rest of us and says that it was our "good karma" to be present during that question because it enables us to receive that specific cure. And being privy to that cure will allow us to help others with the same problem and ourself from a similar struggle. So in turn, I say to each and every one of you reading this book that it is your "good karma" to find your way to all these sacred teachings and it was my "good karma" to be the one to bring them to you.

The following poem was given to me by one of my students after a weeklong Feng Shui training session. Each line reflects my deepest feelings about why I teach and why I wrote this book. It is my testimonial offering from my soul to yours. May "wind and water" always be with you. OM MA NI PAD ME HUM

Go to the people
Learn from them
Love them
Start with what they know
Build on what they have
But the best of leaders
When their task is accomplished
Their work is done
The people will remark:
"We have done it ourselves."

—*Two-Thousand-Year-Old Chinese Poem*

FENG SHUI

HARMONY BY DESIGN

ONE

TOOLS FOR BEGINNING
THE PROCESS

As you start to work with the magical art of Feng Shui you will quickly realize that it is an intricately woven system, rich with metaphors, omens, and powerful symbolism. Move your couch and strengthen your career, hang a wind chime and increase your wealth, change the color of your bedroom and you change your feelings about a relationship. Certain things represent other things, areas of your home oversee different areas of your life, and the ancient concepts of wind and water (Feng Shui) still have a major influence on the outcome of your fate.

The Chinese knew that in order to have a healthy family or a successful business, certain factors on the land had to follow a specific order in alignment with the various forces of nature. Homes needed to stay moderately furnished, uncluttered, and welcoming so the ch'i could flow easily.

They believed that if you wanted to have a life that was "sweet," making offerings to Buddha of sugary cakes would help bring this about. They understood the importance of honoring the earth, for they knew that they were the caretakers of God's soil, and that proper care and maintenance of their land were crucial to their survival. Many of these ancient concepts are simple, yet profound. They have been passed down with honor through the ages and, over time, have evolved into the basic Feng Shui principles that we use today.

The following nine principles are the backbone of all good Feng Shui design. These concepts will be with you throughout the book and, it is hoped, will become integrated into your thinking—for they set the tone and foundation upon which all other Feng Shui adjustments rest.

NINE FENG SHUI PRINCIPLES

1. Satisfy the four conditions.
2. Explore the predecessor law.
3. Strive for balance.
4. Trust your intuition.
5. Reduce clutter.
6. Like attracts like.
7. Raise the percentages.
8. Use the nine basic cures.
9. House maintenance is crucial.

1. SATISFY THE FOUR CONDITIONS: In order for the placement of important household objects, specifically your bed, desk, or stove to be considered "good Feng Shui" (in the Black Hat Sect school of thought), it first must satisfy all these four conditions: 1) *Positioning must be relative to entranceway, not based on compass direction* (this means the position of the bed/desk/stove is relative, based on the location of the door and not on any of the four cardinal directions); 2) *the bed/desk has the largest view of the room* (the angle that the bed/desk/stove is placed in faces the largest view of the room); 3) *the "mouth of the ch'i" is in viewing range* (this means that when lying down on your bed, sitting at your desk, or cooking at your stove, you will be facing the door); 4) *the bed, desk, stove, and person are not in a direct line with the door* (although you will want to have a clear view of the door, you do not want to be in a direct line with its powerful energy force).

2. EXPLORE THE PREDECESSOR LAW: In Feng Shui, it's always important to know who owned the object, the gift, the land, or the house before it came into your possession. The energy of the prior owners also gets passed down with the item in question, along with all their successes and failures. If you are purchasing a house or renting an apartment, try to inquire about the status of the former occupants. Check if they moved for reasons that imply an upgrading in their lives—larger house, job relocation, etc.—or because of a setback such as a job loss, divorce, or illness. These situations, for better or worse, can be a direct result of the Feng Shui patterns that exist in that house. Having that important information will help you decide if you want to step into the former owner's shoes, based on the history that you uncover. Keep in mind that even if you discover bad news, your knowledge of Feng Shui remedies can help you turn the trend of the history of the prior owner and house around.

3. STRIVE FOR BALANCE: The whole premise of Feng Shui is based on the universal yin-yang principles that are said to govern all mankind. In short, these principles espouse the belief that all facets of nature (and mankind) have both negative and positive aspects. This does not refer to good versus bad, but rather to opposing aspects that depend on each other's existence to create wholeness. For example, without night we wouldn't know day, without hot we wouldn't have cold, without winter we wouldn't see summer, etc. **Many of Feng Shui's theories take their cues from nature and try to bring indoors the beauty and perfection of God's original floor plan . . . the environment of our world.** Of all those basic concepts, the importance of balance is probably the most crucial. Striving for balance as you design your space is like bringing these concepts of nature into your home. The way you position the pictures on the walls and the way you align your area rug with the center of your couch are just a couple of examples. Another way of working with balance is through the system of opposites. For example, if you have a long corridor that is causing the ch'i to flow very fast, you might want to place a heavy statue in the hallway to symbolically slow down the ch'i. If a room is too dark and feels very heavy, try adding brighter lighting to "lighten up the room." **Mindful application is the key to balance, design, and good Feng Shui.** Remember, balance does not only have to mean symmetry; it can also mean arranging items in a way that conveys a sense of proportion, although everything may not be "technically" balanced.

4. TRUST YOUR INTUITION: As you begin to work with energy, you will become more sensitive to the different types of environments that are around you. Things that you never noticed in the past will become very obvious. You will react to colors and certain designs in homes and offices that you were never aware of before. You will come to realize that energy can either lift your ch'i up or make you feel moody and depressed. You will become more aware of how your being is affected by the Feng Shui of different places. This refining process of your own senses helps you to develop your own "inner voice," better known as your intuition. Your intuition will help you fine-tune all your Feng Shui adjustments regarding everything from bed placement to choosing colors. Many times throughout your Feng Shui process you will find yourself confused or at a loss about what to do in a certain situation. It is specifically at those times that you need to find a quiet place, close your eyes, and visualize your different options. Meditate on the different choices and let your intuition guide you to the correct decision.

5. REDUCE CLUTTER: Clutter is one of the most common Feng Shui problems found in most homes and apartments. By nature we tend to be "pack rats," saving, storing, and hoarding our memories along with our memorabilia. The main problem with clutter is that it blocks and distorts the natural flow of ch'i. Places that have piles of junk, papers, and old books in them tend to stagnate the ch'i and adversely affect the Feng Shui of that particular area. Even things that are not technically considered junk can affect your personal Feng Shui. For example, if you're seeking a new relationship, first check all your drawers for old love letters and gifts from your ex-partners (especially in your bedroom). These innocent-seeming mementos can keep your ch'i emotionally tied to the past and to all the old memories of times gone by, leaving your ch'i unavailable to draw in new relationships. This doesn't mean you have to throw out all your old cards, photographs, or Fiesta Ware; just make sure that those items aren't preventing you from being on an energy level that will permit you to move forward. Check your house for other "old-baggage items" and throw them away, give them to Goodwill, or let a friend hold on to them till you're truly ready to part with them. The other clutter no-no's are what I call the "guilt gifts." These are the presents that came from our least favorite in-law, youngest child, or the neighbor down the hall. Even though we may have appreciated the gift, accepted it, and sentimentally said, "Thank you . . . how did

you know that I wanted a Chia Pet? I love it!" we know that if we lived to be one hundred years old, we'd still never use it. These are the objects we have to physically and emotionally give ourselves permission to let go of, before they accumulate and dictate our lives.

6. LIKE ATTRACTS LIKE: Some of the laws of nature are very simple, especially the law of energy that states "Like attracts like." Who you are is what you will draw to you. The ch'i in our bodies sends out energy signals that draw in certain people, places, and situations that reflect the inner message in the code of those signals. Through the situations that we repel and attract come our life's experiences, partners, and opportunities. One of the main ways that the ch'i in our bodies is shaped is through the Feng Shui in our homes and offices. This is why you must make sure your environment reflects what you want to pull in. This doesn't mean that in order for you to earn a hundred thousand dollars a year your home has to be expensively furnished, but it does mean that in order for your finances to change, your Wealth and Career areas should be cared for and properly adjusted according to the principles of Feng Shui.

7. RAISING THE PERCENTAGES: This is an important intervention for adjusting the Feng Shui in your home, specifically if you have a section of the Feng Shui map known as the Bagua missing from your *overall floor plan* or if there is a particular area of your life that you want to enhance or emphasize. First, identify the area that is either missing in your overall floor plan or that you want to be strengthened in your life. For example, let's assume that the Relationship area is missing—or, maybe it's not missing from the overall floor plan but you would like to enhance it. The way you raise the ch'i and the opportunities for drawing in a new relationship is by applying this method of support which I call "raising the percentages." This approach means that you go to every room of your home, find the Relationship corner of each room, and make the appropriate Feng Shui adjustment. This method will help raise the percentages of the missing areas by building up the ch'i in the smaller Relationship areas located in each room. You can use this approach for any of the nine areas of the Bagua that you would like to build up and secure.

8. USE THE NINE BASIC CURES: In Feng Shui, although there are many solutions and cures to remedy different problems, there basically are nine main cures

you can easily utilize to adjust the Feng Shui in your home: 1) lights/bright objects; 2) mirrors; 3) sound; 4) life force; 5) heavy objects; 6) color; 7) movement/mobile objects; 8) power/energy objects; 9) water (see chapter 2).

9. HOUSE MAINTENANCE IS CRUCIAL: Our homes are regarded as very sacred places in Feng Shui. They oversee and mirror many aspects of our lives, especially the quality of our health. So it is very important that we maintain our homes just as we maintain the hygiene and health of our bodies. All repairs, refurbishing, redecorating, and housework should be looked upon as a labor of love because each act of improvement is an opportunity for you to change and enhance the quality of your life. This doesn't mean that in order for you to have great Feng Shui you have to perform all the labor and housecleaning yourself (thank God!). It does mean that if you have the luxury to pay for these services, do it with pride, respect, and gratitude to the individuals who are providing the services in your home. On the other hand, make sure that you are happy with the service providers and that they are competent, qualified, and caring to your home and valuables. Hire domestic workers and contractors with the same level of standards and loving care you would use to find a nanny for your infant, a baby-sitter for your five-year-old, or a doctor for your surgery. *Be picky; it's your castle and it's your life!*

YOUR HOME MIRRORS YOUR LIFE

The Feng Shui assessment of your home will begin with a step-by-step walk-through reviewing everything from the location of your front door, to the colors used in each room of your house.

The important thing for you to remember is that all these things affect the way ch'i (energy) flows through your home and workplace. The conducive flow of that ch'i directly affects your own ch'i and the strength of its force. In turn, your personal ch'i will dictate the overall quality of your life and its outcome. You might be asking yourself, "How does all this work?" In simplest terms, the ch'i in your body acts very similarly to the way the energy in a magnet works; it draws to it the same type of energy it magnetizes out. For instance, if your ch'i is sending out energy signals that resonate to a sense of harmony and balance, then it will draw to it things, events, and opportunities that will reflect that feeling. That's why it's so important to work with and balance the ch'i in your environment because it indirectly affects what type of relationships, finances, career opportunities, etc., you will attract. The chart on the following page indicates how ch'i travels through the universe and filters down through many levels, eventually emerging in your homes and workplaces affecting everything ranging from your relationships to your health.

THE CIRCLE OF LIFE

The initial source of ch'i energy is generated from the universe. The stars, the moon, the sun, and other celestial bodies radiate energy that filters down through the stratosphere, and eventually to our planet Earth. The ch'i then divides itself into additional sections as it distributes itself throughout the different countries in the world. As it continues to circulate throughout these countries, it then breaks down further funneling itself into states, cities, neighborhoods, communities, acres, and blocks. Finally it arrives at our apartment buildings and homes, making its way through the individual rooms, circulating around furniture and various objects, and eventually affecting and impacting on the ch'i of all the occupants who reside in these dwellings.

As the ch'i circulates throughout your home, it begins to develop certain forms and invisible energy patterns. These patterns of energy then impact on and shape the ch'i that exists in our bodies. The ch'i in our bodies in turn sends out these energy patterns like a telegraph to the world. The energy then draws to it, like a magnet, certain life situations (e.g., relationships, jobs, etc.) that reflect the same type of energy patterns that the ch'i is sending out. In turn, these different life situations send energy back to our environment, back to our neighborhoods, back to our communities, and eventually back to the universe. This energy fuels and operates the *"Circle of Life."*

The closer the ch'i from the universe gets to the individual, the stronger its effect on human ch'i. For instance, the ch'i that's around your bed will affect you more profoundly than the ch'i that circulates throughout your country of origin. Human ch'i in turn, as it manifests and extends outward, has a direct impact on the world and all the things in it.

By learning to detect how the ch'i flows through and around your house,

THE CIRCLE OF LIFE

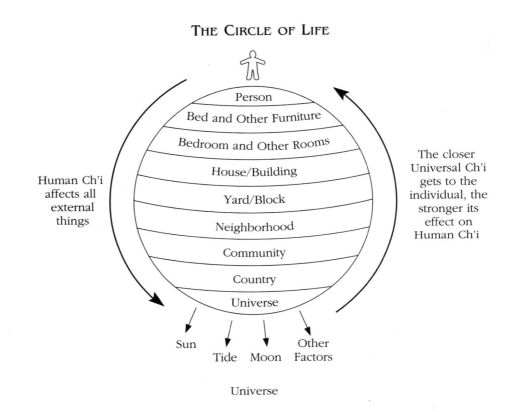

Human Ch'i affects all external things

The closer Universal Ch'i gets to the individual, the stronger its effect on Human Ch'i

Person
Bed and Other Furniture
Bedroom and Other Rooms
House/Building
Yard/Block
Neighborhood
Community
Country
Universe

Sun   Tide   Moon   Other Factors

Universe

This chart is from the Black Hat Sect Lin Yun Temple Teachings. Yun Lin Temple News, vol. 2, no. 4.

you can then locate the areas where energy is blocked, stagnant, oppressive, or flowing too strongly. The assessment of the ch'i in your home, which we call the "Feng Shui of your home," will give you all the information that you need to make the proper adjustments to bring back into balance the things in your environment that are out of the natural order of nature's flow. Bringing things back into order may be as simple as moving your desk into a better energy position, adding extra light to a room, or simply changing the color of your bedroom. By learning how to work with energy through designing the interior of your home, you can ultimately shape and alter the many different situations in your life.

1) THE BAGUA: THE BLACK HAT SECT FENG SHUI MAP

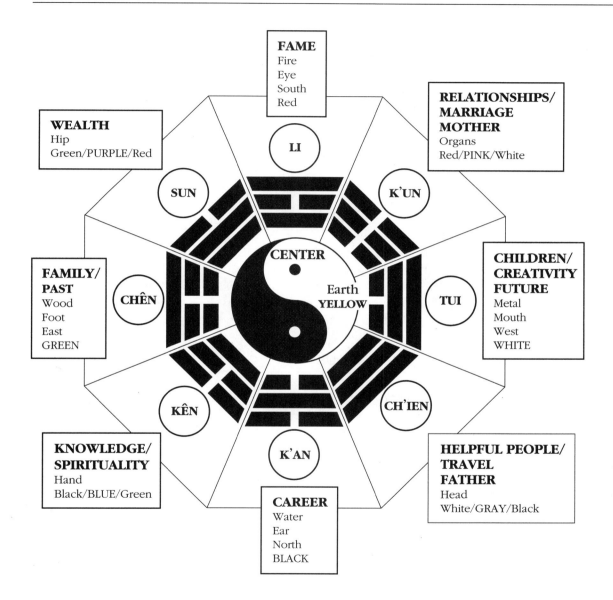

FAME
Fire
Eye
South
Red

**RELATIONSHIPS/
MARRIAGE
MOTHER**
Organs
Red/PINK/White

WEALTH
Hip
Green/PURPLE/Red

LI

SUN

K'UN

**FAMILY/
PAST**
Wood
Foot
East
GREEN

CHÊN

CENTER
Earth
YELLOW

TUI

**CHILDREN/
CREATIVITY
FUTURE**
Metal
Mouth
West
WHITE

KÊN

CH'IEN

**KNOWLEDGE/
SPIRITUALITY**
Hand
Black/BLUE/Green

K'AN

**HELPFUL PEOPLE/
TRAVEL
FATHER**
Head
White/GRAY/Black

CAREER
Water
Ear
North
BLACK

As the energy force moves closer to the individual, it breaks down into nine compartments, eight of which specifically correspond to different areas of your life and one additional area that oversees all issues that are not represented in the other eight areas. The map that we use to illustrate this information is referred to as **the Bagua** (pronounced bah-gwah). The Bagua, meaning eight-sided trigram, is taken from the *I Ching*, the ancient Chinese philosophy that emphasizes the yin-yang principles, which is believed to govern all universal laws. Various healing modalities such as Chinese herbal medicine, acupuncture, and Shiatsu massage were directly derived from these basic laws of nature. Feng Shui itself has its roots in this belief system, for it also tries to assist mankind in understanding different aspects of life. Feng Shui uses our physical environment as a schoolroom to teach us about ourselves and provide us with the tools we need to help with the conflicts and the challenges that we face daily.

When referring to the Bagua, we mean the entire eight-sided diagram in the illustration. When we want to refer to just one section of the Bagua map, we will use the term *gua* (pronounced gwah). There are nine main guas, or areas, in Feng Shui that correspond to various components of your life. In addition, each gua also oversees other specific aspects and attributes. These aspects include corresponding colors, elements, compass directions, areas of the body, and individual family members.

THE FENG SHUI BAGUA

From the perspective of the Black Hat Sect Tantric Buddhism, the Feng Shui Bagua has nine sections. They include: Fame, Marriage/Relationships, Children/Creativity, Helpful people/Travel, Career, Self-knowledge/Spirituality, Family, Wealth, and the Center—all other things.

1. FAME: The *Fame* area of the Bagua is located in the middle of the top section of the octagon chart. Its Chinese name is *LI*, and it represents who you want to be known as or what you would like to accomplish in this lifetime. It refers to fame such as in public recognition, wanting to become a well-known actor, doctor, or businessperson. Equally important, if not more so, Fame can also mean wanting to be recognized for other important roles in our society that

usually do not receive the same type of acknowledgment, such as being a loving mother, a nurturing father, or an inspiring schoolteacher. This area also oversees all issues relating to the *eyes*, and the *middle daughter* in the family. It is ruled by the element of *fire* and is strengthened by the color *red*. Its position on the Black Hat Sect Bagua is *south*.

2. MARRIAGE/RELATIONSHIPS: The *Marriage* area on the Bagua chart sits on the upper-right-hand corner of the eight-sided map. Its Chinese name is *K'UN*, and it most strongly represents the marriage ch'i in your life and your ability to draw on a successful, loving partnership. It is also the area that conducts the energy flow for other types of relationships including dating, living together, and other nontraditional unions. Individuals who choose not to be in a relationship can still utilize this gua as an area that represents their relationship with themselves or their friends. This section also oversees all issues related to the *organs* of the body and the *mother* in the family. It does not have a ruling element but it does resonate to the color *pink*. Its position on the Bagua is *southwest*.

3. CHILDREN/CREATIVITY: This section of the Bagua is located in the middle on the right side of the chart, and it represents the *future* and all the life-affirming things that we give birth to. Its Chinese name is *TUI*, and it represents all your *descendants*, in particular your *children* or the children you plan to have. Any issues or difficulties regarding fertility can be addressed here. In addition, this area oversees all issues of *creativity* including new thoughts, new ideas, art, writing, and inspiration. The creativity aspect of this category allows for all individuals—men, women, and children alike—to utilize this gua because all the energy it generates tends to serve the same general purpose, to manifest the creation principle. The area of Children also represents the *youngest daughter* and is ruled by the element of *metal*. Its corresponding color is *white*, and it oversees all issues related to the *mouth and teeth*. Its position is *west* on the Bagua.

4. HELPFUL PEOPLE/TRAVEL: This section is located on the lower-right-hand side of the Bagua chart. Its Chinese name is *CH'IEN*, and it oversees two main categories in your life, the first being the energy that draws on the helpful people in your life. Helpful People refers to all people we come in contact with who aid and direct us along life's path. They can include friends and family members who support and love us on a daily basis or the counselor who helps

us through a difficult time. Many times these Helpful People show up quietly, without a familiar face or name. They may appear to you as the person who patiently takes the time to give you proper directions or the one who conveniently pulls out of his parking space just when you're in need of one! This section also represents our ability to magnetize opportunities and to be a "helpful person" to others. The other category this section oversees is the area of *Travel.* All aspects and opportunities related to travel (business or personal) are generated from here. The *head* area, the *father,* and the color *gray* are all represented in this gua. Its position is *northwest* on the Bagua.

5. CAREER: This section of the Bagua map is located directly in the center of the bottom of the chart and provides the foundation energy that stabilizes the rest of the guas. Its Chinese name is *K'AN,* and it oversees all matters concerning one's *career, hobbies,* or *skills.* This section differs from the aspects shown in the fame area because it represents what you do as opposed to who you want to be known as. This section generates the ch'i force that fuels the issues regarding the type of work you do or the type of work you aspire to do. For instance, work-related issues like being hired for a job or getting a long-awaited promotion are generated from this gua. Our *careers* and the different work that we do are very important ways that we "provide service" and give some offering back to the world. The way we contribute to society is very personal and can range from raising a family to volunteering at a local hospital. This gua represents the *middle son* in the family and the *ears* on the body. It is ruled by the element of *water* and corresponds to the color *black.* Its position is *north* on the Bagua.

6. KNOWLEDGE/SPIRITUALITY: This area is located on the bottom-left-hand corner of the Bagua chart. Its Chinese name is *KÊN,* and it oversees all types of *self-knowledge* and the ways that we are able to enrich our understanding of who we are. This is the gua that generates the energy that brings us our opportunities and lessons for spiritual growth. It overseas all areas of *spirituality* and when used for practices such as yoga, meditation, self-reflection, and prayer, it can become a very powerful healing area in your home. This area helps us open up and develop our intuition, which is our personal "inner knowing." This section also supports all aspects of *educational pursuits* ranging from academic to informal and nontraditional types of study. The *youngest son* is represented here as well as both *hands* on the body. This gua is not ruled by a

primary element but it does correspond to the color *blue*. Its position is *northeast* on the Bagua.

7. FAMILY: This section of the Bagua is located directly in the middle on the left-hand side of the map. Its Chinese name is *CHÊN*, and it oversees all issues related to your *descendants* and the history connected to the many generations of your family lineage. This area primarily represents biological, reconstituted, and nontraditional family units. This section also includes support groups, religious congregations, and your inner circle of friends that you consider to be like family to you. In addition, it represents and provides the cohesive energy for your *family of co-workers* and all other work-related units or *organizations*. Because it represents the past, all family secrets and childhood issues are stored here. This gua oversees aspects that relate to the *eldest son* and the *feet* in connection with the body. It is ruled by the element of *wood* and it corresponds to the color *green*. Its position is *east* on the Bagua.

8. WEALTH: This area of the Bagua is located in the upper-left-hand corner of the eight-sided map. Its Chinese name is *SUN*, and it generates the ch'i that draws on the energy that oversees *finances* and all the things that we perceive as connoting wealth. Wealth in our society, so often, is associated with greed, excess, and luck. The presence of this gua reminds us that *money*, as complicated as it might seem, is just another type of energy force. Having the amount of money that you need or want should not only be seen as a luxury but as a birthright that we are all entitled to. This is the nest egg of the Bagua, thus a great section in which to store all your valuables: piggy banks, stocks, coins, stamps, savings account book, etc. This section oversees the energy and all issues related to *power*. Shoring up this area will help us to strengthen our ability to draw on the power source that connects us with the abundant universal supply. This will help us develop our internal sense of "healthy power" and release the "unhealthy power struggle" that we often experience from others. The *hip* area on the body, our bone structure, and the *eldest daughter* are all represented here. This gua does not have a ruling element, but it does have a corresponding color of *purple*. Its position is *southeast* on the Bagua.

9. CENTER: The center of the Bagua connects all the eight other sections and is represented by the yin-yang symbol. Its Chinese name is *MING TANG*, and it oversees *all the other issues and life situations* that are not represented in the

eight other guas. For instance, *health*-related issues can be addressed and reinforced in this section. Although health issues are a very big concern for most people, you'll notice that health is not indicated in any of the other eight areas on the Bagua chart. The reason for this is that there are many factors that influence the outcome of good or poor health. Health from a Feng Shui perspective is not seen as something that can be easily adjusted in just one gua. Good health is a result of all the areas in your life and guas in your home being in balance. You can also use this center area to reinforce an issue or a life situation that has already been represented in one of the other guas in the Bagua. This center space oversees *all other family members and areas of the body* that are not addressed in the other eight guas. Its ruling element is *earth*, and it corresponds mainly to the color *yellow*. Its position is in the center of the Bagua chart. (Please note that the Black Hat Sect School of Feng Shui follows the Bagua used in the King Wen era. This Bagua places the south direction on the top, the north direction on the bottom, the west direction on the right, and the east direction on the left.)

These nine areas and their corresponding aspects can be located by super-imposing the Bagua map over the floor plan or layout of your home, apartment, or office space. In order to determine how to correctly position the Bagua map on your space, you first have to establish certain factors such as where the doors and entranceways are located in relation to the rest of your home.

2) DRAWING A FLOOR PLAN OF YOUR HOME

If the mere suggestion of having to draw a floor plan is enough to give you anxiety or intimidate you, you are not alone! Many individuals who are excited about Feng Shui try to start this process and get stuck precisely at this juncture. There are *two main reasons* why this initial Feng Shui step overwhelms many people.

The first reason is the perceived lack of artistic ability. This is a psychological ploy, a distortion that runs with itself and discourages you from moving forward. I call this the *conscious* or the *tangible* reason that delays the Feng Shui process. You do not have to be an artist or an architect to draw a floor plan. A floor plan can be just a simple aerial view of your living quarters. If you are able to draw circles, squares, and rectangles you can easily accomplish this part. You may even have a floor plan of your home which you can use, or you can enlist the help of your partner, neighbor, or friends.

The second reason, and maybe even the more important one, is the subconscious or *intangible reason*. When you first start this process, on many levels you are thinking about working with Feng Shui as a way of making changes in certain areas of your life. Many times, just the thought of making changes (even if it's for the better and truly what we want) is more than enough to stir up a lot of feelings and emotional ch'i on a subconscious level. Those inner feelings unvoiced and unacknowledged can easily get in the way of your moving forward and attaining your goals. One very powerful way of delaying the process of moving forward is by not doing your floor plan. Your subconscious mind knows that the minute you start drawing your floor plan, you have committed to beginning your Feng Shui process. If you can acknowledge your resistance without self-judgment or denial, you are well on your way to overcoming the obstacles that are holding you back from pursuing your objectives.

See if you can try doing one room first. Pick the simplest room or the one that interests you most. Keep in mind that this floor plan *does not* have to be of exact dimensions or to architectural scale. For our needs and level of skill, a rough copy of the floor plan will suffice. Try to be patient with yourself during this part of the process, for it is very similar to assembling a large puzzle. At first you have all these pieces that don't seem to belong together or make any sense, but with time and patience the bigger picture comes together and emerges as a complete image at the end.

The following instructions are designed to walk you through drawing the floor plans of your space and to enable you to start your Feng Shui assessment process. Keep in mind that just as described in the Circle of Life illustration, Feng Shui and ch'i exist on many different levels. We will be assessing the *Feng Shui of three levels of your property*.

1. The Feng Shui of each room
2. The Feng Shui of each floor of your home
3. The Feng Shui of your lot/land or block

Each level includes the nine areas of the Bagua that correspond to various situations in your life ranging from relationships to finances. Looking at all three levels of the Feng Shui of your home will help you develop a profile of the areas that are strongly supported in your life or identify areas that would cause you to be more vulnerable. This profile will enable you to make the proper adjustments and subsequently change the energy in those problematic areas for the better.

First you have to gather the following materials:

A notebook for writing; blank paper or pad for drawing; pencils with erasers; black marker/pen; colored markers/crayons; red marker/pen (use red only when instructed to); and a ruler.

The following illustrations are to be used as a visual guide that will help you to re-create the interior elements of your home, while getting you to pay more attention to smaller details that will later on bring you valuable information regarding the Feng Shui of your life.

Placing the Bagua over Each Room

Step #1: Take a blank sheet of drawing paper and a pencil with an eraser and walk over to the first room you want to start working on.

Step #2: Date top of page and give it a room title. Use separate sheets for each room.

Step #3: Stand in the entranceway of the room that you chose and let your eye travel around the parameters of the four walls. Determine if the general shape of the room is square, rectangular, L-shaped, circular, etc. Draw that shape in pencil on your blank paper. Use the color *black* for the outline of your rooms, house doors, and windows.

Basic House/Room Shapes:

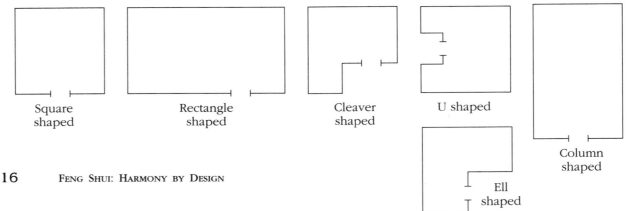

Square shaped

Rectangle shaped

Cleaver shaped

U shaped

Column shaped

Ell shaped

Step #4: Now modify or alter the shape of the four walls according to the specifics that are relative to your room. Check for built-in closets, wings that jut out, structural corners, sections of the room missing, etc. Erase the sections of the walls that require modification and pencil them in.

Step #5: Now indicate where all the doors and windows are located using a *W* for windows and an opening in the penciled wall line for a door.

Door Positioning:

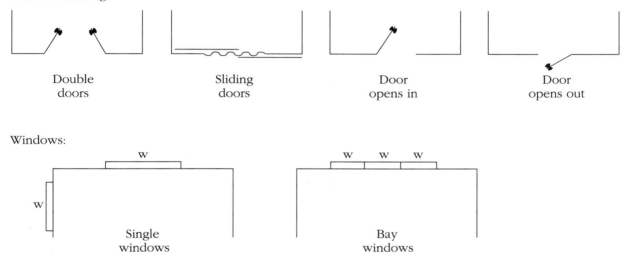

| Double doors | Sliding doors | Door opens in | Door opens out |

Windows:

| Single windows | Bay windows |

Step #6: Using rectangles, squares, circles, etc., draw symbols to represent the *main pieces of furniture* in the room your are illustrating. The shapes you use are not as important as the *general location of the items*. Areas that seem to collect newspapers, junk, or clutter in general should be clearly indicated with a triangle. Here are two sample floor plans.

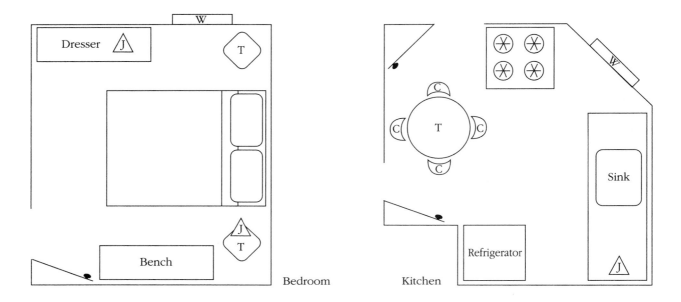

Bedroom   Kitchen

Step #7: Take a final look at the layout of the room. Make sure all the main objects are indicated. Check for other objects such as closets and indicate if the closet is freestanding or built into the room (its door flush with the parallel wall). Add these things to your room plan now.

Step #8: Go back and repeat steps 1 through 7 for each room in your house.

Step #9: If you have drawn each room on a separate piece of paper, collect all the different room plans and start to piece them together by laying them out next to one another. You can also cut out the rooms and place them on a larger sheet of blank paper (do not glue yet). Then add any other modifications needed to make the floor plan more cohesive. If you drew the floor plan on only one sheet of paper, just make the necessary adjustments for cohesion. *Don't worry if your floor plan doesn't fall neatly together.* It doesn't have to be perfect, just good enough to give you a basic overview to work from.

Step #10: Do step #9 for each floor.
Your Feng Shui layout may be different for each floor.
Don't forget to place the Bagua over each floor and align one of the lower three

guas (Self-knowledge, Career, Helpful People) with the *main entranceway to the floor* in question (see page 9).

Step #11: Now add in all common areas such as foyers, hallways, and stairs. At this point you can paste down any loose pieces of the floor plan on the blank sheet of paper.

Hallways:

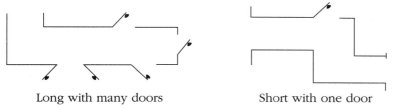

Long with many doors   Short with one door

Congratulations—you made it! You now have a completed floor plan from which to work. The next important part of your Feng Shui process is finding out how to properly place the Bagua map over your plan. This will enable you to locate the areas in your home that oversee the ch'i flow for many aspects of your life, ranging from your financial matters to your personal relationships with others.

3) LOCATING THE POWER SPOTS IN YOUR HOME

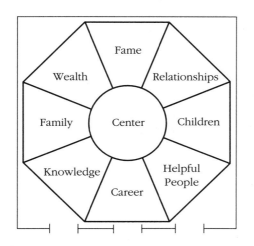

In order to correctly place the Bagua over your floor plan, you first need to understand how to properly position the map in relation to the various *entranceways* into your home, the individual rooms, and the yard around your home.

PLACING THE BAGUA OVER EACH ROOM IN YOUR HOME

Step #1: Pick one room on your floor plan and locate the main entranceway into the room. If the room has more than one entranceway or door, pick the door/entranceway that is used most often by the residents in the house. If both doors are used equally, pick the one that is wider. If they are both used equally and are both the same size, then use the one that the guests use. If your home has two or more floors, do the rooms on the bottom floor first, then work your way up.

Step #2: Choose a pen or pencil in a color (except red) that you haven't used yet. Take the Bagua map and place it directly over the room with the Fame section at the top center and the Career section running parallel with the center of the wall that your entranceway is on. The bottom three sections (Knowledge, Career, Helpful People) ***always run parallel to the wall of the entranceway that you are using***. If you are placing the Bagua correctly over your room, then the doorway can *only* fall into one of the three bottom areas of the Bagua, the Knowledge, Career or Helpful People section (see diagrams 1–4). Sometimes the doorway/entranceway is wide and you'll find that it overlaps two of the three lower guas (Self-Knowledge, Career, Helpful People) (see diagrams 5 and 6). That's okay. If the doorway/entranceway of your room overlaps any other section (e.g., Relationships or Fame areas) than the three named above, the Bagua was placed wrong (see diagrams 7–10).

Go back and try this step again. The only exception to this rule is when the entranceway is located on an inset in an irregularly shaped house (see diagrams 11 and 12). *The proper alignment of the Bagua with your entranceway is crucial,* for it will determine the correct positioning of where the other guas are located in the rest of the room.

Diagram 1

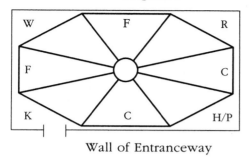

W   F   R

F   C

K   C   H/P

Wall of Entranceway

Diagram 2

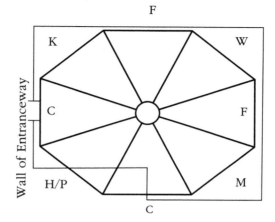

F

K   W

C   F

H/P   M

C

Wall of Entranceway

Diagram 3

Wall of Entranceway

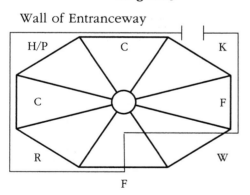

H/P   C   K

C   F

R   W

F

Diagram 4

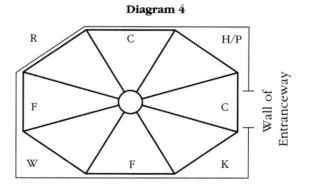

R   C   H/P

F   C

W   F   K

Wall of Entranceway

Diagram 5

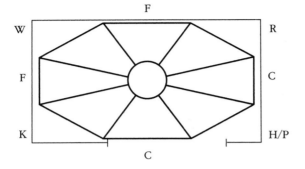

Entranceway overlaps Career and Helpful People guas.

Diagram 6

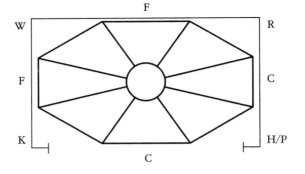

Room with entranceway that crosses over 3 guas (Knowledge, Career, Helpful People).

Diagram 7

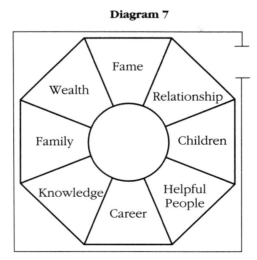

Incorrectly placed Bagua. The entranceway gua can *never* be in the Relationship area.

Diagram 8

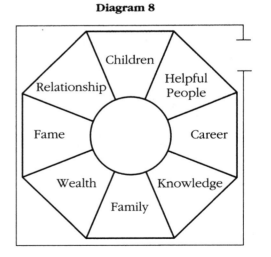

Correctly placed Bagua. The entranceway is in the Helpful People section.

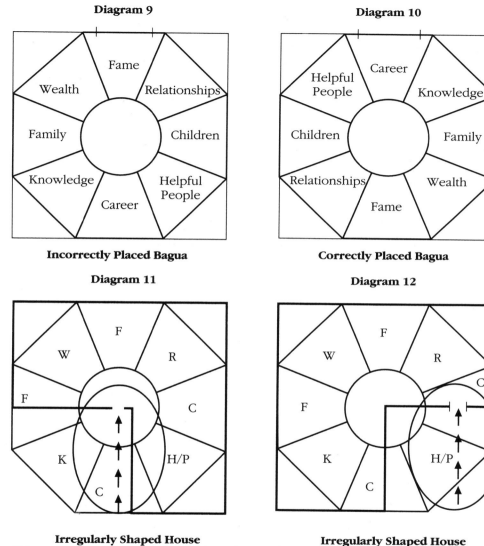

Diagram 9

Fame

Wealth   Relationships

Family   Children

Knowledge   Helpful People

Career

Incorrectly Placed Bagua

Diagram 10

Career

Helpful People   Knowledge

Children   Family

Relationships   Wealth

Fame

Correctly Placed Bagua

Diagram 11

F
W   R
F
C
K   H/P
C

Irregularly Shaped House

This entranceway is still considered to be in the *CAREER* gua, even though it is technically closer to the center of the Bagua.*

Diagram 12

F
W   R
C
F
C
K   H/P

Irregularly Shaped House

This entranceway is still considered to be in the *HELPFUL PEOPLE* gua, even though it is technically in the Children gua.*

* These minor adjustments allow us to include the total property of the house shape into the Bagua layout, thus providing a more accurate account of which guas are missing. We use this system to determine the correct Bagua layout for *irregularly shaped houses.*

Step #3: If the room is not a complete square, stretch the Bagua into longer or shorter shapes to accommodate the different room sizes. As the Bagua stretches to the various lengths and widths of each room, certain guas will be more emphasized, others less. Depending on the size of the room, certain guas will be elongated or reduced. This will influence the amount of ch'i that is able to be generated for a particular life area. Different rooms will draw on a larger amount of ch'i energy for certain aspects of your life, while other rooms will reduce and limit the amount of ch'i energy.

Because the Bagua is in the shape of an *octagon* and most rooms are not octagonally shaped, it can be very confusing at first, as you try to locate the different corresponding sections of your rooms/home. Although there are nine basic areas to the chart, they do not always divide up into *exact* measurements and sections. Throughout this book you will often discover that Feng Shui is not an exact science, and often it will leave us with much room for personal interpretation and flexibility. Keep in mind that we are basically dividing up your

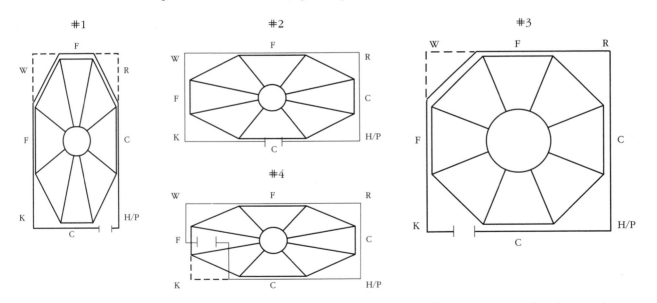

Illustration 1 is "long" on Family and Children (great for a newly married couple). Illustration 2 is great for a business because it's "long" on Fame and Career.

Illustrations 3 and 4 are not good for a business or a home because 3 is missing the gua of Wealth and 4 is missing Knowledge.

room into nine different sections of "invisible energy" (ch'i) and energy does not always adhere to invisible borders or stay confined to imaginary boundaries. Often the ch'i of one gua will spill over into the neighboring gua. So when you are trying to figure out exactly where one gua ends and the next one begins, know that you are looking for a general vicinity and not an exact dimension line.

Step #4: This step is a helpful trick designed to give you another approach to assist you in properly laying out the Bagua. Take a marker or crayon of a color that you haven't already used (except red) and with nine circles divide up the room into nine sections. Let these circles extend past the four corner slants of the Bagua map to the end corners of each room. This format will give you a better sense of the range that each section/gua oversees. Keep in mind that even though the Bagua map is octagonally shaped, we always "treat it" as if it were a square or rectangle as we place it over the room or house.

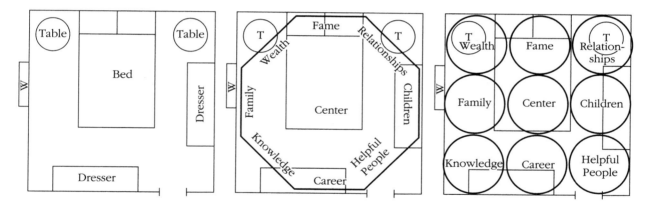

Step #5: Now go back and repeat steps 1 through 4 and apply these instructions to the overall floor plan of the bottom floor of your home. Remember to line up the *FRONT* door of your apartment or house with one of the three Bagua doors, Knowledge, Career or Helpful People. If your home has side, back, or garage doors that are used as the main doorway, *still* place the Bagua using the *front door*. The reason for this is that even though you have chosen to use a particular door, the *original ch'i flow* was designed based on the architectural blueprint and layout using the "original" front door. Use steps 1 through 4 for each floor of your home. If you choose to, you can also do this for your basement or attic areas.

Step #6: This step is for those of you with more than one floor who are having difficulty trying to superimpose the Bagua correctly on each floor. Sometimes additional floors have staircases, foyers, landings, etc., that confuse and complicate the correct positioning of the Feng Shui map. Although all the possible layouts cannot be illustrated here (see page 27), try to deduce the principles behind the solutions and then modify them to meet your particular problem.

PLACING THE BAGUA OVER YOUR LOT OR BLOCK

Step #7: Follow the same instructions listed in step 5 on placing the Bagua. Instead of using the front door to align the Bagua, use the entranceway into the lot, beginning at the opening of the driveway, or front gate (see pages 28–29). If the lot is several acres in size, lay the Bagua map over the lot with the three bottom guas—Knowledge, Career, Helpful People—closest to *your* estimation of where the front entrance is. There are times when situations are not clear cut and you will have to learn to trust your gut and intuition. This is an important step for those of you who have land around your home or are thinking about buying a house with land or a yard. For instance, families venturing into new businesses would want to make sure that the Career area on the lot is intact. A family would want their Children section intact if they are planning on having a child. Architects and contractors can use this information to pick out the best location in which to build your house, while real estate brokers can match auspiciously placed property with specific clients based on their goals. Others who live in more urban areas or cities can identify where their building is located on their block, i.e., in the Career corner of the block, and assess what gua the higher flow of ch'i is being extracted from. All this information will factor into the profile of the overall Feng Shui of where you live.

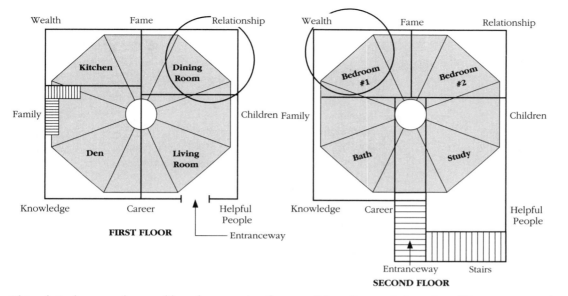

This relatively square home, although possessing the same "shape" on each floor, has different guas overlapping because the **ENTRANCEWAY** to each level is in a different position. For example, the **RELATIONSHIP** area on the first floor overlaps the **WEALTH** area on the second floor.

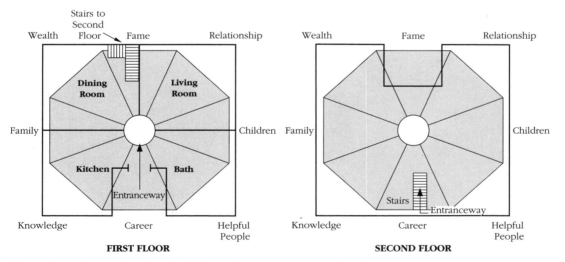

This U-shaped home has the **CAREER** section missing on the first floor but intact on the second floor. In contrast, the second floor is missing the **FAME** area.

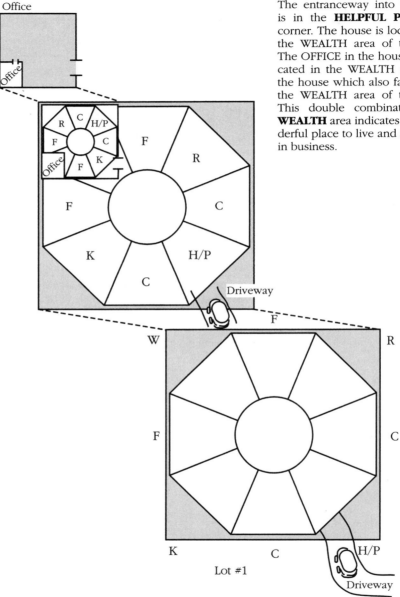

The entranceway into this lot is in the **HELPFUL PEOPLE** corner. The house is located in the WEALTH area of the lot. The OFFICE in the house is located in the WEALTH area of the house which also falls into the WEALTH area of the lot. This double combination of **WEALTH** area indicates a wonderful place to live and success in business.

Lot #1

The entranceway into this lot overlaps two guas, **CAREER** and **KNOWLEDGE.** The house is located in the **RELATION-SHIP** area of the lot. This lot would bring difficulties to a couple who would want to start a family, for it is missing the **CHILDREN** gua.

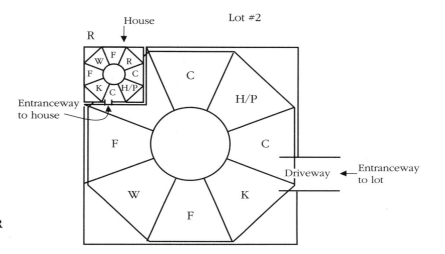

FINDING THE MISSING OR PROTRUDING GUAS

In Feng Shui we think in terms of shapes being either complete or incomplete. Rooms and house shapes that are basically round, square, oval, or rectangular are preferred over other forms. Many times, rooms and homes are designed with corners and sections that are missing. Other times, certain spaces are designed with additions or corners that extend out. The basic rule in Black Hat Sect Feng Shui is that if the addition is less than half the width or length of the room or house, it is a protruding gua (an extra section). Anything larger than that creates a missing gua (a section omitted). In either case, the Feng Shui of that space will be affected for better or for worse—depending on which area of the Bagua gets extended or which area of the Feng Shui map gets reduced. Go back and review your floor plan. Check your rooms, lot, and your overall floor plan for areas that have protruding or missing guas. Also check for oddly shaped rooms such as ells, five-walled rooms, U-shaped areas, etc. Make a note of those areas in your Feng Shui notebook. You will need to go back to these sections and make the appropriate adjustments at a later time.

Congratulations, again! By now you should have a completed floor plan indicating where your Fame, Relationship, Children, Helpful People, Career, Knowledge, Family, Wealth, and Center areas are in each room, floor of your house, and section of your lot. These blueprints are the X rays that we will be using to diagnose all the problem areas of your home that are harboring imbalanced ch'i. In addition, these same blueprints will direct us toward providing the cures and remedies needed to help resolve the detected problems.

Summary

The Bagua and Its Corresponding Aspects

LIFE SITUATION ENGLISH	LIFE SITUATION CHINESE	TRIGRAM	BODY PART(S)	COLOR(S)	ELEMENT(S) *FIVE ELEMENTS	FAMILY MEMBER	DIRECTION
Fame	LI	☲	Eyes	Red	*Fire	Middle Daughter	South
Relationships (Marriage)	K'UN	☷	Organs	Pink	Planet Earth	Mother	Southwest
Children (Creativity)	TUI	☱	Mouth	White	*Metal Lake	Youngest Daughter	West
Helpful People (Travel)	CH'IEN	☰	Head	Grey	Heaven	Father	Northwest
Career	K'AN	☵	Ears	Black	*Water	Middle Son	North
Knowledge (Self/Academic) Spirituality	KÊN	☶	Hands	Blue	Thunder	Youngest Son	Northeast
Family (Descendants)	CHÊN	☳	Feet	Green	*Wood Mountain	Eldest Son	East
Wealth	SUN	☴	Hip/ Bones	Purple	Wind	Eldest Daughter	Southeast
Others	MING TANG	☯	All Others	Yellow	*Earth	All Others	Center

PLACING THE BAGUA WITH MORE THAN ONE FLOOR

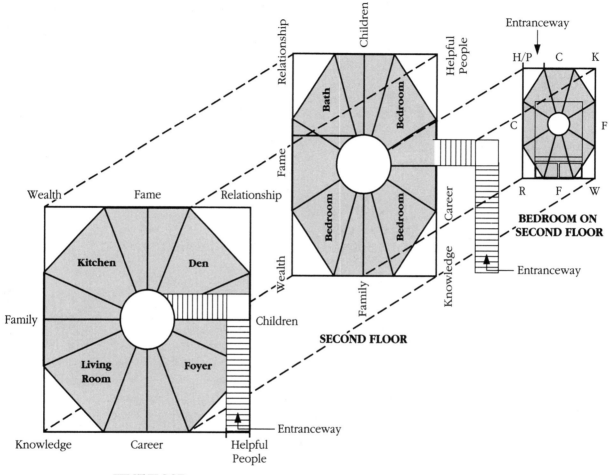

FIRST FLOOR

SECOND FLOOR

BEDROOM ON SECOND FLOOR

T W O

HOW TO ASSESS YOUR SPACE
AND MAKE ADJUSTMENTS

There are three basic ways to begin a Feng Shui assessment of your home. You can apply an objective approach, a subjective approach or a combination of the two. An objective approach applies the Feng Shui principles of the interior factors to adjust the Feng Shui of one's home, without focusing on a specific problem. The objective approach looks for problem areas within the home such as structural imbalances or awkwardly placed furniture and makes adjustments accordingly. The objective approach acts as a *preventive* measure, adjusting imbalances in your home regardless of whether the imbalanced area has manifested a problem in the individual's life. For example, in undertaking an objective adjustment, an awkwardly placed bed would be moved even if it's not apparent how the poor positioning has affected the individual who sleeps in it. For the Feng Shui professional, this approach allows for more anonymity and less disclosure of a client's personal problems. It also encourages individuals who might not be clear on what their specific issues may be to participate in the Feng Shui process anyway.

A subjective approach is much more focused on issues that the individual specifically wants to work on. You come with an agenda to this approach, with an awareness of some of the difficulties in your life that you are struggling with. You have some prior knowledge and awareness of the problems you're facing, and that they have already somehow manifested themselves in your life. For example: You are having a hard time being successful in your career. The way that you would then start this assessment process would be by making adjustments of all issues regarding career and in all the guas in the house, rooms, and lot that oversee career. This approach serves as an *intervention* process, acting after the fact on situations that are already considered problematic. This is a more personalized approach that is specific and to the point.

The third, or combination approach, combines the two processes with what the individual objectively sees *and* personally knows about his or her life. It provides an overall balance by addressing prevention and intervention methods collectively. A combination approach to Feng Shui allows you to work on specific problems in your life as you rebalance the overall flow of ch'i, which makes this method the most thorough and expansive.

Along with your completed floor plan, take your Feng Shui notebook and start on the next part of your assessment process by answering the question below.

Wish List: What Three Things in Your Life Would You Like to Change?

Take a quiet moment, a deep breath, and reflect on issues you are facing right now in your life. Some of them might be old and familiar, while others may be current and new. Think about these issues and then make a list of them. Don't judge, analyze, or edit them, just allow yourself to be as honest as you can about the situations. If you have more than three things on your list, see if certain issues overlap. Narrow them down and pick out the three *most* pressing or important issues to you. List them in your notebook.

Sample Wish List

1. I want a relationship with a woman/man who is loving and nurturing.

2. I want the promotion I am next in line for at my job as a staff supervisor.

3. I want the chronic pain in my lower back to improve and heal.

Your Wish List

1. _____

2. _____

3. _____

This list will help you focus on the different areas of your home that correspond to the specific issues in your life that you want to work on during your Feng Shui assessment process. Over the years this list should change, reflecting those issues relative to the time period in which you are doing your Feng Shui.

THE POWER OF INTENTIONS

One of the most important things in Feng Shui is the concept of INTENTIONS, whether they are personal, those of the Feng Shui specialist, or behind the suggested adjustments and blessings. *Intentions are thoughts that activate the solutions which remedy the problems.* They are a very powerful use of the conscious mind and sacred in your process of change. The more specific you can be, the better. When you are writing or thinking about your intentions, do not be modest when asking for things that you want or need. It is our birthright to want and ask for things. You are not any less of a spiritual being to want financial success or material objects. Actually, it is quite the contrary, because as we become more spiritually enlightened, we naturally draw to us more energy. Money, as discussed in the information on the Bagua, is basically just a powerful form of energy. If being enlightened or being spiritual means doing without, then we would have all been dropped off on a Himalayan mountaintop somewhere to meditate all day and contemplate life. We haven't, and it's not the mission most of us have been called to carry out. If we are asking for things that we believe will truly better our lives, then that request is a sincere intention. Black Hat Sect Feng Shui principles are derived from the philosophy based on Tantric Tibetan Buddhism. One of the main objectives governing its belief system is to alleviate the suffering of all sentient beings (that's us) and to better their lives. That's why Feng Shui was given to us—to be used to improve the overall quality of our lives.

MUNDANE VS. TRANSCENDENTAL SOLUTIONS

Eight out of ten things in our life do not turn out the way we want. We will all encounter different problems in our lifetime.

—PROF. LIN YUN, 1/14/94

It is a belief of Black Hat Sect Feng Shui that there are two basic solutions to most problems: the mundane and the transcendental. Both solutions are seen as equally important but differ vastly in approach and effectiveness.

MUNDANE SOLUTIONS

These are the types of solutions that come from an acceptable, reasonable, and logical "realm of knowledge." They consist of helpful suggestions that are based on information which is familiar and logical to us. These solutions incorporate common sense, good advice, and sound judgment as ways to accomplish your goals and resolve your problems. For instance, let's look at the first INTENTION listed in the above Sample Wish List—"I want a relationship with a woman/man who is loving and nurturing." A mundane solution to this intention may be to: get out more often and socialize at least once a week at a new restaurant or coffee house; take a class where the participants have interests similar to yours; or join a dating service and seek out someone with those qualities. A mundane solution to wish number two, wanting a promotion at work, might be to take some additional classes to improve the skills you need for that particular position. A mundane solution to the third wish, relieving chronic back pain, may be to seek out a new doctor with an alternative treatment plan. These are all solutions that seem like practical, sensible approaches to solving the problem at hand. We believe, in Black Hat Sect Feng Shui, that these types of solutions are helpful and important but are only ***10 to 20 percent effective***! The reason for this is that in life, there are many things that are out of our control and level of understanding that factor into the outcome of a situation. This set of coincidences and variables is better known as karma. *Karma is the result of many factors happening at once to determine a specific outcome.* We have all experienced at one time or another a situation in our lives that did not turn out the way we'd hoped. Although we went back to school and got a degree, many of us still didn't get the job or the promotion we wanted. Many of us who have worked hard all our lives still struggle on a daily basis to make ends meet. Sometimes the outcome of all our actions seems futile and frustrating—especially when we witness other individuals prospering and succeeding with what seems like minimal effort. As we become more enlightened, we begin to realize that our lives are not a clear and direct system of cause and effect, but a system that is contingent upon many incidences and many different factors. This is why we need to employ additional methods of problem solving that incorporate all these various components.

TRANSCENDENTAL SOLUTIONS

These are types of solutions that are more mystical by nature and are obtained from a universal "realm of knowledge" that is often not understood by the average person. These solutions are not easily accepted by the "educated masses," for they suggest remedies to your problems that appear to be incongruous with intellectual reasoning. For example, take the request "I want a relationship with a woman/man who is loving and nurturing." A transcendental cure may be to paint the color of your bedroom pink or place a wind chime in your Helpful People corner. A transcendental solution to "wanting that promotion at work" might be to place a heavy statue in the corner of your Career area. One cure for "relieving chronic back pain" may include placing a crystal ball in the center of your bedroom. In Black Hat Feng Shui, we utilize these solutions and believe that they are the most powerful and are ***100 to 120 percent effective***! Many times these cures are deemed "superstitious" and hokey by individuals who, out of fear and lack of understanding, refute that other types of knowledge and ways of solving things exist. The reason for this is that as a society we are conditioned since birth to accept only what can be proven and validated scientifically. Anything else poses a real threat to the way we have approached logical thinking and makes us feel unsure and not safe. Often those of us who have a hard time accepting these solutions also have a hard time accepting the reality of our limitations as just intellectual beings. As we evolve and expand our understanding of who we are, we are beginning to see that we are physical, emotional, intellectual, and spiritual beings . . . multidimensional and much greater than the sum of all our parts. This understanding of our vastness allows us to incorporate other ways of resolving things and restoring harmony in our lives.

When working with the different types of solutions in Feng Shui, it is often tempting to just employ the transcendental solutions to a specific problem and negate the value of the mundane solutions. But the mundane solutions, although only 10 to 20 percent effective by themselves, become much more powerful when utilized along with the transcendental solutions and vice versa. I will **always** encourage you to exhaust all mundane solutions first, in addition to applying the transcendental cures. Often the transcendental cures need a tangible situation through which to manifest. For example: in the case of "wanting a relationship with a nurturing and loving man/woman," the transcendental solution of hanging a wind chime might lift the energy block that is preventing you from getting in a relationship, but the mundane solution of socializing more often will afford you the access to meeting him/her. That is why they are equally important; they work in tandem and must both be considered and utilized.

FENG SHUI ADJUSTMENT ITEMS

Below is a list of TEN categories that include close to fifty different items that are used in Feng Shui to adjust the ch'i in your home or workplace. The range of items listed reflects the various solutions used in the Feng Shui process. In Black Hat Sect Feng Shui, we call these items "Methods of Minor Additions." Some items are interchangeable, while others are specific to certain types of cures. As we address the different solutions, remedies for various problems, and where to place certain items and for what purpose, I will indicate which items are interchangeable and which are not.

1. Lights/bright objects: These items lift up and expand the ch'i.
   a) Lighting—the brighter the better
   b) Crystal ball—glass/man-made, round and faceted 20mm–60mm (always hung on a red string in dimensions of 9 inches (9″, 18″, 27″, etc.)
   c) Candles/lanterns

2. Mirrors: multiuse
   a) Bagua—Deflects negative ch'i.
   b) Convex—Expands narrow areas.
   c) Concave—Turns oppressive images (e.g., towering buildings) up-side down.
   d) Decorative/framed—Reflects and draws in positive images, ex-pands space, opens up closed or missing guas, etc.
3. Sound: Keeps energy moving.
   a) Wind chimes—brass or copper best
   b) Music—speakers/stereo equipment/instruments
4. Life force: Stimulates ch'i.
   a) Plants
   b) Fish tanks
   c) Birds
   d) Bonsai/trees
   e) Flowers
   f) Pets
5. Heavy objects: diffuse fast energy/hold down issues.
   a) Rocks
   b) Statues/sculpture
   c) Yu—small, round offering bowl with nine rocks inside
6. Color: Enhances and/or softens ch'i.
   a) Using the eight Trigram Colors of the Bagua (see page 9)
   b) Using the five Element Color Theory (red, yellow, white, black, green)
   c) Using the "Six True Colors" (white, red, yellow, green, blue, black)
   d) The Seven Colors of the Rainbow (red, orange, yellow, green, blue, indigo, purple)
   e) Vibrant colors—red, yellow, orange, black—enhance ch'i.
      Pastel colors—soften and hold on to existing ch'i.
7. Movement/mobile objects: disperse negative ch'i and circulate ch'i.
   a) Mobiles
   b) Wind chimes
   c) Tassels—red and gold
   d) Flags/wind socks
   e) Windmills
   f) Fountains
   g) Weather vanes

8. Power and energy objects: convey strength and power.
   a) Firecrackers—ward off negative ch'i.
   b) Arrowheads—power objects
   c) Talisman—spiritual protection

9. Water: circulates ch'i and activates wealth.
   a) Indoor/outdoor fountains
   b) Fish tanks
   c) Brooks, streams and trickling water
   d) Ponds with goldfish
   e) Vases/bowls of water

10. Others: Most important, expand on the basic cures.
    a) Bamboo flutes—lift oppressive ch'i.
    b) Beaded curtains—act as a divider.
    c) Ten Coins of the Ching Dynasty—enhance wealth.
    d) Crystals/gemstones—raise energy and vibration levels.
    e) Fragrances—incense, oils, flowers, orange peels—clear negative energy.
    f) Touch items—objects of art, soft fabrics, nurturing objects
    g) Others—your personal touches; advanced transcendental cures

Interior Factors That Influence Feng Shui

As you start to work with Feng Shui as a form of interior design, you will come to realize that the way you approached designing your space in the past will have changed radically—probably not in terms of your particular taste or style, but more in terms of the amount of consciousness and awareness that you have of the way design and placement affect your life. Aesthetics are very important in interior design, for they reflect who we are on a personal level and create an environment that can either be soothing and comforting to us or depressing and uncomfortable to live in. But aesthetics alone are not enough to create good Feng Shui! Many award-winning homes that are breathtaking, costly, and designed by famous artists do not have good Feng Shui. In fact, as a consultant, I have experienced more poor Feng Shui in expensively decorated homes than in modestly furnished studio and one-bedroom apartments. The good news is, good Feng Shui is not necessary based on aesthetics, good taste, or lots of money. It's based on understanding the principles of how the placement of objects, color, energy, and so forth affects us. Understanding that information makes you an informed consumer, allowing you to make decisions that will not only beautify your home but support and enhance your life as well. Feng Shui puts a "spiritual spin" on our concept of design and reminds us that we are all spiritual beings and that the "essence of spirit" exists in all things created by man and God. The beauty, the care, and the time that went into the universe creating an orange sunset or a red-petaled rose should be the example that we use as a model when we are designing our own space. This doesn't mean that we all have to be incredibly talented and creative designers, but it does mean that we need to create our homes, "our personal environments," with the same sense of importance and respect that the universe afforded to "the bigger environment." The comfort and beauty that we receive from a setting sun or a multicolored flower garden are the healing effects that a well-designed universe has on us. In turn, the amount of consciousness and thought that we put into designing our homes becomes our contribution to keeping the world beautiful and harmonious.

Here are the most important interior factors that influence Feng Shui.

(1) BED

The bed is one of the three most important furniture items in Feng Shui. Because we spend one third of our lives sleeping, the position of the bed becomes crucial as it relates to our relationships, health, and overall well-being (see chapter 3). The general rule for the positioning of the bed is that the individual(s) lying in it should have the largest view of the room, always be facing the doorway, but never be in a direct line with it. This is because the doorway in Feng Shui is referred to as the "mouth of the ch'i," and through this opening the energy enters, creating a powerful force that can wreak havoc on your physical body if you are in a direct line with it. In addition, this position weakens your ch'i, leaving you exposed, vulnerable, and unable to protect or defend yourself from the different situations and curves that life will throw you.

Bed position number 1 is the best. Number 2 is good. In number 3, the bed *must* be moved out of the direct line of the entranceway; if this is impossible, create a divider between the bed and the door or place a Feng Shui crystal on a nine-inch red string between the door and the bed. Number

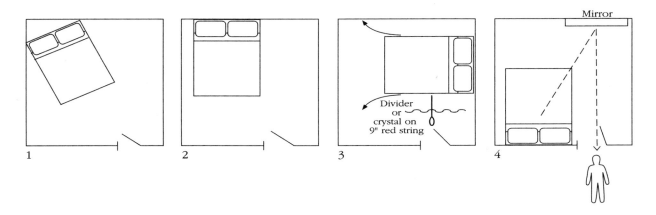

4 has the occupants not facing the entranceway; therefore the bed needs to be moved or adjusted with a mirror to reflect back the view of the entranceway. This places the doorway comfortably in view from that bed position. For a more detailed discussion on bed placement, see chapter 3.

(2) DESK

The desk follows the same set of principles that the bed does; it should always face the door with the widest view of the room. If at all possible, it should be angled in a corner with ample space around it. The desk chair should always

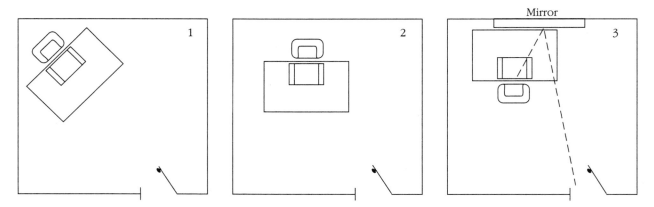

be facing toward the doorway of the room. You should never have your back facing a doorway (see chapter 4).

Desk position number 1 is excellent: it faces the door, it opens to the widest position of the room, and it is in the most commanding position of the office. Number 2 is good. Number 3 has the individual in a very stressful and vulnerable position with his or her back to the doorway. If this desk can't be moved, remedy the problem by placing a mirror in a position that will reflect the doorway.

(3) STOVE

The stove is the most important appliance in your home, for it plays a big part in your overall finances. It is crucial that the stove operate well and that the cook *not* have his or her back to the doorway.

Number 1 stove is in an excellent position. It faces the doorway, and therefore the cook faces the "mouth of the ch'i," the source of the energy flow. Number 2 has the cook's back to the door, so a mirror should be placed in a position that will help the cook see the doorway and not be startled by any surprise guests or noises. In addition, add a wind chime or faceted crystal on a nine-inch red string between the stove and doorway.

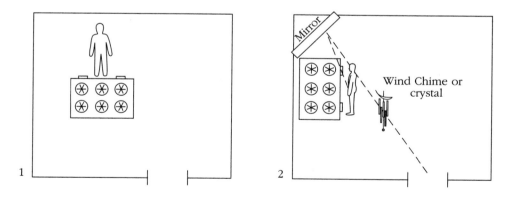

(4) STAIRCASES

Staircases are very important, for they carry the ch'i to and from different floors. Depending on where they are and how they are positioned, they can be helpful and draw the ch'i up to the next floor or they can be disruptive and cause fighting and various health problems. Staircases should be wide and well lit without any obstructions on the steps that might cause a fall. Obstructions, such as toys or shoes, force your body and your ch'i to constantly swerve back and forth to avoid them. This causes a constant sense of avoidance and may affect your ability to deal with things head on or to move up in your career. To remedy this, keep all stairways clear. If your stairways are too narrow they can constrict your energy *and* influence your health. To remedy this imbalance, add lighting and a mirror to expand the space.

When staircases are in a direct line with entranceway doors the ch'i can be siphoned up the stairs too quickly, thus taking away valuable ch'i from other areas. To remedy this imbalance, place a wind chime or faceted crystal on a nine-inch red string between the doorway and staircase; and to anchor the adjustment, place a large plant or heavy object at the base of the stairs.

Stairway number 1: These are called "mandarin duck" stairs because beyond the entranceway the stairs (and the ch'i) split into the pull of the up and down staircases very similarly to the up and down motion the feet of a duck make. This type of stairs is often found in entranceways of split-level homes or homes that have an upstairs and a basement apartment accessed through the same entranceway. Because of the split in energy, these occupants are prone toward bickering, fighting, and having lots of differences. This can cause arguments in the lives of the families living in each apartment, at their place of work, or even among the two tenants living in the same building. Remedies: 1) if the stairs are a short distance from the door, hang a wind chime or crystal ball from the ceiling between the stairs and door, then decorate the railing with a vine or a cloth that connects both directions as one; 2) if the distance between the stairs and the doorway is longer than the tallest person in the house, in addition to the above remedy, add a plant in the entranceway to circulate positive ch'i and cool the residents' tempers.

Spiral staircases: Although they can be beautiful additions to most homes, they are usually frowned upon in Feng Shui. As discussed in chapter 1, each area of your home in Feng Shui has areas that correspond to different parts of the body. The spiral of this type of staircase is seen as a drill bit boring its way

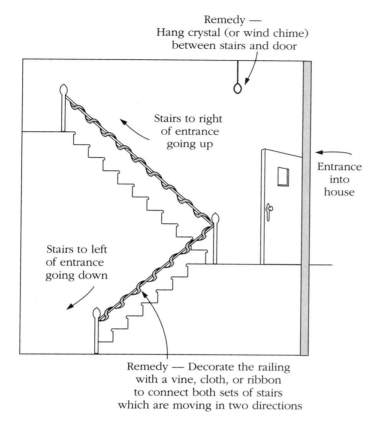

Remedy —
Hang crystal (or wind chime)
between stairs and door

Stairs to right
of entrance
going up

Entrance
into
house

Stairs to left
of entrance
going down

Remedy — Decorate the railing
with a vine, cloth, or ribbon
to connect both sets of stairs
which are moving in two directions

through a section of your home, thus a section of your body. In addition, the holelike opening at the top and between the risers allows for ch'i to escape and dissipate. If one already exists in the space that you live in, adjust it. *Do not* install one after you have moved into a new place, unless you consult a Feng Shui specialist first for the proper ritual and most auspicious date to begin the installation. These types of staircases can give rise to serious heart and respiratory problems. Remedy: add a bright light at the top of the stairs and hang a crystal ball on a nine-inch red string in the center of the ceiling directly above the stairs.

(5) Pillars/Posts/Columns

These types of structures can be quite stately and regal if properly placed in front of a home or government building. If the pillars are far enough apart and allow for ample space for the ch'i and individuals to pass through, then they will lift up and raise the ch'i of that structure. Indoor columns seen often in lofts and basement apartments tend to be more problematic because they usually are blocking an entranceway or obstructing a part of a view. These structures tend to split one's vision, causing the individual's ch'i to become distracted and unfocused. In addition, if the columns are square, they will then have four pointed edges that can create a feeling of threat to whoever sits in line with an edge. The pointed edges in Feng Shui act like a sharp knife or lecturing finger pointing directly at whoever crosses them. This can create a feeling of oppression or threat, or create a constant sense of being reprimanded without just cause.

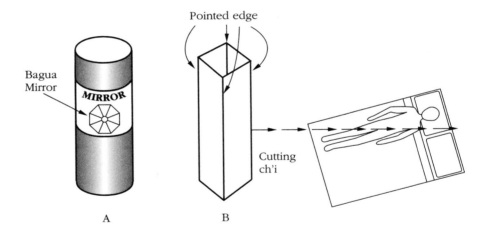

Column A is the better shape of the two columns because, being rounded, it softens the energy. Remedies: Place a Bagua or a round mirror on the column to symbolically create an opening in the structure, which will allow the ch'i to flow through and circulate more thoroughly, or decorate the column with a long tapestry or a faux finish. Column B is much more problematic because it has four pointed corners that jut out in a threatening way to all who are in their path. Remedies: mirror all four sides; soften the edges with hanging material,

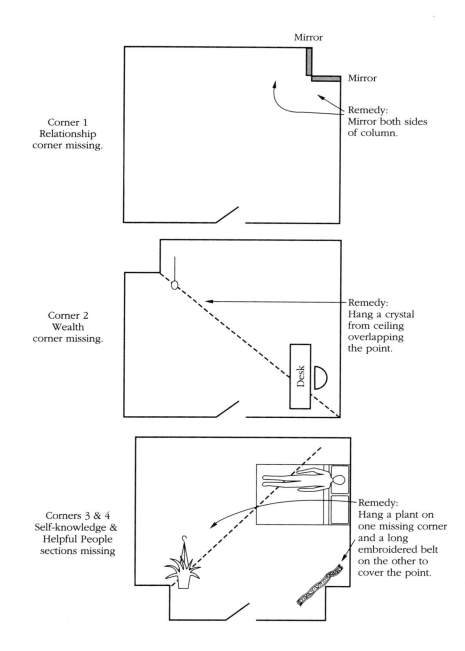

Corner 1
Relationship
corner missing.

Mirror

Mirror

Remedy:
Mirror both sides
of column.

Corner 2
Wealth
corner missing.

Desk

Remedy:
Hang a crystal
from ceiling
overlapping
the point.

Corners 3 & 4
Self-knowledge &
Helpful People
sections missing

Remedy:
Hang a plant on
one missing corner
and a long
embroidered belt
on the other to
cover the point.

decorative tassels, etc.; or round the column off with plastic cones or sheets of thin metal (e.g., reflective aluminum, stainless steel, or mylar).

(6) STRUCTURAL CORNERS

These are corners that are built into the framework of the building but also stick out from corners of your rooms. Many apartments and homes have them somewhere (unless all the rooms were designed as perfect squares or rectangles). Often, you don't even realize you have them until you go searching for them. It is very important to find and identify these structural corners because they indicate that a section of a gua is missing; thus, an aspect of your life is being weakened, receiving less energy or ch'i for that area. In addition, the point on the edge of the column affects your ch'i very much as if someone were aiming the point of a knife at you. It creates "cutting ch'i" energy, which can be very hazardous to your sense of safety and overall well-being. These corners become more dangerous based on what they cross through. If you have these corners, let your eye follow the line of energy that the point is cutting across (see illustrations 2 and 3) and check if the point crosses with your bed, desk, or any area where you spend a great deal of time.

Corner number 1 has the Relationship corner missing. Remedy: Mirror both sides of the column. Corner number 2 has the Wealth corner missing. Remedy: Hang a crystal from the ceiling overlapping the point. Corners 3 and 4 have the Self-knowledge and Helpful People sections missing. Remedy: Hang a plant on one side and a long embroidered belt down over the point of the other. These above adjustments are interchangeable. You can use your own creative ideas; just remember to offset or cover the point. A client of mine hung a beautifully colored kite over the point to disarm the "cutting ch'i" that was slicing through her daughter's bed while she slept.

(7) EXPOSED BEAMS

Exposed beams or decorative logs can be very oppressive and suppress the ch'i of whoever sits under them. The beams that you can't see won't affect you, but the ones that are visible can give rise to a host of problems ranging from headaches to broken ankles. The location of the beam and over what part of the body it hangs will determine the potential problem. When the body's ch'i

Remedy:
Hang two bamboo flutes
on an angle with red tassels.

ILLUSTRATION #1

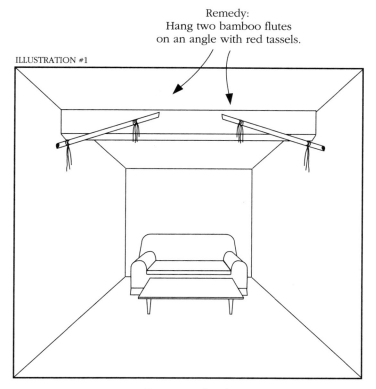

Beams overhead:
Remedy: Move furniture out from under beam;
if not possible, try to position furniture parallel to beam,
then use bamboo flute remedy.

is compromised, people's energy level can be affected, causing them to feel tired all the time and slow down their ability to think clearly. Beams that are over beds, desks, stoves, or entranceways tend to wreak the most havoc. *Bedroom beams* affect health and cause emotional problems. If the beam is over the feet, one can feel slowed down, missing many career opportunities; over the midtorso, problems with the digestive tract or weight; over the head, insomnia and headaches. *Desk beams* stifle creativity and affect work promotions; *stove beams* limit finances; *entranceway beams* limit opportunities for growth and expansion.

Overhead beam remedies: Move furniture out from under the beam; if this is not possible, try to at least position furniture parallel to the beam overhead; to lift the oppressive ch'i, affix two bamboo flutes to the beam hung on an angle with red cord and tassels to re-create the powerful shape of the Bagua (see illustration 1). *Important*: make sure the mouthpieces are at the *lower* end facing upward; decorate or hang a red fringe extending the length of the beam; use copper or silver tubing on the same angle as the flutes depicted in illustration 1.

(8) COLOR

Color is a very important aspect of Feng Shui interior design. The use of color is so vast that I have devoted a whole section to it in chapter 5. For our purposes here, we will briefly discuss the use of color as it relates to the Bagua. Each of the nine areas in the Bagua has a corresponding color. If you want to augment or enhance a particular area of your life, you can go to the corresponding area in your home or room and either paint it its matching color or add something to that area that is made of the same color.

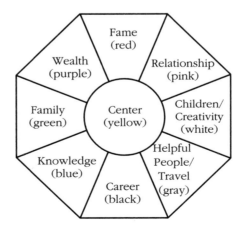

(9) BRIGHTNESS

Good lighting is very important. The sun, the closest star to the earth, is by far the most powerful source of light, for it brings in one of the main life forces provided by nature. Thomas Edison's drive to create indoor light was inspired by the natural light created by God. As with all good Feng Shui, we strive to align ourselves with all the forces of nature to create the beauty and the harmony of outdoors, inside. Adding additional lights, candles, and lanterns to areas that are dull, dark, and without the life force becomes a very effective way of uplifting the ch'i in the area where the lighting is placed.

(10) VOIDS/EMPTY SPACES

Many types of interiors, especially Japanese homes, are beautifully designed around the concept and serenity of negative space. But spaces that are not part of a design layout, such as empty rooms with no furniture or empty corners that are created by angled furniture, can create "dead space" and stagnate ch'i. This does not mean that every open or empty space has to be filled up completely. Try to be aware of the areas that you avoid often and tend to forget about using. These are the areas more often identified during a spring cleaning than during your regular housecleaning rounds. They are the corners that accumulate gigantic dust balls and store lost cat toys. Try to keep them clean and, if appropriate, fill them with colored lights that illuminate the space from below. Light can fill the space without cluttering it. Never fill the voids with clutter; that will just create a host of other Feng Shui problems.

   If you locate these types of spaces in your home, try to be creative and fill them by placing a small table behind the furniture piece with a vaseful of fresh flowers, or add a colored spotlight behind the chair to lift the ch'i and add the energy to the corresponding area of the Bagua in that room.

(11) CEILINGS

Ceilings should be high, well lit, and not give off an oppressive feeling. If the ch'i above your head feels compressed, it can create a variety of problems very similar to those created by overhead beams. Low ceilings subconsciously lower our expectations in life and make us feel "small and unworthy."

As a remedy for low ceilings, you can add mirrors or mirrored tiles to the ceiling and also to one full wall, or place several mirrors on different walls around the room. In addition, placing bright lights that face up or painting the ceiling a bright, uplifting color will also enhance the flow of ch'i.

(12) Doors

The doors in one's house represent the mouths of adults. Too many doors in an apartment will elicit many different "adult opinions," which can lead to a lot of quarreling and differences. Overall, the doors are important because they are the entranceways or the "mouths of the ch'i" that funnel the life force into different parts of the house. If they are not placed in an even or proper alignment, the doors in your apartment can adversely affect your health. Door positioning also refers to open entranceways without doors.

Good door positioning includes single doors that can be opened completely without obstruction, two doors that directly face each other and are *completely* aligned, and two doors that are opposite each other but never overlap.

Bad door positioning includes two doors directly facing each other where one is much bigger than the other. Often referred to as "Big Eats Little Doors," this is not a good door arrangement, especially if the smaller door leads to the more significant room (e.g., master bedroom versus closet). This creates an imbalance of authority for the individuals who sleep in that room. One remedy is to add a mirror to the outside of the larger door to symbolically double the image of the entranceway of the smaller door.

Two doors that face each other in a corridor or hallway and are slightly or severely unaligned are referred to as "Bad Bite Doors." This alignment cuts out a section of one's view as one approaches the parallel door, thus creating an optical imbalance similar to the way a "bad bite" can grate on a jawline in the mouth. This alignment can be harmful to one's health and cause career difficulties and family rifts. Constant exposure to this imbalance can cause a myriad of emotional problems. One remedy for "Bad Bite" doors is to hang a mirror or picture on each side of the overlapping wall to soften the edge of the frame of the door and re-create a balanced image on each side.

Too many doors in a relatively small area or hallway will disburse and dissect the ch'i in too many directions. Too many doors plus too many opinions equal lots of arguing. This arrangement can also weaken the kidneys and bladder, and cause other health-related problems. If there is a door at the end of a long hallway facing you and it leads to a bathroom or bedroom, problems can be further exacerbated, weakening the reproductive organs. The best remedy for too many doors is to add a *brass* wind chime to the center of the hallway to rebalance the ch'i and, in addition, add a Bagua or a round mirror to the door at the end of the hallway. This will serve to slow down and reflect back the force of the fast ch'i flow funneling down the hall affecting sleep, nerves, and intestines.

"Heart Piercing Doors" is the name given to a layout that has inadvertently placed three doors or doorways in a row. This design allows ch'i to flow too quickly causing stressful relationships, vulnerability along the intestinal tract, and problems related to the heart. A crystal hung between each doorway on a nine-inch red string, which will slow down and regulate ch'i, will remedy this situation.

"Slanted doors" are located on a wall that is tilted or slanted, due to intentional architectural or interior designs or to a snafu. These doors, from a Feng Shui perspective, are very dangerous and can portend unexpected set-backs, accidents, or difficulties. The angle of the door skews the ch'i, distorting it and thus creating a lot of unpredictable occurrences. If the wall that the door is on can be leveled or structurally righted, this is the best remedy. Otherwise hang a crystal on a nine-inch red string on both the inside and outside of the door or doorway.

(13) WINDOWS/SKYLIGHTS

In the same way the doors are the "mouths of the adults," the windows represent the "mouths of children." A good window-to-door ratio is three to one. More than that can cause an imbalance of ch'i, giving rise to many unproductive disagreements and fighting. Windows also represent the eyes of the body and are very significant when it comes to any vision-related problems or eye surgery. It is important that the windows be kept clean, with no broken panes, and in good working order, opening and closing easily. Be wary of small windows or not enough windows in a house, for the windows are what let in healthy, circulating ch'i.

Skylights follow the same rules as windows and spiral staircases. Keep them clean, clear, and *do not install them after* you have moved into an apartment unless you do a specific blessing ritual with a Feng Shui expert, in addition to picking an auspicious date. Opening up an area of your wall or roof is considered akin to performing surgery in Feng Shui, so it is important to do it with mindfulness and proper spiritual preparation.

To help mediate problems, add a plant in front of several of the windows to help circulate ch'i, or hang a crystal ball.

(14) FIREPLACES

Fireplaces can be a wonderful source of energy, for they impart warmth, comfort, and a sense of transformation. It's important for health purposes to keep them clean and working properly. It is best if they are located in the center of a room, for they are a very dynamic energy force that can negatively affect other areas of the Bagua and your life. If the fireplace is in the *Relationship* corner of the room or the house, this layout can cause many different types of relationship problems including fighting, bickering, and divorce. Place a mirror over the fireplace and several plants around it to help offset any negative fallout.

(15) AESTHETICS

Aesthetics are a very personal thing, left to the individual decorating taste of the occupants of each home. They should not be contingent upon one's finances but on one's ability to apply mindfulness and thought to the concepts of color, the placement of furniture and objects, and the care and maintenance of one's space, however big or small that may be. When you use interior design concepts and balance them with a working knowledge of energy, small spaces seem big and large places, grand. When you honor the space in which you live, you are actually honoring the piece of Mother Earth on which your home and life are built. The patch of land underneath us sends ch'i from the earth, from which all things in our life are nurtured and fed.

(16) OTHERS

The "other factors" are specific and personal to the individual and the contents in his or her home. They vary based on different situations. For the beginner's purposes, focusing initially on the fifteen Interior Factors That Influence Feng Shui and the Nine Feng Shui Principles in chapter 1 will provide a very solid and concise start. Use your intuition along with your gut feeling to make other adjustments that might not fall into the above categories. These "other interior factors" are what help you personalize the process.

HAVE PATIENCE WITH YOUR PROCESS: DON'T GET TOO OVERWHELMED

In chapter 1, the drawing of your floor plan was presented as the first juncture where many individuals will get stuck. Actually making the Feng Shui adjustments in your home runs a very close second. Just remind yourself that you are in a *process* and if for practical reasons you need more time, give it to yourself. The adjustments suggested previously are best done if completed within three weeks, six weeks, or at most, three months from beginning to end. Most of these situations or problem areas go hand in hand and are connected energetically with one another, so the changes that you implement need to be made during a specific time frame in order for the Feng Shui to fully make a complete shift. When all the different energies regroup during the same period, they create a more clear and conducive shift.

However, if you don't get around to making all the changes within the time frame above, still pursue the process! You just may need more time to acclimate to the changes as they start to affect your life. The main drawback to taking a longer time is that you are breaking up the continuity of the process. When the continuity becomes a bit choppy, it is harder to connect with the "coincidences" that start occurring in your life because of the Feng Shui work that you are doing. This might make you feel that nothing is happening or changing on an energy level, but keep in mind that many of the shifts are subtle and take time to unfold.

When you're working with energy, no matter what efforts you make, if the energy needs more time to kick in, it will take it.

During a consultation at a client's house, I made some adjustment recommendations based on the Feng Shui needs of her home. I suggested approximately six or eight different Feng Shui adjustments. I explained to her, as I do to most of my clients, that sometimes energy takes time to shift and its resistance to change may surface in many ways, some of which are blatant and others more covert. Many times the delays or problems that arise are reflective of one's own resistance to change on a subconscious level. This client had a small studio apartment in New York City and by the time I finished the consultation, she said to me that she would have all the adjustments in place by the end of the next day. I reminded her that sometimes the adjustment process takes more time and did not all have to be done within twenty-four hours.

Two days later she called me and said the day after she hung up her wind chime, it fell down from the ceiling and broke. She told me that she fixed it and immediately hung it back up again. To her surprise, it fell and broke again, this time permanently. With no free time in the week that followed, it took her ten more days before she had the time to purchase another wind chime. After ten days the ch'i in her home finally settled down and, in a calmer state of mind, she happily hung up her new wind chime and it stayed up. Her rush to make too many adjustments too quickly was not in alignment with the time frame that the ch'i needed to move into action.

Check when obstacles arise and ask yourself as honestly as you can, Is the obstacle about my avoidance and my procrastination or is the energy telling me to slow down and hold off for a few days? *Generally speaking*, if you tend to procrastinate about other things in your life, the resistance probably lies within you. If you have a tendency to rush anxiously through things because of a busy schedule or the need to be compulsive, the delay is probably the energy signaling you to slow down.

Remember: Your home mirrors your life *and* the energy patterns that you send out to the world. Try to decode the messages that your energy is sending out, for hidden in those signals is another aspect of who you are, waiting to be embraced, acknowledged, and transformed.

SUMMARY

Chapter 2 covered a lot of information on different items to incorporate into your Feng Shui assessment process. The summary given below will help you review the chapter and place the information into a sequence that will assist you in the next stage of your process.

1. Take out your Feng Shui notebook and/or folder.

2. Decide on your type of approach: subjective, objective, or combination (pages 33–34).

3. List three areas of your life you'd like to work on (page 34).

4. Be clear about your intentions (pages 35–36).

5. Review your wish list (step 3) and list all mundane solutions for each item (page 36). Take notes and schedule things you can do, and the type of help you can enlist.

6. Familiarize yourself with the ten different categories of Feng Shui adjustments.
   1) Lights/bright objects
   2) Mirrors
   3) Sound
   4) Life force
   5) Heavy objects
   6) Color
   7) Movement/mobile objects
   8) Power/energy objects
   9) Water
   10) Others

7. Familiarize yourself with the sixteen Feng Shui interior factors (page 40).
   1) Bed
   2) Desk
   3) Stove
   4) Staircases
   5) Pillars/posts/columns
   6) Structural corners
   7) Exposed beams
   8) Color
   9) Brightness
   10) Voids/empty spaces
   11) Ceilings
   12) Doors
   13) Windows/skylights
   14) Fireplaces
   15) Aesthetics
   16) Others

8. Combination approach to your assessment
   a) Review your wish list and make a mental note of the specific problems, keeping aware of how they may be exacerbated by the imbalances caused by problematic interior factors.
   b) Take out your notebook and, on separate pieces of paper, list each room or common area at the top of each page. If you have more than one floor, list the floor.
   c) Then make three columns on each page and give each column a title: Interior Factors; Problems; and Remedy/Adjustment Items. Then take out your floor plan and systematically go through the list

of interior factors and see if they are factors of concern in any of your rooms or common areas. If so, list each problem and remedy you intend to use.

9. Remember: You are just listing the information now, not making all the adjustments.

10. When your list is finished, go back to your floor plan and draw in little symbols of what and where your adjustment items will be. Put these little indicators directly on your floor plan, using your red pencil. Let all adjustments and changes be indicated in the color red.

11. When you are done with this, congratulate yourself and move on to the next chapter.

EXAMPLE CHARTS
BEDROOM—SECOND FLOOR

INTERIOR FACTORS	PROBLEM/ISSUE	SUGGESTED REMEDY/ ADJUSTMENT
Beam over bed	Affecting health	Hang two bamboo flutes
Relationship corner missing	No relationship	Hang mirror on wall

HALLWAY—FIRST FLOOR

INTERIOR FACTORS	PROBLEMS/ISSUES	SUGGESTED REMEDY/ ADJUSTMENT
Spiral staircase	Spirals through career center of house; might be affecting my job opportunities	Hang crystal and add bright light

THREE

HEALTH, WEALTH, AND RELATIONSHIPS

In the last chapter we addressed various internal factors that influence the Feng Shui of your home. In this chapter we will begin to look at specific rooms, their locations, and how they have an impact on your health, wealth, and relationships. One important catchphrase to keep in mind when undertaking the Feng Shui process is: ***The first room you see will have the most impact on your ch'i.***

This room will usually have the strongest impact on our energy. Identify the room that you see first and assess if its impact on your energy system is a strengthening or a weakening one. In general, common rooms such as your living room, den, or study are good rooms to be placed in a direct line with your entranceway. These rooms tend to convey a feeling of relaxation and imply that they are a place in which to socialize and think as well. Other rooms such as kitchens, bedrooms, and bathrooms tend to condition ch'i in ways that are less favorable and more taxing on one's energy system, as we will discuss later in the chapter.

The Four Most Important Areas in Your Home

Although all the rooms in your home are very important in constructing a Feng Shui profile of your space, the four areas that will have the most profound impact on your *health, wealth, and relationships* are your *entranceway, kitchen, bathroom, and bedroom.*

Entranceways

The entranceway and *everything leading up to it* is a direct reflection of who you are. The entranceway acts as a transitional space that bridges your home with the environment outside. Take some time and review the path that leads up to your doorway. What do you see along the way? Can you improve on it? Add color to the wall or door? Add some artwork in the hallway? Check the mat. Is it welcoming? If you don't have access to your entranceway, try keeping some dried, colorful flowers outside your door or place a cornucopia basket of fresh fruit in the corner of your doorway. Be as creative, simple, complicated, or original as you like. The Feng Shui objective is to create an entranceway that is inviting. If you are in an apartment house, check to see if your doorway is opposite an incinerator chute or near an elevator shaft. Both will cause some unnecessary problems.

In Black Hat Sect Feng Shui we refer to all entranceways as the "mouth of the ch'i." We call it this because the entranceway is the means by which the ch'i travels into your home and into its various rooms. The "mouth of the ch'i" is as vital to good Feng Shui as a clear and open trachea is to proper and robust breathing. When breathing, it wouldn't matter much if you had two large and healthy lungs if you only had a very small mouth through which to access air. Feng Shui is very similar. You might have a very spacious or beautiful home but a very small or congested entranceway, so the ch'i will not be able to get through and circulate into different areas inside. It becomes very important to keep all entranceways clean, clear, well lit, and have doors that open inward to the biggest part of the room. If your entranceway is narrow or if you would like to uplift and stimulate the ch'i flow, add a *brass* wind chime to the ceiling (so that the door hits the wind tag when opened) or put pleasant-sounding bells on the doorknob. Also, check to be sure your entranceway is *not* directly opposite a back door or a distant window. This arrangement will cause the ch'i to escape too quickly, exiting the house before it can accumulate and disburse. Hang a wind chime or a faceted crystal between the entranceway and the back door or window to stop the ch'i from dissipating.

Entranceway Adjustments

1. ENTRANCEWAY NEAR ELEVATOR: If your entranceway is directly beside the building's elevator, the ch'i in your entranceway will constantly fluctuate and not be able to accumulate with any sense of stability. Where the elevator is located and what "gua" your door is located in will determine which area in your life will be most affected. For example, if the doorway falls in your career section, you may experience many fluctuations in your career. Your career might follow the "up-and-down" motion that the ch'i follows due to the vertical movement of the elevator. One remedy is to place a rock or a *heavy object* such as a large vase just inside the doorway to hold down the ch'i energy, thus stabilizing your career. If your apartment directly faces the elevator, in addition, add a Bagua mirror to your front door to deflect the unstable ch'i of the elevator.

2. ENTRANCEWAY NEAR INCINERATOR CHUTE: If your entranceway is opposite or very close to an incinerator chute, you may experience lost opportunities or the inability to hold on to new beginnings before they root. One remedy is to place a Bagua mirror or a concave mirror on your front door to disarm the effect of the incinerator.

3. DOORS THAT OPEN OUT INSTEAD OF IN: In Feng Shui, the doors into homes and rooms should open *into* the space, bringing good ch'i in to be distributed throughout the house. If your door opens out instead of in, the process may be reversed, siphoning out energy from the living space and draining the occupants of valuable ch'i. One remedy is to have the door rehung or place a wind chime inside the entranceway and position a mirror outside, past the doorway to reflect and signal the ch'i back inside the house.

4. NARROW ENTRANCEWAYS: When an entranceway is long and narrow, it limits the flow of ch'i, causing an array of problems. "Narrow-mindedness" and rigidity can be reinforced by this entranceway as well as the feeling that your finances are being choked. On a physical level, respiratory problems, asthma, and difficult births are common outcomes when a person's entranceway is

long and narrow. One remedy is to add bright lighting and beautifully colored paints to the hallway area. A large mirror on the first wall you see to double the size of the space is also effective, as is a brass wind chime on the ceiling to lift and circulate ch'i.

5. DOORS THAT OPEN TO THE SMALLEST PART OF THE ROOM: Doors that open to the smallest part of the room tend to limit the ch'i flow and can affect the residents' emotional well-being and eventually manifest into a variety of physical problems. The neck and the head will be most susceptible to strain and injury, with stiffness and headaches being the most common ailments. One remedy is to move the hinges and the door around to face the largest part of room or place a mirror on the first wall you see to the left or right side coming into the room. Make sure that the mirror is full sized, reflects the larger part of the room, is as close as possible to the doorway, and does not cut off the head of any of the occupants when they are reflected in it.

6. ENTRANCEWAY THAT FACES A BLANK WALL: This type of entranceway into your home can be very oppressive and give you a constant message of "no hope" regarding your future and personal dreams. The "blank wall" entranceway, sometimes referred to as the "brick wall" entranceway, also minimizes and limits one's opportunities in life, especially regarding career matters. Hopelessness and lack of motivation are very common with this type of layout as well as headaches, neck pain, and sinus congestion. One remedy is to mirror the obstructing wall, to open it up to hope and opportunities. Add good lighting and a wind chime to circulate the ch'i.

7. DOOR THAT FACES A SPLIT VIEW: When you enter into this home's layout you do not see a complete blank wall but a vertical half wall that splits your view, causing one eye to focus on a wall a shorter distance away and the other eye to focus on one farther away. This will cause an imbalance of the optic nerve, sending mixed and confused messages to the brain. After repeated exposure to this type of layout, occupants may develop similar imbalances throughout all areas of their lives. Your emotional state is the most susceptible to this entranceway, and melancholy, bouts of depression, and anxiety disorders can result. One remedy is to add a mirror to the closest wall which is splitting the view or hang on the wall a picture that is multidimensional and illustrates depth and range. Pictures of flowing waters, mountain ranges, or sunsets are the best choices.

KITCHEN

The kitchen is a very important room in the home because it represents the element of fire, which fuels the energy force that activates our wealth. The old adage "Your health is your wealth" is particularly true in the Chinese culture. In fact, in Chinese, the word for wealth (Fu) sounds very much like the English word food (T'sai). The kitchen is looked upon as a sacred place where the cook is revered and "kitchen gods" are worshiped.

These beliefs are simple yet profound because they emphasize the importance of the food we eat and its impact on having healthy ch'i in our bodies and, in turn, a happy and prosperous life. The kitchen itself should be well lit and, if at all possible, be the room that absorbs the most natural sunlight. Eating your meals in the room with a view of the sun rising (breakfast) or setting (dinner) can be very auspicious. The natural energy of the sun can activate the flow and distribution of ch'i and create harmonious energy patterns to start and finish your day. The kitchen table should be uncluttered, with an even number of chairs placed around it, and located *out of the direct line of the entranceway*. The primary residents should occupy the seats that have the best view of the doorway. The cabinets that store the food and pots and pans should be organized, neat, and easily accessible. This will help you maintain a well-organized checkbook and financially related systems such as money markets, CDs, IRAs, etc. Fresh flowers and fruit-filled bowls on the table enhance the ch'i and suggest abundance. Refrigerators should be kept clean, defrosted, with the interior lights always working, and the refrigerator should not be directly next to or directly opposite the stove because the stove represents the fire element and wealth and the refrigerator (and sink) represent the water element. Water puts out fire, which will affect the energy needed to stimulate your finances. If your stove is beside your refrigerator, add a mirror to the stove area, which will deflect the image of the refrigerator and sink. The kitchen should not be too small in size or else money will feel very tight and limited. Mirrors on the walls will help open and expand the space. The **stove** and the area around the stove should be well lit, ventilated, and uncramped. If possible, there should be no oppressive overhangs such as microwaves or low air vents. The **stove** itself should be clean and all four burners should be in working order. All the burners should be used regularly and used in rotation, so that the Wealth energy will not stagnate. The burners represent wealth, so the more burners that are used, the more money will be earned. Doubling the amount of burners (through adding mirrors behind or on the side of the stove) will also increase your "money ch'i" and improve your finances. Although gas ranges are best, you can still apply these principles to electric stoves, hot plates, and the rice cookers.

Most important is the positioning of your stove (or the unit that you cook on) in the kitchen. The stove should be positioned in such a way that the cook has a direct and clear view of the doorway, *without being in a direct line with it*. The cook should *never* have his/her back to the door. This type of placement creates circumstances in which the cook can either be startled by a visitor entering through the door or be unaware of things that are going on behind his/her back. This is significant because the energy and the vibration of the kitchen will strongly influence the food that is prepared, cooked, and eaten there.

The kitchen ch'i can easily become unbalanced if the cook is tired and stressed out or if a lot of arguing tends to occur in that room. The negative energy that those situations emit becomes imbued in the walls, furniture, *and* food you eat and serve. Even an invited dinner guest who was not part of the conflict will still ingest the type of energy that surrounded the food when it was prepared. When you cook, be mindful of the energy you are exposing the food you eat to, for food is a powerful source of energy that not only fuels our ch'i but also nourishes us physically, spiritually, and emotionally.

If the kitchen is the first room you directly see when you enter your home, it can shape and influence your eating patterns for the worse. Consciously and subconsciously, we are all programmed to identify kitchens with food and eating. Walking into a space and constantly having our food memory triggered can cause a host of problems ranging from overeating and snacking to digestive and eating disorders. Children who grow up around kitchens that are right in the entranceways or with adults who are preoccupied with food are most susceptible to developing food-related problems.

Be sure to check the Bagua placement of your kitchen and locate the wealth corner of the room. Make sure you are not keeping your garbage pail in that corner, otherwise you may have a hard time holding on to your money. Having your garbage pail in the "wealth corner" of the room may imply that you are symbolically "throwing away your money" every time you take the garbage out.

Kitchen Adjustments

1. KITCHEN LOCATION: If the kitchen is the first room you see when you enter your home, you may develop food, digestive, and eating disorders. Frequent snacking and weight problems are also indicated. One remedy would be to hang a mirror on the outside of the closed kitchen door. If there is no door, place a wind chime or curtain to act as a divider between the entranceway and the kitchen.

2. CENTER OF THE HOUSE: If the kitchen is located across the center line of the house, the occupants' "physical ch'i" will be weakened along the center line of their bodies because the "fire element" of the kitchen is too strong in this position. This layout in a house or an apartment can cause stomach and intestinal problems such as gastritis, indigestion, ulcers, and other digestive-related illnesses. One remedy would be to hang a wind chime over the area where the cook stands and place a mirror on the outside of the kitchen door, which will symbolically draw the kitchen away from the house's center.

3. STOVE NEAR THE DOOR: A stove located too close to a back door that leads to the yard will result in money being lost and blown away. The constant opening and closing of the back door fans the "money ch'i" and causes it to dissipate and dwindle. Placing a divider between the stove and the back door as well as a heavy object (like a cast-iron cauldron) on the top of the stove will remedy this situation. In addition, adding a wind chime to the area above where the cook stands will help circulate the ch'i.

4. STOVES NOT FACING THE ENTRANCEWAY: The stove is one of the three most important interior factors in Feng Shui. Its proper positioning is crucial in terms of finances and income. Having the stove not facing the entranceway also means that the *cook's back is to the door*. This layout creates tension and can limit the occupants' ability to earn a comfortable living. One remedy is to move the stove to a more favorable position facing the door or place a mirror near the cook which will reflect the door and bring the entry clearly into view. You may also hang a faceted crystal on a nine-inch red string between the stove and the doorway to offset the problem.

5. STOVE WITH A BEAM OR STRUCTURAL COLUMN OVERHEAD: When a stove has a beam of any type hanging over it, the beam will limit and depress the finances

of the occupants of the house. The beam creates an energy shift which causes the ch'i around the stove to depress the fire energy that generates one's wealth. Two bamboo flutes on or in front of the beam will remedy this, but remember to hang them on a diagonal, creating a Bagua shape with the mouthpieces at the *lower end*. Make sure each flute has two red tassels, one on each end.

When the cook is facing the door and has ample light with good ventilation, we consider this "good Feng Shui." Although many factors enhance one's wealth quotient, this particular layout positively contributes auspicious ch'i to the occupants' financial potential.

BATHROOMS

The bathroom is also a very important room in the house, for it is governed by the element of water and water is most closely related to money and to our emotions. The bathroom is a very active area in which ch'i constantly flows in and out several times a day. It's the room that is most often used by a variety of individuals (family members, friends, and guests) who would not usually travel through other parts or rooms of your home. Ironically, for all the traffic and visitors it hosts, it is still the room that suggests and warrants the most privacy. This is a dichotomy of sorts, but in other ways it's a perfect analogy to the way we deal with our money and our emotional issues. Both these areas of our lives are influenced by other people and situations but remain the areas we are most inclined to be private about and not discuss. So it would be quite fitting and no coincidence that "money flow" and emotions are stored here. Because there is so much water energy accumulated in this room (sink, tub, and toilet), it's especially important to make sure that all the pipes and faucets are well maintained and kept drip free.

When leaks and drips occur, they should be fixed immediately; otherwise, you may start to experience money losses and financial problems. This room affects finances very differently than the "money energy" of the kitchen does. In the kitchen, the money ch'i is drawn in through the stove and burner area for attracting wealth. In the bathroom, the money energy is contained in the energy of the water and only affected adversely, when there are leaks or drips present.

Because of this, it is important to be mindful of the powerful effect that flushing the toilet has on your finances. All this might sound a bit funny, but when a toilet is flushed, the force of the water being pulled down creates a very powerful energy vortex. That sucking motion can drain your finances, particularly if your bathroom is located in the Wealth corner of your home. If you are building a house, try to construct the bathroom in any location other than the Relationship and the Wealth areas.

When designing a bathroom try to place the toilet out of direct view upon entering the room. If this arrangement is not feasible or a bathroom with a toilet visible from the entranceway already exists in your home, place a plant or some type of dividing object to distract one's attention from the commode upon entering the bathroom. This will act as a preventive measure, reducing the amount of "ch'i strikes" against your wealth and financial Feng Shui.

Regardless of where the bathroom is located, it's always good to keep the door closed and put the lid of the commode down before you flush. This will prevent the ch'i from escaping and all your money from being flushed away. If it's not always possible to keep the door closed, due to children or pets, keep a beaded or material curtain outside the entranceway to disburse the ch'i. Create a beautiful space that reflects your respect for privacy, personal hygiene, and the sacredness of the "water rituals" that take place there on a daily basis.

Daily routines such as bathing and brushing are purification processes that keep us clean, relaxed, and refreshed. These are some of the "self-care" functions that help us feel good about ourselves. Taking baths by candlelight and burning incense during showers turns these daily routines into special moments we give ourselves. Doing these rituals in a well-maintained space, freshly painted with small touches like dried flowers, special soaps, or colorful towels, reflects the care we show for ourselves. In turn, energy gets conveyed to the issues regarding our finances and positively affects how we feel about and draw in money. If we have "stressful energy" around making money it can be turned into a lighter, more pleasant experience. On the same note, the water energy also affects our emotional stability. When you are going through a difficult time, make especially sure that all the drips and leaks in the house are repaired. These water-related problems will shake up your emotional state and leave you feeling unstable and unable to cope with life's foibles.

Bathroom Adjustments

1. BATHROOM LOCATION: When the bathroom is the first room you *directly* see upon entering your home, it is usually not considered "good Feng Shui,"

because the conditioning process that occurs to one's ch'i tends to specifically affect issues of health *and* wealth. The continual view of one's bathroom places a lot of strain on the occupants' bladder and kidneys, causing those "water-related organs" in the body to be subconsciously overworked. The visual message also affects the urinary tract by giving the brain a false signal to constantly urinate. Place a mirror on the outside of the door and keep the door closed at all times.

2. BATHROOM FACING A KITCHEN: Your bathroom should not be directly facing the kitchen or be located inside of the kitchen area. This is not good Feng Shui for several reasons; first and foremost is that having the bathroom in such close proximity to the kitchen is poor and improper hygiene. Two separate functions take place in each room, and neither one is compatible with the other. The other reason is that the kitchen is ruled by the element of *fire*, and the bathroom is ruled by the element of *water*; water puts out fire and both, when placed together, can be very combative. This combination will weaken the digestive tract and individuals can develop stomach and intestine-related disorders. Place a full-length mirror on the outside of the bathroom door, always keep the door closed, and hang a faceted crystal on a nine-inch red string in the center of the ceiling in the kitchen area. If the bathroom door is in a direct line with the kitchen table or the stove, hang the crystal between the bathroom door and the stove/table instead.

3. BATHROOM FACING A BEDROOM: If your bathroom door is *directly* facing your bedroom or if you have a bathroom in your bedroom and its door crosses past any part of your bed, this is not considered good Feng Shui. The bedroom is represented by the element of *wood*, and the bathroom is represented by the element of *water*. Wood naturally seeks water for its growth and will draw on water energy, pulling the energy toward it and away from its original source. This will create an energy leak causing money problems as well as health-related problems of the digestive tract. In addition, if the bed overlaps any part of the bathroom door, the person lying closest to the bathroom and whatever body areas overlap the entranceway will be most affected. Place a mirror on the outside of the bathroom door and hang a faceted crystal on a nine-inch red string between the bathroom and the bed. Keep the bathroom door closed at all times.

4. BATHROOM IN THE CENTER OF THE HOUSE: If the bathroom is located along the center line of your house, it will adversely affect the Feng Shui of your finances. All your money will be flushed away and, in general, you will have a hard time with business-related opportunities. The center of the house is also the center of the Bagua and represents all the other things in your life that are not represented in the other eight guas. Keeping this area stable is very important and significant for your life's Feng Shui. Place mirrors on all four walls and hang a crystal on a red string nine inches long from the center of the ceiling to remedy a centrally located bathroom.

5. BATHROOM AT THE END OF A LONG CORRIDOR: When the bathroom is located at the end of a long corridor, with its door directly facing you, it tends to weaken the occupants' intestinal and reproductive systems. The length and narrow shape of the corridor tends to accelerate the ch'i, causing it to pick up speed as it moves swiftly down the hallway. This creates a forceful push of energy that can be very disruptive to the bathroom ch'i, even if the door is closed. Keep the bathroom door closed and place a mirror on the outside of the door to slow down and deflect the ch'i. In addition, add a brass wind chime or a faceted crystal on a nine-inch-long red string to the center of the hallway to break up the force of the ch'i.

6. TOO-SMALL BATHROOM: If you have a relatively small bathroom, your ability to remain focused and feel directed will be constricted. Many individuals do their best thinking in the bathroom, using this private time to rethink the important and mundane issues of the day. A limited space will not generate the ch'i that supports this process. One remedy is to make the room comfortable and beautiful! Add candles and fresh flowers. Install bright lighting and maintain proper ventilation. Paint the room a light, cheery color, add mirrors to expand the room, and hang a wind chime from the ceiling to circulate and raise the ch'i.

7. BATHROOM LOCATED IN THE WEALTH AREA OF THE HOME OR ROOM: If your bathroom is located in the Wealth area of your home or room it will strongly impact on your ability to generate and hold on to money earned. The water element of money, combined with the forceful vortex created by the flushing of the toilet, will have you constantly "flushing your money away" and the "wealth ch'i" that goes with it. One remedy would be to keep the door closed and the lid shut (especially during flushing). In addition, place a rock or any

heavy object such as a large floor vase near the toilet to counteract the flushing motion and hang a faceted crystal on a nine-inch-long red string in the center of the bathroom.

BEDROOM

Although all the rooms in your home are important in Feng Shui, the bedroom is probably the room that is the most significant regarding health and relationship issues—mainly because we spend one third of our lives sleeping, which translates to being in our bed/bedroom for one third of our lives. While we are sleeping, our bodies use that time for resting, refueling, and repairing. As we sleep, the energy in our body moves into a relaxed state, making it very susceptible and impressionable to the energy that exists around it. If the energy in the bedroom conveys a message of nurturing and love, then the body will bask in that comforting vibration all night. If the bedroom conveys a message of chaos and clutter, then that's the energy your room is giving to your body, and in turn, that's the energy your body is conveying to your health and relationships.

Keep in mind that in the world of energy, "like attracts like." If you want to strengthen, enhance, or draw a special relationship to you, make sure your bedroom reflects all the things you would want in that relationship. Then try to create the room so that it conveys those same feelings. After a while, the feeling of your room will be picked up and absorbed by your energy while you are sleeping. This, in turn, will help shape your personal ch'i, drawing to it the same type of energy and things that will mirror the type of energy that you are sending out.

When designing your room by the principles of Feng Shui, it is important to keep certain concepts in mind. The three most important factors that go into good bedroom Feng Shui are: 1) the correct positioning of your bed; 2) the overall feeling that your bedroom conveys; and 3) the condition of the Relationship corner in your bedroom. Your bed should always face the doorway without being in a direct line with it, and your door should always open to the largest part of the room. This places you in the most commanding position of the room and gives you a firmer grip on your relationships and their related issues. Check if the headboard is loose or shaky and, if so, repair it immediately; otherwise you may fall prey to a rocky or unstable relationship. In addition, a poorly placed bed will also create a host of problems related to health and general well-being, ranging from insomnia to depression. Do an impromptu check under your bed and see what is being stored there. If it is very dusty or there are clothes stored there that are never used, it's really time to clear it out. Energy tends to stagnate and not circulate under those conditions. If the objects have sentimental meaning like old love letters or pictures of past lovers, they will further block your "love life" energy. If you really want to shift the energy in this room, get rid of these mementos completely or at least store them somewhere else outside the house. Check the items that you are sleeping over and that exist around you because they will all affect and influence your relationship energy. To really get a fresh start after a relationship ends, get a new mattress or at least buy some fresh, new sheets for a fresh, new beginning.

The room itself should be uncluttered, free of loose magazines and unread books. *No work-related material, especially computers, should be kept in this room.* The bedroom should *only* be used for sleeping and making love. Any other objective creates a duel energy that gives the room and your ch'i mixed and confusing messages. An occasional book now and then is okay, but check out the subject matter first. If the book is a horror story or a love saga about someone whose partner has left him or her suddenly this is not a message to be on your mind before going to sleep. The energy of any book will stay with you long past the time you are reading it. If your goal is to get into a long and happy relationship, then you need to read loving, positive words before falling asleep.

The same principles apply to having a television in the bedroom, especially if you watch the news and all the negative messages that it relays to you each night. Even if you don't watch the news or use your computer for work-related matters, these units give off high levels of electromagnetic energy, even long after they have been shut off. Studies have shown that prolonged exposure to these electromagnetic energy fields can cause many immune-related illnesses. In addition, smaller electrical units such as clock radios, telephones, and answering machines, should all be kept at a safe distance from one's head and body (approximately four feet or more) during sleep time. Electric blankets should not be used at all or only turned on to heat up the bed *before* bedtime and disconnected once you get into bed.

Make your bedroom a wonderful sanctuary that reflects who you are and what you want in your life. Light and sound lift the ch'i, so be sure that your overhead lamp has a bright bulb in it (100 watt), even if you only use it once in a while just to find your socks. Have softer, more complimentary lighting available such as colored bulbs and candlelight, along with special music for relaxation and romance.

Mirrors are a great addition to any bedroom, but try not to have one placed directly across from your bed. Your ch'i tends to rise up at night and could be startled unexpectedly by its direct reflection. Other uses of mirrors that are more favorable include hanging a mirror in a narrow entranceway to open up one's opportunities or placing a round mirror in the Relationship corner of the bedroom to promote compassion. If you're experiencing communication problems in your relationship, try hanging two round mirrors on opposite walls, facing each other, to dispel any misunderstandings or conflicts.

Last but not least, the condition and objects in the Relationship corner of your bedroom are *very important*. Take your Bagua out, place it over your bedroom, and locate the Relationship corner of the room. Check to see if it is altered in any way, if the section is missing completely, or if there are any problematic "interior factors" that need adjustments. If so, make the necessary changes suggested in chapter 2. Make sure that the corner is clutter free and decorated with mindfulness and clear intentions. Add to it fresh flowers, candles, pictures of you and your partner. Check that the art on the walls reflects the energy of what you want to draw into your life. Pictures of your family or artwork depicting a morose scene might be wonderful from a personal or artistic point of view, but it is not the best message to convey in the Relationship/Marriage corner of your bedroom. You don't have to get rid of these things completely; you just may need to place them in a more conducive spot in the house. If the size of your room allows you to place your bed in the relationship corner of the room *and* have it meet all the requirements of proper bed positioning, then you have a very special Feng Shui arrangement that will positively contribute to your goal of obtaining a healthy and happy relationship. Please remember the importance of ***mundane solutions,*** especially when it comes to relationship difficulties. If you're seriously looking for a relationship, then try to be open and take part in different types of activities that will connect you to other people. If you are in a relationship and you are experiencing some difficulties, don't forget to utilize the myriad of counseling and other related services that are available to you. If you are really determined to change a pattern of energy that is no longer working for you, then make sure you pull out all the stops and do whatever is necessary to bring to you the happiness you deserve.

Bedroom Adjustments

Good versus Bad Bed Positioning

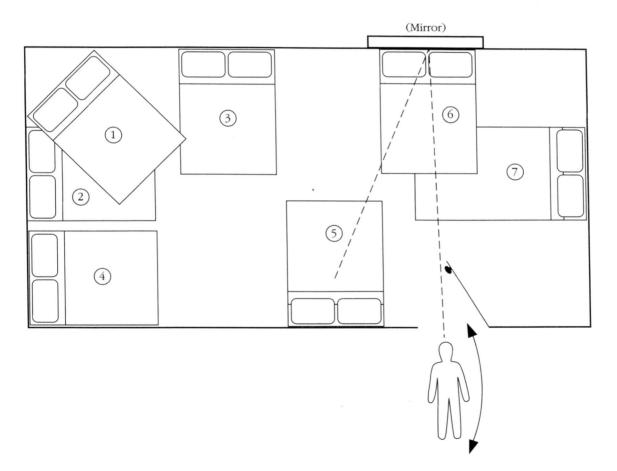

Good Bed Positions: Bed positions 1 through 4 are all good Feng Shui positioning. Bed number 1 is in the best position because it not only faces the door but it also has the widest view of the room without being in the entranceway. Beds 2 and 3 are in the next best position; although they face the entranceway correctly, they do not have the widest view of the room. Bed number 4 is the least favorable of all the best bed positions because although it faces the entranceway, it does not have the widest view of the room, in addition to having limited space around one side of the bed. This arrangement can throw off the equality in the relationship and oppress the ch'i of the individual who sleeps on the side with less space. A remedy would be to move the bed over to center it on the wall and place a mirror anywhere in the room that would allow it to reflect a clear view of the entranceway.

Bad Bed Positions: Bed position number 5 is the best of the worst bed positions because although it doesn't allow occupants to face the doorway, the situation can be easily remedied by placing a mirror on the wall where spot A is located. This will create an alternate angle, allowing the occupants to see the doorway in the mirror's reflection. Bed positionings 6 and 7 are the most *dangerous* of all because both beds are in a direct line with the doorway, or the "mouth of the ch'i." The mouth of the ch'i is a very powerful area through which the energy force passes several times a day. That energy force can wreak havoc on the body, especially the parts of it that are parallel to the entranceway. In addition, the body's positioning in bed 6 has the sleeper with his or her feet facing out the door—not a very good omen because this position is indicative of the feet-first way in which corpses are usually carried out. One remedy is to move the bed out of the entranceway and into a more auspicious position. If this is not possible, place a divider between the bed and the doorway or hang a faceted crystal on a nine-inch red string between the bed and the door.

Note: If the door in the bed-positioning illustration had been featured on the left side of the bedroom in the Knowledge gua, the rules would remain the same by just reversing the various bed positions.

1. BEDROOM LOCATION: If the first room you *directly* see when you enter your house is your bedroom (or your bed, if it is a studio apartment), you will tend to be lazier, more tired, or preoccupied with sex. Keep the door closed and

place a mirror on the outside of the door. If the room has no door, place a wind chime or a faceted crystal on a nine-inch red string between the door and the bed.

2. MASTER BEDROOM BELOW CENTER LINE OF HOUSE: Draw an imaginary line through the center of your house. If your bedroom is located below this line, it is in a weaker energy position than if it were located above it. The farthest area from the front door is always the best position for the master bedroom. This affords the occupants the most control over their domain and creates a climate of stability and security in their relationships. If the master bedroom is below the center line, to regain control and stability of your relationship and life hang a mirror on the wall closest to the center line to symbolically pull the room back into the upper part of the house.

3. BEDROOM THAT IS NEXT TO OR FACES A BATHROOM: If your bedroom is next to your bathroom, generally this is not a problem unless you sleep with your head against the wall that connects the two rooms. The constant movement from the water energy of the bathroom tends to create an imbalance that can throw off the body's delicate chemistry (most of our body is made up of water). This can create many different physical and emotional problems. You can move the bed to another wall, or if there is no other option, hang a crystal over the bed on a nine-inch red string, paint the wall a different color from the room; and incorporate a transcendental cure to reinforce the adjustments. If the bedroom door directly faces a bathroom, disburse the energy by placing a wind chime or crystal on a nine-inch red string between the two rooms. If the bathroom is located off the bedroom and the bed crosses with the bathroom door, this is not good Feng Shui. This arrangement can affect all the areas of the body that cross with the doorway, making the residents especially susceptible along the digestive and urinary tracts to infections and illnesses. If you can, move the bed or place a crystal or divider between the bed and the door. In addition, keeping the bathroom door closed and putting a mirror on the outside of the door will deflect any negative ch'i.

4. BEDROOM WITH A MISSING OR OBSTRUCTED RELATIONSHIP CORNER: If your bedroom has the Relationship corner missing, your ability to form a stable relationship can be affected, or stress can be placed on the relationships you

are already in, creating problems that can lead to separations and divorces. A mirror on the wall to open up and re-create the missing space or a crystal hung from the ceiling approximately six inches from the corner point will remedy a missing Relationship corner. Add a lush plant or fresh flowers to activate the relationship ch'i.

5. BEAMS, PIPES, OR STRUCTURAL COLUMNS OVER THE BED: Beams or any type of overhang that is visible over your bed can be very divisive to a relationship, especially if the beam only falls across one partner in the couple. Conflicts, disagreements, and communication problems can arise causing everything from petty fighting to divorce. In addition, beams in general are an oppressive factor, but when located over a bed they can really affect the quality of one's health. The part of the body that the beam crosses over tends to be the most vulnerable to health-related problems ranging from headaches and insomnia to leg and digestive disorders. Move the bed out from under the beam or turn the bed around and position it parallel to the beam. Either way, hang two bamboo flutes on the beams that are most problematic. Make sure the flutes are hung with red string and two red tassels, on an angle with the mouthpieces at the bottom (see page 49). Bless flutes with the Three Secret Reinforcement outlined in chapter 7.

6. BEDROOM IN THE RELATIONSHIP AREA OF YOUR HOME: If by chance or choice your bedroom happens to be located in the relationship area on your overall house floor plan, this arrangement can be very auspicious for the individuals who sleep in this room. If you have determined that the room is in fact located there, then take the Bagua map and locate the relationship corner of that **room**. The area where the Relationship corner of the house overlaps with the Relationship corner of the room becomes a very *powerful spot* in one's home. Make all the Feng Shui adjustments that the room requires and create a beautiful corner where your "relationship ch'i" can thrive and blossom.

7. BED UNDER A SLOPING CEILING: If your bed happens to be under a sloped ceiling, this arrangement can be very oppressive to your ch'i and greatly affect the area of the body that the slope passes over. If your head is under it, headaches, emotional and financial pressures, and strange, uncommon ill-nesses can be the result. If your feet are under the slope, you may experience difficulty moving forward in your career and in your relationships. If it is not

possible to move the bed out from under the slope, mirror the sloped ceiling to lift the oppressive ch'i or hang pictures on the slope that show depth and movement (such as scenes of water, horizons, or mountain ranges).

8. BEDROOM THAT ENHANCES FERTILITY: Although many factors, both physical and karmic, go into the reasons why some individuals can conceive while others cannot, from a Feng Shui perspective, there are several things one can do to enhance the fertility ch'i of the bedroom. One remedy is to place your bed in the children's gua of your bedroom and hang a faceted crystal (on a nine-inch red string) in that area along with some "children-friendly" objects such as stuffed animals, toys, and children's books. This will stimulate the ch'i in the children's area of your bedroom and create a welcoming environment for the incoming child.

SUMMARY

At this point of the Feng Shui assessment of your home, you have gathered a wealth of information regarding the different kinds of internal and overall room factors to look for and consider. Review the charts below and add to your Feng Shui assessment list the additional changes you will need to make. Keep in mind that all the adjustments will require an additional step to seal and enhance their effectiveness. This final, but all important step is called the *"Three Secret Reinforcement."* This closing procedure will be discussed in detail in chapter 7.

ENTRANCEWAYS

Good Ch'i

1. Entranceway is wide, open, and well lit
2. Books, artwork in entranceway
3. Opens to largest part of room
4. Painted bright, uplifting colors
5. Positively reflects who you are
6. Welcoming to all who enter

Bad Ch'i

1. Narrow entranceway
2. Dark entranceway
3. Clutter in entranceway
4. Directly faces a back door/ window or obstructive wall
5. Near an elevator
6. Near an incinerator chute

KITCHENS

Good Ch'i

1. Bright and cheery
2. Clean and uncluttered
3. Stove/cook face door
4. Located in wealth corner of house
5. Sun-filled room
6. Occupants enjoy spending time here

Bad Ch'i

1. Beam over stove
2. Cook doesn't face door
3. All burners do not work
4. Stove opposite refrigerator or sink
5. Bathroom is located in kitchen area
6. Located in center of house

BATHROOMS

Good Ch'i

1. Well maintained
2. Door is kept shut
3. Lid on toilet is kept down
4. Plants/flowers
5. Well lit and ventilated
6. Colorful and welcoming

Bad Ch'i

1. Water leaks/faucet drips
2. Bathroom located in wealth corner
3. Commode is in direct view
4. Running toilets
5. Bathroom crosses bed area
6. First room you see

BEDROOMS

Good Ch'i

1. Bed faces entranceway
2. Bedroom "feels good"
3. Reflects who you are and what you want in a relationship
4. Has diverse lighting
5. Beautiful Relationship corner
6. Flowers and plants

Bad Ch'i

1. Bed crosses doorway
2. Missing Relationship corner
3. Beam/sloped ceiling over bed
4. Clutter/clothes/papers/books
5. Computer/work in bedroom
6. Shaky headboard

F O U R

DESIGNING WITH CONSCIOUSNESS: LOW-COST–HIGH-GAIN TIPS

Often people are very intimidated by the idea of designing their own home. They believe that a beautifully designed home is contingent mainly on good taste, style, a creative sense, and lots of money. Well, I'd be remiss if I denied that those things aren't important factors, but important to only one type of approach to designing interiors. Another way to create a wonderful place to live or work in is to design your space according to the principles of **energy**. Feng Shui design teaches us different ways to use placement as a form of art and energy as a tool for design. When you "*design with consciousness*," you employ a very different approach to creating a special place—a place that not only is wonderful to come home to, but also supports your life's goals. Many of us do not have the luxury of additional funds to furnish or redecorate our homes the way we would ideally want to. The beauty of Feng Shui is that it allows you to make small and simple changes that produce many big and dramatic effects in your life. Its objective is to help you make your home the best it can be, within a *budget* that you can comfortably afford. Then, as we begin to rebalance and shift the energies in our own homes, slowly, one house at a time, we collectively contribute to an overall shift in the energy of the whole planet. By just simply focusing on your own space, caring for it, and making it the best it can be, you will inadvertently assist the planet in taking a quantum leap forward. As we move rapidly into the twenty-first century, take pride in knowing that you directly participated in helping the planet restore its original alignment with the healing forces of nature.

As you have seen in the last chapter, it only takes the specific placement of furniture and a few interior factors to enhance or decrease your health, finances, or relationship opportunities. In chapter 3, we emphasized the most important rooms in your home—the entranceway, kitchen, bathroom and bedroom areas—and how the different layouts in those rooms can affect your life. In chapter 4, we will take a look at the other rooms that are used less frequently or for more specific functions. In addition, we will explore other Feng Shui principles and design tips that can be applied to all the areas of your home, helping you to create a space that has been . . . *"designed with consciousness."*

LOW-COST–HIGH-GAIN DESIGN TIPS

1. Establish reference lines.
2. Use objects as dividers.
3. Remember the theory: Less is more.
4. Diffuse long structures.
5. Avoid blank walls.
6. Always face the door.
7. Check above your head.
8. Remove sharp edges.
9. Personalize your space.

ESTABLISH REFERENCE LINES: When hanging pictures, artwork, or mirrors, try to use the "sight lines" of the main individuals who occupy your home to provide a reference line for the correct height to hang the item. Often we hang objects on walls without much thought and place them either too high or too low. This common design error causes the top reflection of an individual's head to be cut off or a part of the mouth or throat to be cut off at the bottom. This is not good

Feng Shui, for it can create imbalanced ch'i, which can cause headaches, or it can cause you to be cut off from your emotions and have many career and relationship opportunities pass over your head. If there is more than one adult in the house, try to average out a height that would accommodate the sight line of all individuals. If there is more than one picture in the room, take a look around the room making a complete circle, and check to see if they are generally in the same height line.

USE OBJECTS AS DIVIDERS: When you want to divide a room to create a work space or a play area for children, instead of installing a wall or a very tall screen use half bookshelves, tall plants, a row of pottery, or pile up old clothes trunks for an extrafunky look. Tapestries or sheer or beaded curtains can be hung from the ceiling and used as a wonderful divider, while still letting air and light through. Be creative, work with different objects that you wouldn't usually think would go on the floor or would be hung from the ceiling.

REMEMBER THE THEORY LESS IS MORE: Take a walk through your rooms and check the amount of space around the different pieces of furniture in your house. Look for the areas that seem a bit cluttered and confined. Especially check around your bed, desk, stove, and living-room furniture. Take notice if these areas are tightly packed in; if they are, try to create some space or get rid of the excess furniture or clutter. In Feng Shui, it's better to have less furniture and more room than more furniture and less room. The ch'i needs room to circulate properly in order for it to support and enhance your life. If you are having a difficult time moving around your home comfortably, you will probably have a hard time negotiating certain aspects of your life as well.

DIFFUSE LONG STRUCTURES: Long, narrow structures in Feng Shui tend to accelerate energy and create a dominant energy force, causing adverse situations for the residents who live in that house. If you have a corridor, hallway, or driveway that extends fifteen feet or more, you can slow down the ch'i by dividing up the structure in intervals. Every five feet, hang a picture on the wall, change the direction of the floor tiles, or place a small throw rug on the floor. If the structure happens to be your driveway and facing your house, then place flagstones or flowerpots every five feet to reduce the speed of the ch'i outside.

Fast ch'i can cause everything from missed opportunities to strange illnesses and freak accidents.

AVOID BLANK WALLS: Take notice of the wall space that you face going in and out of *all* the entranceways and rooms of your home. Check and see if, when entering and leaving a room, you face any blank walls. If you do, place a mirror, tall floor plant, artwork, etc., on or against the blank wall that you face. In Feng Shui, it is very important that our homes convey to us a perpetual message of hope and encouragement. When we are constantly faced with a blank wall, our ch'i is conditioned to believe that there is no opportunity up ahead, nothing to look at or forward to. A blank wall makes us look away, thus causing our ch'i to be thrown off balance or to one side. Every wall does not have to be filled with objects. It is most significant when the wall in question is in an entranceway or at the end of a hallway.

ALWAYS FACE THE DOOR: It is a Feng Shui *"faux pas"* to sit with your back to the door. Position the significant pieces of furniture (bed, desk, stove, couch, dining chair), to face the door (not in a direct line with it). Having your back toward a doorway implies that "things can go on behind your back" without your ever knowing. Not facing "the mouth of the ch'i" (entranceways) is an uncomfortable and subordinate position for your ch'i to be in. We have all heard the sayings "being talked about behind one's back" or "being a back stabber"; they both have negative connotations. Even if you are living alone and there is no chance of anyone entering the apartment while you are there, your ch'i will still be affected by having your back to a doorway. The areas of your life that can be affected can range from your finances to your health.

CHECK ABOVE YOUR HEAD: Check for large pieces of furniture that tower over your head while you are sitting at a desk or sleeping in your bed. These objects will compress your ch'i and throw the balance of your physical energy off, creating a sense of stress, pressure, and lethargy. Large, formidable pieces of furniture also tend to absorb a lot of the ch'i in a room, drawing it away from other needed areas. If these pieces of furniture are a dark color or made out of a dark wood, they will drink up the energy even more. In bedrooms, check armoires and closets; in other rooms, check for tall bookcases, overhead shelves, and of course, structural beams.

REMOVE SHARP EDGES: Sharp edges in Feng Shui act like threatening fingers—harassing, accusing, lambasting, and pointing at the target of their wrath. These sharp edges can show up on structural corners, coffee tables, desks, etc. Not all of them are potentially dangerous—just the ones that are in a direct line with a place in the house where the occupants spend a lot of time: for instance, a sharp desk corner that directly faces the entranceway to the room, pointing at everyone who enters the room. These angles are of most concern when the line of their points cuts through one's bed, desk, favorite chair, etc., and directly impacts on that individual's ch'i. With your eyes, follow the line of the point and see if it passes through any significant area. If it does, try angling the furniture piece, placing a cascading plant to cover the edge or hanging a crystal ball (on a nine-inch red string) between the point and the person. In general, try to purchase furniture that has more rounded edges, in shapes of circles, ovals, or half circles. These shapes tend to soften the energy and create a smoother flow of ch'i.

PERSONALIZE YOUR SPACE: Make sure that your home feels and looks like *YOUR* home. Bring personal items in that reflect your likes and interests. If you are a sports enthusiast, make sure that you have a couple of books on baseball or tennis displayed on your coffee table. If you enjoy sewing or needlepoint, hang your artwork or quilts on the wall. Graduated? Show off your degrees and proudly hang them on the wall. Locate the little things that reflect who you are and display them with high esteem. This doesn't mean that designing a space should be a free-for-all, where everything and anything goes. Golf clubs thrown haphazardly in the hallway blocking an entranceway is not only bad design but bad Feng Shui as well. ***Don't use your lack of design skills as an excuse for lack of mindfulness!*** If you combine your common sense and your Feng Shui knowledge with clear, **CONSCIOUS INTENTIONS**, you won't go wrong. If you need extra help, don't hesitate to enlist the advice and the opinions of friends and professional designers, but in the end *make sure all final decisions are yours*. I've been to numerous homes where clients had previously hired interior designers, spent tons of money, and had them pick out the design scheme, only to realize later on that they hated it.

Significant Others: Satellite Rooms That Help Support Your Feng Shui Process

Dining Room

The kitchen is where the food is prepared, but the dining room is where the food is eaten. The dining room has a dual vibration that gracefully combines the social energy of the living room with the nurturing and food energy of the kitchen. This room can be a very dynamic place, especially if it is used often for daily meals and frequent gatherings. The energy that is exchanged here not only nourishes us through the food we eat, but also stimulates our intellect and supports our intrinsic need to be social and be part of a group. Because so many different energies are activated in this room, it becomes very important that the Feng Shui be well balanced and supportive to all who dine there.

The dining table in this room should be either round, oval, or octagonal, with an *even* number of chairs or seats around it. Make sure that the chairs are comfortable. Often we buy furniture that is beautiful to look at but not very comfortable to sit or eat on. Check that there is enough elbow room between the seats and behind the chairs. This will allow for enough personal autonomy, along with ample interactive space for comfortable eating and good conversation. Make sure that there are no broken or unbalanced chairs or table legs. If there are, your guests will not feel on an equal footing and the main residents of the house will draw to them shaky opportunities and unstable finances. To ensure a commanding stance over finances, the breadwinners of the house should always occupy the chairs that face and have the best view of the entranceway. Try not to clutter the table with excessive plates and dinnerware when eating meals or entertaining guests. Centerpieces and candles can be a beautiful addition to any table, but make sure that they are not too tall or they will divide the table in half and be distracting to guests' ch'i, thus causing unnecessary anxiety. Make sure the room's atmosphere is conducive to the length of time that your dinner will span; larger dinners, including dinner talk, serving time, main courses through desserts and coffee, can last for several hours. If you enjoy entertaining, use the dining room frequently, or just want to keep your wealth ch'i stimulated, place a **faceted crystal on a nine-inch-long red string** or a **wind chime above the dining room table**. Check that there are no beams or obstructions over the table or over the area where anyone sits; and make sure that the table is not directly in the entranceway. If it is, either move the table or adjust the overhang by using two bamboo flutes (see p. 49). If you cannot move the table out of the entranceway, try hanging a crystal (on a nine-inch red string) between the table and doorway to deflect the impact on the occupants' ch'i. Suspending lamps and chandeliers is okay, as long as they don't hang too low and obstruct the view of the diners. The dining room is a place where people come together to eat and socialize; the time that is spent there preps the group and sets the tone for the rest of the evening.

Remember the importance of **CONSCIOUS INTENTIONS**! If you want a relaxed, informal gathering, make sure your dining room conveys that message. If you want to create a more formal dinner atmosphere, straight-backed chairs, your best china, and preset tables may convey that message. Any visible artwork or pictures should reflect comforting images or encourage creative conversation. There should be no loud music or irritating stimuli: these powerful energy factors tend to overactivate the ch'i in the room causing the diners to feel hurried and rush through their meals. If your dining room is the room where you actually sit down and eat the food that you have prepared, then be sure to create a room that is relaxed, friendly, and allows for perfect digestion.

LIVING ROOM

The living room is a good room for the occupants of a house to first see upon entering. It should clearly and loudly convey the message "Relaxation and leisure time welcomed here." It's the room where you go to put your feet up, read a good book, or watch some television. It should be comforting, soothing, and remind you at all times that you're "off duty" and on a long sabbatical. Keeping a consistent theme of "rest and relaxation" in this room is very important. Because in our lives today we are faced with so many responsibilities, ranging from work to raising children, when we establish a space in our lives where we can go and be reminded that *life is not all work*, then we have created an important place where our ch'i can be replenished and unburdened.

Because the living room is such a wonderful place to be, we are often tempted to bring our work and stress-related things to this area. But bringing work into this area can create mixed messages on an energy level, so caution should be used when considering using this space for alternative things. The living room should reflect who you are and the ways in which you enjoy comfort. If you enjoy watching old movies, reading a good book, or listening to rock music, then your space should be designed so that your VCR tapes, CDs, or favorite novels are easily accessible. If you watch a lot of television, make sure that the TV is aligned evenly with the chair or couch that you view it from. So often I enter a client's home and find their TV off to the right or left, clearly out of comfortable view from where the client usually sits. A TV can have a mysterious way of moving when nobody's looking and little by little wind up out of the original spot where it was initially placed; and even though its new position makes it uncomfortable to watch, we tend to adapt to the discomfort, straining our necks and our eyes, tolerating anything to avoid getting up to reposition it.

Think about what comfort and relaxation mean to you and make a list of what would bring the best of those intentions to fruition. Have fun and get as outrageous as you'd like. Don't let money be your excuse or obstacle. After you reread your list, you might be surprised to find that money has more to do with purchasing things than with life's little comforts. Many times it's the little things that are important and nurturing to us, like having our favorite blanket to keep our feet warm or that old easy chair that we love to snooze in. Bring the "little comforts" in and you'll create a special room, designed just for you. The living room should not be overly crowded, although furniture should be comfortable and welcoming. Artwork should consist of pictures that enhance relaxation such as: scenic pictures of sunsets, mountains, or cascading waters. If entertaining guests is important to you, then make sure your living-room arrangement is conducive to socializing. Check that the chairs or couches are arranged in a way that guests can easily face one another and converse. Coffee tables, end tables, and nesting tables should be available for guests to place their drinks and snacks on. If you're hosting a party, try to be aware of where you serve your food and beverages. These areas become a central place where people tend to gather and mingle. So it's important that the ch'i be circulating well and that the display of food and drinks be visually appealing to the appetite as well as the eyes. To raise the ch'i of the party (and the guests), add flowers to the tables and place wind chimes in all four corners of the room. Have diverse lighting that can easily be changed to fit the mood of the evening. Three-way bulbs are a great addition to living-room lamps, for at the turn of a switch they can create low "mood lighting" for romantic evenings, medium lighting for book reading, and bright lighting for socializing with friends.

CHILDREN'S BEDROOM

The way that we design children's rooms is also most important because children's ch'i is very impressionable, especially during their early formative years. Their ch'i, just like our ch'i, is shaped and affected by the environment in which they live. Homes that are chaotic and stressful will create energy patterns that will shape their lives and ultimately last them a lifetime. When we apply **CONSCIOUS INTENTIONS** to what *their needs are* and how the Feng Shui of their space is impacting on them, then we are truly being mindful of all their needs. The most important thing in a child's bedroom is the positioning of the bed and the type of bed. The same positioning rules that apply to adult beds apply to children's beds. The child, while lying in bed, should be facing the doorway, able to easily view anyone who is entering the room. If this is not the case, place a mirror opposite the entranceway on an angle which will allow the child to see the reflected doorway. This gives the child a sense of command over his/her own space and helps build independence and a strong sense of autonomy.

If your child sleeps with his/her head close to the entranceway or with any part of his/her body crossing the entranceway, anything from behavioral problems to hyperactivity and depression can result. The force of the ch'i from the entranceway can quickly offset a child's delicate equilibrium and sense of stability. It is also best if you can place the child's bed against a solid wall that doesn't connect with a bathroom or kitchen wall. The water and fire energy that dominates these two rooms will be too disruptive to children's ch'i, weakening their health and diminishing their ability to concentrate well. Make sure that there are no large, oppressive pieces of furniture or bookcases towering over their heads, especially while they are sleeping, for this will create a feeling of being overwhelmed and pressured in their young lives.

Bunk beds, although a great space saver, can wreak havoc on a child's ch'i, especially for the child who sleeps on the bottom bunk. The overhang of the upper bunk depresses the child's ch'i, causing the ch'i to alter and be limited from its fullest potential. The child who sleeps on the upper bunk will exhibit similar problems (although not as severe) because the bed is too near the ceiling, cutting down on the energy around the child's body. If bunk beds are absolutely necessary, then to offset these problems, mirror (or use mylar on) the *bottom* of the upper bunk and the two closest side walls that run perpendicular and parallel to the beds. This will allow for the child's energy to expand and be less constricted during the sleep state. If the space in the room allows, place the bed in the "children's area" of the room. Although this is not a mandatory adjustment, when possible, it provides a wonderful alignment process for the child.

The children's gua in their room is where they draw their energy from. It should be well kept, uncluttered, and *reflect the personality of the child.* Hang a wind chime, mobile, or faceted crystal on a nine-inch red string and let your child help you decorate and make this a special area for him/her. Try to be aware of the type of posters that are hanging on your child's wall. What are the messages they convey? Violence? Horror? Freddy Krueger or the Lion King? Remember, everything in that environment has a vibration and gives out a message that contributes to shaping one's ch'i. Assess the messages that your child is receiving throughout the night, for that's the energy that will shape his/her whole being throughout the day. If you feel changes are in order, try to negotiate and in good faith see if you can reach a compromise where your child at least understands the reasoning behind these decisions.

All artwork and mirrors should be *hung at eye level based on the height of the child* and not on the eye level of the adults who are hanging things up. **Think about it: If all the mirrors and wall hangings in your bedroom were a foot or two over your head, how would that make you feel?** Out of place? Disoriented? Small? Answer: All of the above! The furniture should be age appropriate with a design pattern that allows the child to grow up and not be locked into an immature look. This is especially important to keep in mind if you are purchasing custom-made furniture or expensive bedding or are constructing closets and shelves. Children change, and it's crucial that their personal environment be somewhat flexible and accommodate to their journey. If the bedroom is being used for homework as well as a playroom, then a separate study area should be created in the room. Desks are best placed in the Knowledge section of the room, with the child facing the doorway. The child should not study with his/her back to the door. If no other desk position is possible, then place a mirror on the front or side wall of the desk so that the child can clearly see the entranceway. Either way, place a crystal on a nine-inch red string in the Knowledge gua of the room to assure the best possible learning environment. Make sure the room is well lit, bright, cheery, and filled with uplifting colors. All these factors will stimulate and nurture your child's ch'i. Get your child involved in the Feng Shui process as much as possible. When I asked my seven-year-old niece, Jovan, what she liked most about her room, she said that she was able to choose the colors of the paint. And choose she did; she had one wall painted red, another wall blue, one yellow, and the fourth wall white. She was very definite about her color choices, and that sense of definiteness is truly reflected in her personality. The more children understand, from a young age on, how to apply "mindful intentions," the more we will help them raise their level of "conscious awareness" in their lives. This is one of the greatest gifts we can impart to our children, for it empowers them by teaching them how to fully participate in shaping their own dreams and destiny.

GUEST ROOM

The guest room is the one room in the house that is usually not used very often, except by guests during holidays, family gatherings, and summertime visits. Because this room is not frequented daily, special care should be taken in arranging the design of this space. Areas like this that are not used often create dense and stagnant energy patterns. These patterns, if left unchanged, can adversely affect the Feng Shui of the occupants of the home. Try to be mindful and apply all the same Feng Shui principles to this room that you are using in the other main areas in your home. Check the bed positioning and make sure that the sleeper has privacy, ample drawer and closet space, and the best view of the door, without being directly in line with it. From a Feng Shui perspective, the proper bed positioning sets the "vibrational tone" of the room, and all the other patterns that contribute to "good Feng Shui" will follow. The ripple effects will create an atmosphere that your guests will appreciate and find comforting. Make sure that the room reflects your care and welcomes the guests who board there. Small comforts such as clean towels, extra blankets, and a new box of tissues go a long way. If these little comforts are provided by the hosts, without the guests having to ask, even better. This conveys a very welcoming message that says, "I thought about your needs, even before you arrived and wanted you to feel at home and be as comfortable as possible." To really make the room special, add a vase of fresh flowers, a bowl of mixed fruit, or a carafe of their favorite beverage. Conscious intentions are what create the best Feng Shui, even for transient guests.

Keep in mind that, even when this room is not being used, it still affects the main residents' Feng Shui. Lack of circulation of the energy in this room will weaken the ch'i of the area that this room oversees. To remedy this, first check your *overall floor plan* and locate the area of the Bagua that the guest room overlaps. For example, let's say that it overlaps the Helpful People corner. Go into the guest room and find the Helpful People corner of that room and, in that area, hang a mobile or a wind chime to keep the energy moving. Add some plants, birds, or a fish tank to the room, to bring in the powerful life force. In addition, these "life force" adjustments act as a lure, encouraging you to bring your energy, on a daily basis, into this room to care for their needs. This arrangement allows you to frequent this room more often than you would normally and bring your energy to this part of your home and, subsequently, your life.

ATTIC/BASEMENT/PANTRY/STORAGE ROOM

These rooms do not have to be problematic if they are kept clean, well ventilated, and organized. An **ATTIC** that is used for storage should be cleaned out every six months. Because it is the highest place in the house, the attic represents all the things that are metaphorically "hanging over your head." It's important that you be aware of all the items you are storing, especially if they are items from your past. Old memorabilia can be fun to save, but make sure that there are no painful memories or unresolved issues attached to these belongings or you will also hold on to those feelings on an energy level. This type of energy is emotionally charged and can cause headaches, depression, and an overall sense of feeling pressured in your life. If the attic has a pitched roof, hang a crystal ball on a nine-inch red string in the highest part of the pitch. If the attic is being used as an office or guest bedroom, make sure the bed or desk is not placed under the slant of the roof's walls. If the slants are unavoidable, try mirroring them and hanging two bamboo flutes (see p. 49) to offset their oppressive angles. Either way, install a ceiling fan to keep the ch'i circulating and to raise the energy levels of everyone living in the house. Many of my clients from the East, especially Thailand, use the attic to house their altars and offerings to Buddha. This is because the attic is seen as the highest place in the house, worthy of the honor of housing Buddha. Placing Buddha there is the most respectful homage they can pay.

The **BASEMENT** represents the foundation of our lives. It's the area that we stand on and that all the other floors are built over. It's important that it be well maintained and devoid of potential Feng Shui problems such as clutter (stagnant energy), water leaks (money/emotional distress), and dark, dingy areas (health problems). Remember that ch'i rises. All energy imbalances that manifest themselves in the basement area will slowly rise, permeate the rest of the house, and affect the overall Feng Shui of all the occupants. If this part of the house is used for storage, make sure it is well lit and properly ventilated. If it is a finished basement used for other things such as exercising, a TV/game room, or an additional bedroom, hang a crystal on a nine-inch red string at the top of the stairs and a wind chime in the center of the room to help the ch'i circulate.

The **PANTRY** and **STORAGE ROOM** are great for organizing specific items such as nonperishable food, winter/summer clothing, old books, etc. Make sure that these rooms remain organized, and use sealed and labeled boxes for clarity. Food items should be consumed regularly and stored properly to avoid insect and moth problems. Check cans for expiration dates and boxed foods for staleness. Keep shelves clean and frequently dusted. Remember, **food picks up the vibration of the energy that surrounds it**. If it's being stored in dust and chaos, it will pick up the energy of "unimportance," and it will be spiritually depleted long before it even reaches your kitchen. Check what area these rooms oversee (on the Bagua), and if they are areas of concern to you, add live plants, red tassels, or wind chimes to rebalance the stagnant energy.

STUDY AND DEN

A **STUDY** or **DEN** is a great addition to any home. They usually indicate that there is some space to spare in the house and that reading and education are important priorities. These are great rooms to see first upon entering your home. They encourage learning and expanding one's knowledge base. The Chinese believe that education is one of the five main factors that influence a person's life (see chapter 6). In Black Hat Sect Feng Shui, we also feel that it is very important, so important, that a whole section of the Bagua (Self-knowledge) is devoted to education. Make sure these rooms are not cluttered and that bookshelves or large pieces of furniture do not tower over the person studying. It is good to store books and other educational materials in this room, but try to keep them free of dust and mildew. Books tend to hold an exorbitant amount of energy. A book accrues years of energy starting from the person who originally wrote the manuscript, all the way through to the individual who purchased it. If you multiply that by forty, fifty, or one hundred books, the energy sources really add up and can weigh down and suck up all the energy in a room. This could create a room in which it is hard to concentrate and study.

To design the best possible atmosphere, make sure that the occupant has a comfortable chair and that his/her desk is facing the door, **without** being in a direct line with it. Make sure the Knowledge area is organized and, to ensure good study habits and wisdom, hang a crystal there on a nine-inch red string or add a beautiful wind chime. If at all possible, try not to clutter up the space, especially the center of the room. The center area of every room is known as the MING TANG and is a very powerful source of ch'i energy. Add proper lighting and thriving plants, not only to support but also to stimulate the circulating ch'i. Keep the desk organized and uncluttered. Messy workstations translate into unclear and unfocused thinking. Remember, the ch'i of the room sets the tone of what will or will not transpire in that space. Check if the room is reflecting your objectives; if not, make the necessary changes.

HOME OFFICE

Many of us have our offices located in our homes. This arrangement works best if you are able to have your office in a separate room or in an area such as the basement or attic. Being in an area that can be closed off, locked away, and not passed through during nonwork hours will help you create a physical boundary that will assist you in separating out your ch'i. As I addressed in previous chapters, the motion of ch'i is very fluid. It flows and sways in and through your home, mixing its energy with the other energies there. Office and other work-related energies have a very different focus than the more domestic energies of the kitchen, bedroom, living room, etc. When you mix these two kinds of energy together, without proper division, you can run the risk of depleting the ch'i on both sides. *Often, with this arrangement, you'll find that your work life will override your personal life, and your personal life will spill over into your business activities.* It's hard enough for most people, during stressful or busy times, not to take their work home with them (literally or figuratively) when they work outside their home, but when you work inside your home it becomes nearly impossible. So, in order to achieve good home-office Feng Shui, it is most important that you first create physical, then emotional boundaries around your office and your work time.

This means no offices in the bedroom! Try not to mix those energies together, for doing so will deplete both your work and love life. If you are not able to have an office in a separate room, then try to contain your office and where you do your work to a certain area of a room. You can create boundaries around the designated area by erecting dividers such as a half-folding screen (make sure it doesn't go all the way up to the ceiling, or it will close you in), a four-foot-high bookshelf, or a row of plants. All these objects will suggest a line of delineation, especially when coupled with your "conscious intention" of why you are placing it there. Make sure the lighting is good. Try to avoid fluorescent lights, especially the ones that are directly over or near your head (desk lamps). These lights flicker at a very rapid rate that can affect the rhythm of your brain waves and cause tiredness by keeping your brain signals in an alpha-brain state. Try to personalize your space with diplomas on the wall, special objects, favorite pens, etc.

The next important adjustment in your home office is the correct place-ment of your desk. Your desk should face the entranceway to the room, without having it (and you) be in a direct line with the doorway. If the size of the room allows, place the desk on a diagonal, in the farthest corner facing the entranceway. This is the most commanding and powerful position for the desk to be in, for it conveys a sense of authority and mastery over one's domain. If by chance you're able to place your diagonal desk in the wealth area of the room, your wealth ch'i will increase even further.

Make sure that the desk area is clear and well organized to foster clear thinking and circulate ch'i. A cluttered and chaotic desk in the wealth area will work in reverse, causing a host of business problems ranging from missed appointments to decreased revenue. Actually, wherever the clutter is located in the office will determine which area of your business will be most affected.

The location of computers and typewriters should follow the same rules as proper desk placement. They should also be positioned so that the typist faces the doorway. If this is not possible, then place a mirror in front of the person at the desk or computer so that it reflects a clear view of the entrance-way. To further ensure a well-run business, place a crystal on a nine-inch red string over the desk area and a wind chime in the career area. Try to use your knowledge of Feng Shui to personalize the adjustments specifically needed for your business. If you want to stabilize your income, make an adjustment in the wealth area. If you want to bring in more clients to increase your revenue, make an adjustment in the Helpful People section. If you want to increase your business by becoming better known, then you should make your adjustment in the Fame area. Use the "Feng Shui Adjustment Items" section in chapter 2 and pick the method that you feel will best activate your "intention." Fresh flowers on the desk or in the knowledge area will lift the individual's ch'i and stimulate good business smarts. Green plants that are healthy and lush will signify growth, new beginnings, and MONEY! Ask yourself what type of energy message your office is conveying. Make sure that message reflects your goals and intentions.

On a recent Feng Shui consultation, I recommended to a client of mine, who is an artist and does collage work, that she create her art directly on the walls of her office, using the walls as she would four large, blank canvases, instead of hanging already created pieces made by someone else. I had her personalize the walls in her space by decorating them with her art and with things that inspired her the most. In addition, she got to have loads of fun doing the very thing we were told not to do for most of our childhood: ***"Don't draw on the walls!"***

Remember, even if this is an office that clients never come to, treat it with the same importance in terms of design and maintenance as you would if it were the Oval Office and you were the president. Your business has to reflect your respect for your work *first*, before you think of its effect on any client or consumer. Make it special, if it's special to you.

The Chinese have used a variety of symbols throughout the centuries to depict good omens that draw auspicious luck and opportunities to all who are privy to their messages. Listed below is a group of symbols and patterns that depict fortuitous omens. Consider using them as part of your decor by expressing your conscious intentions through the various design patterns that you use in your space. You can incorporate these symbols in your artwork, wall hangings, fabric patterns, and furniture motifs.

Feel free to make up your own symbols and patterns and let them represent special meanings to you. Design your home with them or place them around your home in areas that you pass through on a daily basis. Let your symbols represent your wishes because once the symbol and its meaning are programmed into your subconscious mind, symbols bypass rational thought and therefore bypass our judgments and secret fears of not ever getting what we want.

AUSPICIOUS PATTERNS AND SYMBOLS*

Pattern	Meaning
1. Elephants	Wisdom
2. Pine tree	Longevity and endurance
3. Vase	Peace
4. Phoenix	Grace and wisdom
5. Fish	Success
6. Lotus	Endurance and uprightness
7. Water ripples	Wealth and heavenly blessings
8. Clouds	Heavenly blessings and wisdom
9. Gold Pieces	Wealth
10. Yin-yang	Unions and balance
11. Flowers	Prosperity and love
12. Tortoise	Longevity
13. Old coins	Wealth
14. Bats	Good luck
15. Cranes	Fidelity, honesty, and longevity
16. Deer	Wealth and luck
17. Fu dogs	Protection and loyalty
18. Dragon	Power, authority and strength
19. Fruit	Good luck and health
20. Old Man	Wisdom and longevity

* Evelyn Lipp, *Feng Shui for the Home* (Union City, CA: Heian International, 1990), 65.

SUMMARY

This chapter has covered all the "satellite rooms" in your home that have a significant impact on your personal ch'i and the Feng Shui of your life. In addition, we have reviewed the nine main low-cost–high-gain tips for designing from a Feng Shui perspective. Use the guidelines below to serve as a reminder of the important points to emphasize and avoid in regard to the Feng Shui of each room. **In addition, when designing your area, make sure that you remember to personalize your space, use your intuition, be creative, and—most of all—have some fun!**

DINING ROOM

Good Ch'i

1. Used often for meals
2. Dining table—round, oval, octagonal
3. Main occupants face the door
4. Relaxed atmosphere
5. Uncluttered table
6. Encourages conversation

Bad Ch'i

1. Table crossing doorway
2. Irritating stimuli/loud music
3. Cramped quarters
4. Unsteady table and chairs
5. Beams over table
6. Tall centerpieces

LIVING ROOM

Good Ch'i

1. First room you see
2. Comfortable and restful
3. Furniture pieces face one another
4. Encourages socializing
5. Diverse lighting
6. Host's chair faces door

Bad Ch'i

1. Work is done here
2. Can't relax here
3. Too much furniture
4. Accumulates clutter/newspapers
5. Not often used
6. Messy room

CHILDREN'S BEDROOM

Good Ch'i

1. Child and bed face door
2. Bed is against a solid wall
3. Desk faces door
4. Artwork/mirrors hung at child's eye level
5. Well lit, bright, and cheery
6. Child included in design decisions

Bad Ch'i

1. Stressful environment
2. Bunk beds
3. Towering bookshelves/furniture
4. Clothes/toys out of reach

5. Violent or scary posters
6. Not child friendly

GUEST ROOM

Good Ch'i

1. Proper bed positioning
2. Welcoming
3. Plants/life force
4. Thoughtful comforts
5. It "feels like home"
6. Anticipates guests' needs

Bad Ch'i

1. Bed under a slanted wall
2. Lack of ventilation
3. Seldom frequented
4. No drawer/closet space
5. Lacks privacy
6. Uncomfortable bed

ATTIC/BASEMENT/PANTRY/STORAGE ROOM

Good Ch'i

1. Cleaned out every six months
2. Ventilated year-round
3. Organized
4. Well lit
5. Painted in light, uplifting colors
6. High ceilings

Bad Ch'i

1. Cluttered
2. Water leaks
3. Mold and mildew
4. Dark, dingy areas
5. Accumulates junk
6. Disrepair

STUDY/DEN

Good Ch'i

1. Good first room to see
2. Books and related material
3. Desk faces door

4. Located in a quiet area
5. Conducive to learning
6. Knowledge area is clear

Bad Ch'i

1. Poor lighting
2. Large, towering bookcases
3. Desk is wrong size (too big or little)
4. At street level
5. Uncomfortable chair
6. Dark decor

HOME OFFICE

Good Ch'i

1. Located in a separate room
2. Personalized objects in space
3. Desk faces or is catercorner to entranceway
4. Computer faces entranceway
5. Live green plants (silk or dried okay)
6. Wealth corner augmented

Bad Ch'i

1. Located in bedroom
2. Cluttered workstation
3. Messy desk area

4. No boundaries around work
5. Fluorescent light on desk

6. Tight, small place

FIVE

USING COLOR TO ENHANCE YOUR LIFE AND CREATE HAPPINESS

There are several different theories that are used in working with the colors of the interior and exterior of your home. Some are from Black Hat Sect Feng Shui, others from different sources. Each will provide you with an approach to working with a specific color sequence for healing and adjustment purposes. We will explore three different avenues of working with color systems. As you read about the different options, see which sequence feels the best to you. You might find that over time and under different circumstances, one color sequence works better than another. Feel free to move in and out of the systems as you see fit. If certain color sequences don't seem appealing or appropriate to you, *give yourself permission not to use them if they do not feel right.*

For example, if I suggest that pink is a good color to paint your bedroom in order to enhance a failing relationship, and you really hate the color pink, **please** don't paint your bedroom that color. The objective of Feng Shui is to try to bring balance and harmony into your life; if you are working with colors that you truly don't like, you would be doing the opposite of what the goals of Feng Shui would want you to do. As a Feng Shui specialist, I would never encourage you to live with colors you "*could not live with*." Why should you? There are so many color schemes and other types of adjustments for you to choose from; find one that not only remedies the problem but appeals to your sense of aesthetics as well. Trust your intuition, listen to your inner voice, and make that voice your authority—then have some fun picking out your colors!

The transformational power of Feng Shui is derived from its keen ability to understand and decode the healing aspects of nature and then re-create those healing aspects indoors. Through understanding what makes a forest of trees soothing or a beautiful sunset inspiring, we can attempt to recapture the magic of the outdoors and bring that magical force inside. One of the most profound healing aspects of nature that affects our lives on a daily basis is the presence of color.

Color is probably the most plentiful and visible of all the gifts that we have received from nature. It's the first thing we see when we open our eyes as a baby and it's the last thing we see each night, before we go to sleep. It affects everything from our choice of clothing to the range of our moods. The more we understand how colors have an impact on our lives, the more we will realize that if we take our cues from Mother Nature, "the world's greatest artist," the more we will come to understand the innate properties that govern our healing and our world.

Almost everything in nature is defined by color: the hot yellow sun, clear blue waters, midnight blue skies, red roses, green pastures, purple eggplants, pink grapefruits, and so forth. Even our emotions are conveyed more thoroughly by adding a visual description of color to them. How often have you heard our moods described as *green* with envy, *red* with rage, or feeling sad and *blue*. Even our skin colors have been described as "*white* as a ghost" or "*green* around the gills." Color has an impact on our lives and creates rich, saturated images that encourage us to react and emote. It is no coincidence that the universe used the world around us to illustrate the vast use of the color spectrum to beautify our world, stimulate our senses, and nourish our spirits.

According to various spiritual teachings, before human beings incarnated into a physical body, the soul part of their being existed previously on an ethereal level. The soul itself, on that ethereal level, is made up of units of sparkling white light. This "light" is described often by individuals who have recounted memories of their "near-death experiences." A very bright light is what they saw last, as they were passing over to the other side. These units of white light (which is really our soul) are often referred to as an "individual's vibration" and are as unique and specific to each person as a set of fingerprints or a strand of their DNA. Each person's vibration acts as a personal computer, storing all the relative information that is needed by that individual for this lifetime. The information stored ranges from the kind of relationships we will draw to us to the type of lessons we are here to experience.

When white light breaks down into the seven colors of the rainbow in the body, these areas are referred to as "**energy centers**." The Sanskrit word for energy center is *chakra* **(sha-cra)** which, loosely translated, means spinning wheels of light. One of the ways these spiritual energy centers get fueled and nourished is by absorbing their corresponding *colors* from the environment. The colors from our environment act as nature's "food for the soul," specifically created to feed the chakras. The mechanism that the physical body uses to absorb the energy from color is called the *aura*. The aura is the subtle light that glows, surrounds, and interpenetrates the physical body, acting like a sponge, absorbing color from the environment and feeding it to the chakras. That is why the presence or absence of color in our lives is so important, for without it we starve our souls and deplete our energy system. As far back as 1878, Dr. Edwin D. Babbitt published his classic work, *The Principles Of Light And Color*. After many years of research on color therapy, he concluded that different colors can be used as healing agents because of their reparative effect on different illnesses.*

Now, in the 1990s, we are just starting to realize the impact light and color have on our health, and especially on our psyche, with the recent diagnosis of the disorder **SAD** (Seasonal Affective Disorder). The core of the illness is that certain depressions are seasonal and are due to a lack of natural sunlight, the lack of which changes the body's chemistry causing a specific type of depression that is treatable by using natural and/or artificial light on the patient. Doctors and scientists have finally acknowledged the significance that light has in our lives and our physical and mental health. Although many of these doctors and scientists haven't yet begun to address the spiritual aspects of the healing power of color and light, we are much closer to bridging that gap through understanding the use of Feng Shui in our lives and homes.

There are many systems of color that are available to us to use in healing

---

* (Mary Anderson, *Colour Healing*, New York: Samuel Weiser, 1979), 14.

our lives and creating happiness. In this chapter we will address the Creative Color Cycle according to **Black Hat Sect Feng Shui** and its spiritual leader, **Master Thomas Lin Yun**. In addition, we will review the Affective Color System and explore the **Chakra Energy System** and see how the use of its color system can affect our lives and change our patterns of energy.

FENG SHUI, COLOR, AND THE INTERIOR OF YOUR HOME

The color that exists in the interior of your home has the most significant impact on your life and your Feng Shui. This is because these colors, especially on the walls, change so infrequently. Over time, the consistency allows these colors to form specific energy patterns that lock into a certain vibrational pattern of ch'i. Depending on how compatible colors resonate with one another and then with you, these patterns will then either support and enhance your ch'i or depress and eventually stifle it. The colors or lack of colors in your home have a significant impact on your ability to create an environment that will either nourish your spirit or drain your energy. I have been on more consultations where the lack of color, more than any other issue, has been the main Feng Shui problem. When color is a problem, it is usually because there is not enough of it, rather than too much. Most people are afraid of using and *"playing with color."* It tends to be the most "reacted to" of all the adjustments I suggest because colors elicit **FEELINGS** and **EMOTIONS**! Most of us prefer to avoid our feelings and emotions, because doing so keeps us in control and out of touch with our true selves. This need to remain neutral is often reflected in the way we design our homes and shun the use of color. This tendency can be seen in the choice of paint colors that we use on our interior walls and the fabrics we choose. The more neutral the colors (beige, tan, browns, ***not whites***), the more subdued the ch'i will be in your home. This is not meant to imply that all use of neutral colors is bad. Quite the contrary: often neutral hues can be used creatively as a backdrop for other busier or more intense colors. In addition, using neutral colors along with specific "conscious intentions" can create an ideal setting if you are choosing to design a room that is low-key and calm. I am more concerned when these neutral colors are used repeatedly in most of the rooms of the house. That's when I believe that collectively they send out a slow and anesthetizing energy that stagnates everything. Keep in

THE CREATIVE COLOR CYCLE CHART

GUA	PRIMARY COLOR	SECONDARY/TERNARY COLORS	SUPPORTIVE COLORS
Fame	Red	None	Purple
Relationship	Pink	None	Red/White
Children	White	Off White/Warm White	Yellow
Helpful People	Gray	None	White/Black
Career	Black	None	Gray
Knowledge	Blue	None	Black/Green
Family	Green	None	Blue
Wealth	Purple	None	Green/Red
Center	Yellow	Orange, Tan, Gold, Brown	Red

mind that every room in your home oversees a different part of your life. If these parts of your life are the parts that you are trying to change through Feng Shui, and you discover that you basically have a neutral color scheme running through your home, you should then seriously consider adding color to your space. If doing it all at once feels too overwhelming, try choosing just one room at first—then, as you feel more comfortable over time, venture out into other spaces.

I finally convinced my friend Spanky, in Seattle, to paint her bedroom, which was beige, colors that were more energizing and vibrant. Halfway through the paint job she started to panic and was overcome with emotions. Although she had picked out two very beautiful colors, lavender and light green, she found the combination of colors overwhelming to the point that she not only hated the effect, but claimed it made her sick. The painting of her bedroom evoked many feelings for her which, in turn, triggered some issues she had to deal with regarding her life and relationships. You can look at the colors she picked out as a wrong choice for her *or*, from a Feng Shui perspective, you can acknowledge that the color adjustment, and choices, was exactly what she needed to elicit and move her through those particular issues. Interestingly enough, as much as she hated the colors, she never did quite get around to painting over them. Now almost a year later, after she has processed many of those issues, she is ready to repaint and finish the job.

Color is and can be a very powerful healer. As you begin to become more aware of its impact on your day-to-day life, you will come to appreciate and honor the life-sustaining gifts that it brings to you.

The first method we will address in working with color is **the Creative Color Cycle from the Black Hat Sect Feng Shui Bagua Map**. Each of the nine guas of the Bagua has a primary color, some have a secondary color, and others have two supportive colors (see p. 103).

USING THE CREATIVE COLOR CYCLE TO IMPROVE YOUR FENG SHUI

The primary color enhances and uplifts the ch'i of the particular gua it oversees. The secondary or ternary colors also enhance the energy of the gua in a similar way. The supportive colors often work more indirectly, creating a supportive cushion around the color and placing it in a creative cycle flow. As the color chart reveals, some of the preceding and succeeding colors of the various guas run into one another because each gua is fluid and tends to move in a continual flow. In addition, the moving motion of energy acts as a pillar, supporting and nourishing each gua that it surrounds, generating the ch'i flow from either side of the gua. This method is best used for: **1) replacing a missing or awkwardly shaped gua or 2) as a Feng Shui adjustment for enhancing the ch'i of any specific gua/life situation**. For example, if your bedroom has a missing Relationship corner due to a built-in closet or a large structural column, you can paint the walls around the closet or the structural column the color pink. Pink is the corresponding color in the Relationship gua on the Bagua. Even though the Relationship area is technically missing, bringing its corresponding color to the area will transcendentally re-create the missing area. After you paint the area, bless it with the *Three Secret Reinforcement* to secure and activate the adjustment.

Another way to utilize this color sequence is by inserting a colored object in the gua as an adjustment item instead of actually painting the whole section a given color. You can use a ***purple vase*** as the "color adjustment" for the Wealth corner of the room. The Wealth corner resonates to the color purple. The vase (or any other significant object) will activate the *Wealth area* through the vibration of its *purple color*. This in turn will serve to raise the level of the ch'i that is connected to the resident's finances. Color can be used transcendentally just as you would use any wind chime or crystal ball, especially when you couple it with the *Three Secret Reinforcement*. When you use this type of "item adjustment," remember to be mindful of the type of item(s) that you are using and make sure that it resonates appropriately with your objectives and INTENTIONS. For instance, if you choose to place a large **WHITE** lamp in the **CHILDREN/CREATIVITY** section of your living room to enhance your creativity ch'i (WHITE oversees the Children/Creativity area), make sure you check in on your feelings about the lamp first. Ask yourself if you really like the lamp. Does it reflect your sense of creativity, or do you find it aesthetically boring? Did someone whose creativity you admire give the lamp to you as a gift? Or, did you inherit the lamp in your divorce settlement from a partner who was never really supportive of your creativity? This is what I call "**mindful thought**." The more you become aware of the energy around the objects in your house, the more you will be able to create your own happiness and affect your own destiny. This doesn't mean to imply that you need to love and revere every object or piece of furniture in your home. But it does suggest that you should choose with care any items that you intend to use specifically for adjustment purposes.

Remember to follow these seven simple steps to help you shift the ch'i, when you're using color as a transcendental cure to adjust a problem or dilemma in your life.

1. Identify the problem.
2. Clarify your "conscious intention."
3. Find the corresponding gua the problem relates to.
4. Locate the appropriate color cure.
5. Pick the type of color adjustment or item you intend to use.
6. Decide in which room(s) you will apply the cure.*
7. Reinforce all cures with the Three Secret Reinforcement (chapter 7).

---

* When you're deciding to implement a cure, the type of cure (vase vs. painting a wall) will help you determine which room to make the adjustment in. For example, a *green* vase with flowers might work much better with your decor in the *Family gua* of the living room than the *Family gua* of the study. Pick the room in your home that works best for you and the adjustment in question. The only caveat to this general rule regards relationships and relationship-related issues. Those adjustments seem to work best when they are made in the Relationship area of the bedroom. Feel free to adjust as many guas in as many rooms and areas as you like. Multiple adjustments for one particular problem help to "raise the percentages" (see chapter 1) of resolving that problem.

Your "conscious intention" will help program the cure for the specific goal that you wish to achieve. In addition, by blessing the cures with the *Three Secret Reinforcement* (chapter 7), you turn an ordinary "purple vase" from something decorative into a transcendental Feng Shui cure.

EXAMPLE CHART FOR APPLICATION OF THE CREATIVE COLOR CYCLE

PROBLEM/SITUATION	CORRESPONDING GUA	CORRESPONDING COLOR	SAMPLE ADJUSTMENT	ROOM
Difficult time finding a relationship	Relationship	Pink	Vase with pink roses	Bedroom
Problem with blood pressure (health-resolved issue)	Center	Yellow	Paint ceiling in bedroom yellow	Bedroom
Lost job/unemployed	Career	Black	Hang artwork with a lot of black in it	Kitchen
Want to increase wealth ch'i	Wealth	Purple	Add 3 purple throw pillows to couch in wealth corner	Living room
Improve Study Habits	Knowledge	Blue	Hang mirror in a blue frame	Den/study
Reputation tarnished at work	Fame/family	Red	Hang red curtains	Kitchen
Family disputes	Family	Green	Burn green candles	Living room
Difficult time conceiving	Children	White	Place a large white lamp on table	Bedroom
Wanting to purchase a used car	Helpful people	Gray	Describe the type of car you want and place a note in a gray box	Den

FENG SHUI, COLOR, AND THE WHITE HOUSE

Several years ago I was interviewed for a magazine article and was asked to assess the Feng Shui of the White House. After reviewing several photographs of the Oval Office, the Treaty Room, and the Lincoln Sitting Room, I began to notice a particular pattern developing regarding the choice of colors that were picked out by President Clinton and the First Lady, Hillary Rodham Clinton. All three rooms had color schemes that included deep reds and golds, Prussian blues, and some greens. They had asked their decorator to help them create a White House that reflected the president's personality, as well as the youth and vigor of his administration. The request resulted in many changes in the interior color scheme of quite a few rooms in the White House. The Oval Office, previously occupied by former president George Bush, was transformed from a room painted in softer colors of pale blue and cream to the stronger, more intense hues of Prussian blue, crimson, and gold. The Treaty Room, which was the Cabinet Room for the last half of the nineteenth century, was repainted from its prior color of pale green to a more vibrant color of deep red. The Lincoln Sitting Room used the abundance of its natural sunlight to cast a warm, golden glow throughout the room. All these color choices were beautiful and accurately reflected the mood of the White House and its long history as a living museum.* From a Feng Shui perspective, however, although these colors are beautiful and powerful, they are also very intense. Intense colors, such as crimson, are also very magnetic and draw to them an exorbitant amount of ch'i energy. This in itself is not bad, but upon reviewing the Chinese astrological charts of President and Mrs. Clinton, I discovered that even though they are approximately one year apart in age, they were both born in years that were dominated by the Fire element. The element Fire resonates to the color **red**. While it makes sense that they would both instinctually gravitate toward choosing crimson colors, the amount of those colors used, coupled with the large amount of **Fire** in their birth years, inadvertently drew to them a lot of chaos and friction. The choice of colors of this president clearly indicated to me his desire to be well known and to carve out a place in the history books. **Red**, the color of **Fame**, also oversees one's reputation and (on an energy level) draws ch'i to it, as a fly is drawn to fly paper. Too much use of this color can create a "lightning rod effect," drawing to it much hostility, aggression, and even violence. This has been evidenced over the last several years of the Clinton presidency, as we witnessed at the White House gunfire, suicidal pilots, and an unprecedented number of personal and political attacks on both the president and his wife. To remedy this problem, as a Feng Shui specialist, I would recommend that the Clintons reduce the amount of **red** in their decor and/or introduce other colors such as black (the color of the water element) or even more greens (the color of the wood element). This would help place the energy that exists inside the White House back into a color sequence that is less antagonistic and more conducive to the well-being of the president, his family, and the country as a whole.

* (Marian Burros, *House Beautiful*, March 1994.)

ENERGY, EFFECT, AND COLOR

Color can have a profound impact on moods and energy flow. Certain colors can enhance one's ch'i, while others depress and limit one's energy. The following is a list of mood or energy objectives and their corresponding colors.

ENERGY COLOR CHART

EFFECTS ON MOODS AND ENERGY	COLOR
Lifts energy	Yellows, reds, turquoise, bright colors
Slows down energy	Browns, rusts, all dark colors
Softens energy	Light pinks and greens, corals, pastel colors
Draws energy	Reds, golds, rich purples
Neutralizes energy	Whites, beiges, tans
Enhances creativity	Oranges, turquoise, teals, vibrant blues
Enhances spirituality	Purples, violets, white
Warming colors	Reds, oranges, yellows, yellow-green
Cooling colors	Blues, blue-green, lavender
Romantic colors	Pinks, reds, oranges, warm greens
Sexual colors	Reds, black, oranges, hot pink
Grounding colors	Reds, browns, tans, beiges
Power colors	Golds, black, burgundys, reds, royal blue
Soothing colors	Greens, blues, peach

As a general rule, these colors affect people's energy in similar ways. Feel free to explore them, give them some thought, and decide for yourself how they make *you* feel. The more you personalize the various steps of the Feng Shui process, the more your home will truly reflect you and all your needs. The best way to choose color for your home that fits your personal needs is by first thinking about what your favorite colors are. Make a list of them in your Feng Shui notebook and, next to each color, write a few words or lines about how that color makes you feel. Use as many adjectives as you like. The point of the exercise is to get you in touch with the feelings and energy behind the color choices. Then, without deciding which colors will go in which rooms, go to your favorite paint store and collect paint chips in a variety of different shades of the colors you are exploring. Take those paint chips home and review the various colors asking yourself, How do each of these various shades make me feel? When you come across a color shade that matches the objectives behind your color choices, you'll know that you have a match. Now you can discard the excess paint chips and peruse the colors you've chosen and the various feelings that they evoke, then decide which rooms in your home would benefit greatly from those colors and their specific effects on energy. This color exercise is a wonderful process that really helps you tune in to your feelings and get to know yourself and your needs much better, thus creating a home that really reflects who you are and acknowledges your desires.

A few, quick energy painting tips are: Try to avoid painting all your rooms the same color, especially white or off-white. Color acts as a great divider, helping the ch'i flow know where one source of energy begins and another one ends. Without this division, energy can scatter, dissipate, and affect one's personal boundaries. This may cause a "spilling-over effect" in one's life where, for example, business runs into personal life or individual merges with partner in a relationship, and tends to "lose sense of self."

The color white and shades of it should be used sparingly in one or two rooms at the most because ch'i cannot absorb the color white and tends to ricochet and bounce off the walls causing everything from anxiety to insomnia. A good application of the color white is on ceilings, doors, trim, or moldings; white in these locations breaks up the color on the walls causing the ch'i to slow down a bit, have definition, and become absorbed in the space. One last pointer: Adding new colors or painting over all-white spaces at first can feel very overwhelming. Your ch'i was conditioned by the energetic patterns created by your most recent paint job and might initially react not only to the color change but also to the change in energy. Give yourself at least two to three weeks to decide if you really don't like the new paint scheme or if you just need time for your energy to shift and become comfortable with it.

> My dear friend and very talented artist, Pat Dawkins, always reminds me of the "color story" when she painted her hallway an incredibly rich color of turquoise. She said the moment she first rolled it on to the wall she felt her whole being open up and she became instantly energized. In the meantime, a friend who was helping her paint became more and more anxious and overwhelmed by the color. Even neighbors and friends stopped by and couldn't help but comment, "Maybe it's too much." She personally loved the color, held firm, and over the years she was continually inspired by its richness and never regretted her choice for one day.

THE CHAKRA ENERGY SYSTEM AND THE HEALING POWER OF THE COLOR SPECTRUM

The **Chakra Energy System**, as mentioned above, is the energy system that exists in our bodies and is governed by seven different energy centers and their corresponding colors on the color spectrum. Each chakra oversees different characteristics and aspects of our life. Below is a chart that depicts the chakras, where they are located in the body, and their matching colors. By understanding just a little bit about the chakras and their unique system of color, it is easy to see how significant an impact color has on everything psychological, emotional, spiritual, and physical that is a part of our lives.

Although these "little computer centers" have the awesome responsibility of keeping us alive and our vibration moving twenty-four hours a day, they actually require very little from us to keep active and functioning. **The main source of their fuel is gathered and absorbed from the *different colors* that we come in contact with through our environment, nature, food, clothing, and interior and exterior surroundings.** Learning to harness and access these energies through color will empower us to make the necessary internal changes that will help change our lives for the better.

For many of you reading this book, this is probably the first time you have heard about the chakras. Rest assured, though, that you have always had them within you and they have worked for you in the same way they have worked for others who have known about them. The main difference now is that you are *aware* of their existence and have the *choice* to consciously utilize their power to help shape your life and your personal ch'i. Just as our automatic nervous system works without being told to and our lungs breathe air in and out for us without thought, our bodies naturally absorb color from everything that is around us. As long as you are alive and breathing, you can rest assured that your body is soaking up a substantial amount of color from the environment. But different issues, experiences, and karmic lessons in our lives manifest differently for different people. This means that each of us doesn't have the same amount of "color fuel" in each chakra as the next person. For example, one person might be very strong in the first center (SURVIVAL CENTER—RED) and have no problems taking care of him/herself and earning a good income (first center issues). This "might" mean that his/her first center is relatively balanced and has enough red energy to support *those specific issues*. That same person might have other issues present for them in other chakras or might have an imbalance in the first chakra regarding other issues that reside there. Different days and different situations on the same day can affect and change the energy current or color force in each chakra. One day, in the morning, you may feel that first center is strong with no obstacles to stop you from completing your favorite art project, then, later on that day you might find yourself having a difficult time trying to finish painting a spare bedroom. The ch'i in the chakras is fluid and flexible, moving and changing with the changes in your life.

Below is a chart that depicts the chakras, where they are located in the body, and their matching colors.

1. SURVIVAL CENTER

The **first chakra** is located at the **base of your spine**, and its energy pattern resonates with the color **RED**. It oversees all issues that have to do with survival, such as your ability to take care of yourself, provide proper housing,

THE SEVEN MAJOR CHAKRAS

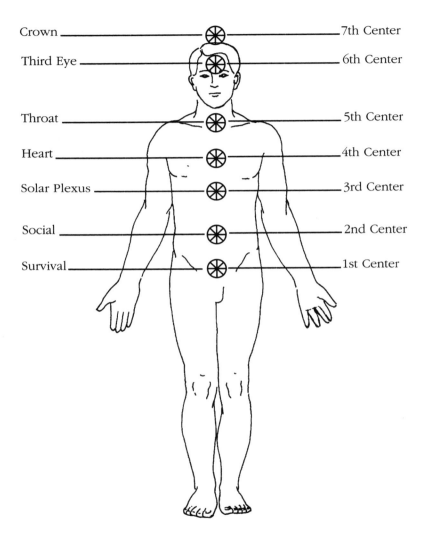

Crown ———————————— 7th Center

Third Eye ———————————— 6th Center

Throat ———————————— 5th Center

Heart ———————————— 4th Center

Solar Plexus ———————————— 3rd Center

Social ———————————— 2nd Center

Survival ———————————— 1st Center

THE CHAKRA ENERGY SYSTEM AND ITS CORRESPONDING FACTORS

CHAKRA	LOCATION	COLOR
1) Survival Center	base of spine	red
2) Social Center	2″ below navel	orange
3) Will Center	solar plexus	yellow
4) Heart Center	center of chest	green
5) Throat Center	throat	sky blue
6) Third eye Center	between eyebrows	indigo
7) Crown Center	top of head	purple

and attend to your basic needs regarding food, work, and emergency situations. It oversees issues regarding money and your ability to follow through on most projects and complete them. It's also our root center that provides the grounding energy needed to stay clear and focused in life. This center oversees all physical and health-related aspects of the genitals, legs, knees, feet, and sexuality in relation to *procreation*. When the Survival Center is **balanced** you feel rooted, able to follow through and complete simple tasks such as doing the laundry or cleaning the kitchen with relative ease. Your confidence is up and you feel secure in the way life needs to unfold. This center also oversees all issues having to do with the MOTHER. When it is **underactive**, you tend to be overly dependent on others to the point of codependency or have a difficult time earning money and taking care of yourself. When it's **overactive**, you tend to be a caretaker, caring for everyone else's life but your own. You might have a lot of responsibilities and/or children to care for.

2. SOCIAL CENTER

The **second chakra** is located approximately **two inches below the navel**, and its energy pattern resonates with the color **ORANGE**. The energy in this center is very absorbent; it collects information regarding your culture, your family dynamics, and your sense of who you are in the world. It oversees all issues related to how you *feel* about yourself and how you came to understand who you are through your life's experiences. The Social Center is the center where we come to define ourselves in relation to others. The way that this center evolves results in the development of either clear and healthy self-boundaries or personal boundaries that are distorted and do not honor who we are. This center is the "**feeling center**" and oversees our **emotions** and all things related to them. Because of the sensitivity aspect of this center, it tends to be the area where we hold on to all our childhood issues and traumas ranging from abandonment to incest. All addictive behavior (drinking, bingeing, drugs, etc.) is stored here. Sexual energy, intimacy, and raw creative energy is activated from this chakra. This chakra oversees all physical and health issues related to the lower intestines, ovaries, and lower back. Issues related to the FATHER are addressed and retained here. When this chakra is in **balance**, you feel balanced emotionally and comfortable with who you are in the world. When it's **underactive**, you are usually shut down emotionally, cut off from your own feelings, and depressed; you will also often feel lonely and have a difficult time accessing your creative energy. When this center is **overactive**, you will tend to overcompensate, trying to control the energy through excessive eating or frequent sex. You are extremely empathetic and can inappropriately take on the emotional states of others. Your sense of passion and creativity is used for pleasing others rather than for your own approval.

3. WILL CENTER

The **third chakra** is located in the **solar plexus area in the opening where the rib cage parts**, and its energy pattern resonates with the color **YELLOW**. This center oversees the energy force behind our "will" and our ability to focus our energy in a specific direction or on a definite purpose. This is the center where our intellectuality and our ability to reason are stored—where we can step back and take an objective look at a situation using rational thinking. From this center we analyze, process, and distribute our thoughts, form new ideas, and tap into our own willpower. It is this center that activates our drive and moves us toward our goals, getting us over inertia or stagnant energy. It's the center that holds on to all our **fears** and **anger**. This center also oversees health issues related to our stomach, intestines, liver, gall bladder, adrenal glands, and middle back. When this center is in **balance**, we are focused and able to move forward with our life's goals and challenges. When this center is **overactive**, we tend to be very willful, controlling, and often manipulative, trying to always get our way by misusing our will through forcing things to happen. When this center is **underactive** we tend to not have much energy, lack the ability to get going on projects, follow through on goals, and think clearly. We also tend to act powerless and without any sense of healthy discipline or willpower.

4. HEART CENTER

The **fourth chakra** is located in the **center of the chest**, and its energy pattern resonates with the color **GREEN**. This is the center where we are able to feel love for ourselves and unconditional love for others. From this center we connect with the oneness that unites us with all living things including other people, nature, the animal and mineral kingdoms, the universe and a higher power. This is the center from which we derive our true personal power, security, confidence, and trust. This chakra is also the energy center that oversees all aspects of healing. All things that we do with our hands are generated from the Heart Center, for it connects directly to the two minor chakras located in the palms of the hands. In terms of health, it oversees our upper back, chest, shoulders, arms, hands, lungs, and all physical and emotional issues of the heart. When this center is in **balance**, we have a strong sense of who we are and what our connection is to the bigger picture of humankind. We are able to be empathetic, kind, and love unconditionally. We have a healthy, well-balanced sense of our personal power and instead of abusing it, we use our power to empower others and create good. When this center is **underactive** we tend to be unable to connect with ourselves, others, and the world as a whole. We feel insecure and lack confidence and a sense of spirituality about our lives. When this center is **overactive** we tend to lose a sense of ourselves and merge with others, overidentifying with other people's problems and life situations. We tend to be "all over the place," with no "personal center" to return home to.

5. THROAT CENTER

The **fifth chakra** is located in the **center of the throat** and resonates with the color **SKY BLUE**. This is the center of our identity and oversees our sense of who we are as individuals. This chakra's issues of identity differ from the "Who am I?" issues of the second chakra (the Social Center) because this energy center is an active center and it doesn't collect information as the Social Center does; instead, it actively shows the world "who we are" by acting it out through our identity. This center is the higher vibration of the second center; it oversees communication and all aspects and types of creativity from artwork to writing. All issues related to authority, teaching, leadership, and organizational and managerial skills are generated from this center. Anything having to do with the voice, singing, or speaking also comes from here. This center oversees adolescence because it is during that period in our lives that we form our identities and show them to the world. This energy center oversees all physical and health-related issues regarding the throat and neck. When this chakra is in **balance**, we are able to comfortably assert and be advocates for ourselves, showing the world our creative skills and ability to oversee projects and responsibilities with ease. When this center is **underactive**, we cannot express our feelings, creativity, or a sense of who we are to others. We tend to withhold and repress our adult self, while feeling stuck in issues that are related to our adolescence. When this center is **overactive**, we can get very rigid and authoritative, trying to control other people and situations by being demanding and giving orders. We are bossy and act like everyone's parent, wanting all things our way.

6. THIRD EYE

The **sixth chakra** is located **on the forehead, between the eyebrows**, and its energy pattern resonates with the color **INDIGO**. This center is called the "third eye" because it is the "eye in our mind" that oversees all aspects of our intuition. Our intuition is the part of us that is our "inner knowing," and sometimes we refer to it as "having a hunch" or a "gut feeling" about something. It's the part of us that "knows something" without fully understanding why or how we know. It is the center of truth because it is from this center that we intuitively see an outcome or a particular situation for what it's worth, without attaching our emotional needs or wants to it (the "emotional center" is the second chakra). This is where we store and access the energy we use to activate our "psychic sight and clairaudient" capabilities. This center oversees all physical or health issues relating to the eyes, ears, and nose. When this center is **balanced**, we are open to receiving intuitive information and trust our gut feelings about people, places, and things. When this center is **under-active**, we often mistrust our own feelings about things and seek out other people's opinions as truth for our own lives. We play down or block our "self-knowing," so that we don't have to deal with the truth of a situation. When this center is **overactive** we try to deal with and get everything done through the use of intuition. We rely on our intuition often inappropriately as a means to avoid dealing with the real world. Although we may be very insightful, we tend not to function very well in the physical realm. Oftentimes we are late for appointments, spacy, ungrounded, unable to connect with our bodies and certain responsibilities.

7. CROWN CENTER

The **seventh chakra** is located at the **top of the head**, and its energy pattern resonates with the color **PURPLE/VIOLET**. This center oversees our connection to our destiny and to our specific path here on earth. The Crown Center acts as our own personal compass, directing and pointing us toward the next part of our journey here. The energy emitted from this chakra acts as a transmitter, drawing and repelling people and situations that are relative to our path. In the esoteric realm, this center connects us to our "higher self" and provides the energy source that is used for creative visualization. This chakra also connects us with the gifts that our soul is here to contribute to the world. It oversees all physical and health-related aspects of our skull, brain, and pituitary functioning. When this center is **balanced** properly, we feel a clear sense that we are on the right path in our lives regarding work, relationships, and self-actualization. We are also able to easily use the powerful gift of creative visualization that is activated here to establish and achieve success, money, happiness, and the ability to heal ourselves. When this center is **underactive**, we are not in control of our lives or our destiny and have no sense of higher planes of existence or spirituality. When the crown chakra is **overactive**, we tend to feel all-powerful and misinterpret our life's path, believing that it is our destiny to control other people's lives. We can be self-delusional, mega-lomaniacal, oppressive, or tyrannical.

There are many ways to access color through the world and our environment. The six main ways that we absorb color through our **AURAS** and **PHYSICAL BODIES** are by means of: **interiors, environments, nature, clothing, food, and meditation or color breathing**.

Home and work interiors have a profound effect on our chakras. The colors that we **paint** our walls, **carpet** our floors, and choose for our **furniture fabrics** and other **materials** in our surroundings all activate, balance, or depress our ch'i, depending on what colors are used and the specific needs of the individual's chakra. When at all possible, pick colors for your home and office that you can connect to and make you feel energized and happy. Make sure that you feel that you can live with them over a long period of time. Remember that these color patterns usually don't change often, so try not to create color schemes that are too neutral or too intense. If you like the color deep purple, instead of painting four walls of a room with it, (which would be very overwhelming) try bringing it into the fabric of your couch or part of the design on your bedspread. You can introduce it into your surroundings through objects such as lamps, vases, and knickknacks. On the other hand, try to avoid creating an all-neutral-colored home because neutrality lends itself to apathy and indifference. Usually individuals who paint their homes in these colors are trying to neutralize themselves and not have too many intense feelings about something in their lives. Now, I know I'm taking a risk by saying that because off-white and neutral-colored walls are considered a "great look" in many design circles, but I stand firm in my convictions that somewhere, regarding something, that individual is cooling down certain feelings because *color invokes feelings; no color invokes neutrality*.

However, if you're partial to neutral colors or if you already have these colors on your walls, *please don't panic*. Try to introduce some color into the space by either painting just one room or one wall. If that doesn't work, try hanging colorful artwork or pictures on the neutral walls. Then, think about my suggestions to you, give what I said some thought, and see if it rings true for you. If it doesn't, let it go. Make sure that *you* have the final say and the final decision about all changes that you make.

I was once on a Feng Shui consultation and upon first entering my client's home, I noticed that every wall in his apartment was painted off-white. He was a vibrant, enthusiastic person who didn't seem to be too affected by the lack of color in his space. Before I commented and explored the color scheme with him, I immediately asked him what type of work he did. He responded, "I am an artist and I work with paints all day long." I quickly realized that he was probably saturated with color at work and that he "needed" his home to be in neutral colors to balance out and calm his ch'i. The home environment that he created helped him achieve the perfect yin-yang balance of the color spectrum, *for him.*

Think about your total color quotient and assess it from a total point of view that has you looking at all the places that you come in contact with throughout each day. If you don't have much color in your "collective environment," you probably will not have a very "***colorful life***." It's your choice!

Other **environments** that we come in contact with every day also can affect the balance of our chakras. The main differences with these environments are that we usually don't have much control over how they are decorated or what colors they are painted, even though they can affect us for better or for worse. These environments can be transitional places such as bus stops, grocery stores, a friend's apartment, or a doctor's office. The way we feel in these places—safe, pressured, nurtured, or uplifted—will determine the state of our ch'i and the balance of our chakras. Allow yourself to think about how a certain place feels to you. Then try to take notice of where in your body you feel those feelings. This will begin to put you in touch with which chakras are reacting to what colors and what situations. For instance, while you are waiting in a doctor's office, take a look around and look at the color scheme in the waiting room. How does it make you feel? Do you like the colors? Hate the colors? Do they calm you? Give you anxiety? Start interpreting and describing the colors with specific adjectives of how they make you feel or react. This will help you build skills and develop a sensitivity to your reaction of how your environment affects you, not only through the colors that surround you, but also to the overall Feng Shui of a place. Use your knowledge and your newly acquired sensitivity to color to consciously help you make decisions about which grocery store you choose to shop in, which restaurant you choose to dine in, even which chair you choose to sit on. If the circumstances permit, honor your energy system and base your decision on the chakra colors that you feel you might need more of that day.

Another common way we absorb energy is through the vast amount of color available to us through **nature**. The universe has provided us with as much color as it has provided us with air to breathe. We are surrounded by **green trees, blue skies, yellow sun, red flowers**, and **animal** and **plant life** that abound with beautiful color. It is no coincidence that the world was created with color as an integral part of everything we see. Color lifts our spirits, affects our moods, and energizes our soul. We absorb the color energy just by being outside and around nature. Take notice of which colors of nature you respond to most favorably. Do you gravitate toward cool blue waters or a forest of trees to find peace and relaxation? Which colors, although beautiful, do not get your attention? Be mindful and aware of the colors around you and how they might be affecting you without your even knowing it. Figure out the colors that soothe you, stimulate you, and make you feel alive. Think about some of your favorite places or things in nature. Make a list of them. Ask yourself what it was about those places that was peaceful, comforting, etc., then think of the colors associated with those images and how they affected you. Take a snapshot of one of your favorite places or a similar photo/painting that depicts the same attributes and *colors*. Place copies of that image in strategic spots where you come into frequent contact with them. *Make eye contact* with the photo as often as you can and feel yourself drawing in the energy and the balancing effect of its color. *Make eye contact with similar colors in your environment* to further enhance your healing experience. Absorb the colors into your body through your eyes, focusing them on the color needed using clear, conscious intentions to help you to visualize your body being filled with its healing ability.

Clothing is also a very powerful way to consciously work with color because our clothing is the closest form of color energy to our **body** and our **aura**, through which we absorb color energy. Besides that, our wardrobe provides us with a daily opportunity to adjust our different needs for color energy. It's not a permanent state of color, and it can change and fluctuate with our moods and imbalances. Use this flexible system with consciousness and you can lift your spirits out of the doldrums one day and help stimulate your creativity the next. Consciously connecting to your chakras will allow you to make the right color choices that will not only make you look good but feel good as well. **Color and clothing can "make the person"** *or* **. . . make the person *invisible.*** The more you tune in to yourself and connect to your color needs, the more you can give your soul the best nourishment it deserves. Each of us has had the experience of trying on clothing that made us look washed-out or drained, then frantically switching to other outfits until we found the one that looked right—breathing out a sigh of relief as we hurried off to work.

THREE WAYS TO CHOOSE THE CORRECT COLORS FOR YOUR DAILY NEEDS

THE FIRST WAY IS: go to the closet where you keep your clothes and run your hands over the different outfits that you have to choose from for that particular day or event. Take notice of which outfit draws your attention and calls out to you. Then *feel with your eyes* and the energy in your body how that outfit would make you feel if you wore it on that particular day. If several outfits appeal to you, do this exercise with each one until you find the right fit, then decide.

THE SECOND WAY IS: specifically pick out an outfit (colors) that will help you with a situation or an issue that you are aware of and need help with. For instance, if it is laundry day and you absolutely don't have the enthusiasm or the energy for the task, you could choose to wear something **RED to activate the first energy center** which will ground you and help you complete the task, or if you need to have a heart-to-heart talk with someone, wear something **GREEN to activate and open the heart chakra**.

THE THIRD WAY IS: by doing a **Chakra Meditation** and specifically receiving information regarding a problem or situation in your life and locating the *colors* you would need to restore balance (see the end of this chapter). Don't be afraid to use color! Not liking a certain color is not a good enough excuse not to use it; instead, find a more discreet way to incorporate it into your wardrobe that won't have you crawling out of your skin. If RED is not your FAVORITE color but you need it on a particular day, try wearing underwear, a scarf, or a handkerchief that is that color. A little color goes a long way. You don't need a lot of it to shift your energy, just enough to make you consciously connect to the energy behind the color. Decorate yourself with the same care you would take if you were designing a sacred temple. ***Remember, your body is the temple that your soul resides in while it is in your care. . . . Honor it, love it, and nourish it with color.***

Food is another way we can influence our chakra energy. Traditionally, when we think about the nutritional value of food, we are referring to the vitamin, mineral, or caloric contents of the food. But when we are dealing with balancing the chakras and our ch'i energy, we evaluate the nutritional value of our food through its color scheme and its corresponding elements. Certain foods based on their color and/or the energy they impart activate different chakras and contribute certain healing energies to various ailments.

One method of assessing foods in terms of their color and healing ability is through the **Five Element Theory**. According to this system, most foods can be broken down and divided up into five groups representing the elements of **FIRE, EARTH, METAL, WATER, and WOOD**. Depending on where your imbalance is and what particular illness you may have, certain foods/diets can be eaten or "prescribed" to help remedy the imbalances.* This particular system for working with food and healing is a little bit more involved and requires much more study than what I am prepared to explore here in this chapter. If this method interests you, then I encourage you to read other books that deal specifically and eloquently with this topic.

Another more tangible method of bringing color energy in through food is by using the chakra system of color. By eating foods that are associated with the seven colors of the chakras and the rainbow, you can ingest the colors that nature infused for us in the various foods we eat for healing and rebalancing our energies. For instance, if you are dealing with emotional issues regarding your childhood or your family, you can try eating more oranges or carrots to help you cope better. If you check the chakra charts above, you will notice that childhood issues are "***second-center issues***," and the second center is the **Social Center**, which resonates with the color **ORANGE**. Thus, orange-colored foods will help balance those emotional issues. Be aware that sometimes a center is referred to as "overactive" and actually needs less of the color that it resonates with. On the other hand, take notice of your food cravings to see if you are gravitating toward any one particular "food color group." Your energy might be telling you that something is out of balance or being stirred up in that particular chakra. Be your own detective; get to know your own energy system and explore how much or how little of any one of these colors you might need. *Ingesting the colors through food is a common way we restore*

* (Annemarie Colbin, *Food and Healing*, New York: Ballantine, 1986.)

balance. Whenever I teach my meditation classes on the chakras, I always try to have a bowl of red fruit or fruit juices available for my students to snack on when hungry. I learned this trick back in the early eighties from my first mentor, Nancy Rosanoff, a wonderfully gifted teacher and psychic in the New York area. She would always have some red grapes around for her students during full-day workshops on Psychic Development and the Chakras. Several months into our work, she finally confessed that she provided the **red food** to assist us in staying grounded during a full day of doing meditation and psychic work. **Red** stimulates the first energy center, the **Survival Center**, which provides us with grounding energy. **Think about the foods you eat and need, then consciously make choices that will appeal not only to your appetite but also to the hunger of your soul.**

Meditation or color breathing is yet another way that your body can absorb color into your energy field and into your chakras. There is really no wrong way to meditate, so for those of you who haven't had prior experience in meditation this is the perfect opportunity to begin exploring this type of healing. There are many different types of meditation and as many different ways to meditate. Some individuals may choose to close their eyes, sit in a comfortable position, or even lie down. Keep in mind the objective of meditation is to help you create a quiet space and time where you can go inside of yourself, shut out all the noise in the world, the chatter in your mind, and connect with your spirit and your Higher Power. Some people use meditation to block out all of life's distractions, release the tensions of the day, and be completely mindless. This clearing process allows the body, mind, and soul to reconnect and merge back together to the oneness that they originated from.

Others may choose to use their meditation time to specifically contemplate a particular situation or issue in their lives. They creatively use the serenity of the sacred space within themselves to help them reconnect to their intuition and receive some guidance from above. Others prefer what I call "**open-eye meditations**." These are the things we do that expand our energy and create the same wonderful, calming effect on our mind, body, and soul. Some examples of "open-eye meditations" are: taking a walk on the beach; painting, sculpting, or working on any form of art; taking a candlelit bath; doing yoga; or listening to your favorite music. All these various "time-outs" honor our spirit and allow our thoughts to be transformed and healing to occur. Each method gives our energy system the opportunity to clear, realign itself, and become more receptive to the nourishing colors that exist in our environment.

Using your breath to inhale the colors around you is another powerful way to bring the colors of your environment into your being. Make eye contact with specific colors in your environment that you feel you may need based on the information provided above on the chakras. Then act as if you are able to transform the colors off of the objects and into the air, breathing in each color, letting your entire body absorb the color and the energy it emits. For example, if you are stuck in traffic and are feeling anxious and ungrounded, try looking around to see if you can find a corner stop sign, a red flower, or a red-colored car. Make eye contact with the object and take a deep breath, visualizing that you are breathing in the color red and that the color is filling up your first center located at the base of your spine. Your first center oversees the energy that grounds your spirit *and* your body, especially during stressful times. Bringing in the color that the first center needs will help restore balance to that energy center and to all its corresponding issues. You can use this method of color breathing for all the colors and the chakras.

The methods that we can use to harness color and improve our ch'i are vast, but all tend to seek the same common denominator to make the various methods effective. That common factor is what I call "***Mindful Application of Thought***." It is the ability to apply your thinking mind and focus it in a specific way, for a specific result, without having to use much of anything else to create an outcome. Now, I know some of you may be saying to yourselves that this is ridiculous or sounds like a form of mind control, but the fact of the matter is that we are just beginning to realize how little of our brains we actually do use (*some of us even use less than others*). As a society, we are starting to further expand our level of consciousness, almost guaranteeing that we will be using more of our brain capabilities and functions. When you are working with energy such as in color work or Feng Shui, your belief in a higher force along with your **conscious intentions** are really the only tools you need to begin to create a change.

Your thoughts are powerful. Learn to use them responsibly with consciousness, and you can change your life and create your happiness.

One very effective way to infuse color into your chakras is through a meditation process called ***Color Breathing***. Color Breathing is a process that allows you to use the flow of your breath, along with ***Creative Visualization Techniques***, to bring the seven colors of the chakras into your body to fine tune and strengthen your energy field.

Below is a simple Chakra Color Meditation that was designed to recharge and strengthen your energy system on a daily basis. Find the time of day that works best for ***you***. Some people choose fifteen minutes every morning before they start their day, while others choose the night time just before bed to practice their meditation. There is no correct way, do not worry about doing it wrong. With practice it will become easier, especially if you try to create a routine that will keep you consistent and structured. If you have difficulty remembering all the chakras at first, it often helps to have a friend guide you through the meditation or record the instructions on a tape recorder to play back each time you meditate. Remember to leave pauses during the parts in which you will require quiet time to do the various steps. This meditation should take you a minimum of fifteen minutes and over time, gradually expand as you add more breathing time to each color in the meditation.

COLOR BREATHING MEDITATION

1. Find a comfortable spot that is quiet and traffic free. Close your eyes, relax, and take a deep breath and exhale. Again, take another breath in, then out. Focus your awareness on your breath. Allow your breathing to naturally find a comfortable rhythm and pace.

2. With each breath, feel your body relaxing and with each exhalation, feel yourself releasing all the tensions of the day and all the worries on your mind.

3. With your eyes closed, bring your attention to the open area approximately six inches above the top of your head. In your mind's eye visualize a beautiful ball of pure white light circulating above the top of your head. As you continue to breathe, the light becomes brighter and brighter with a warm luminescent glow.

4. Visualize yourself slowly breathing this beautiful light in through an imaginary opening located on the top of your head. Slowly, using your

breath, breathe this light through your eyes and ears, into your nose and mouth, continuing to breathe the light down your throat, into your heart, lungs, down each arm, through each hand and out each fingertip. Continue to breathe the light through the intestines, each organ, down the spine into the legs, past the knees, through the feet and out the toes.

5. With each full breath in, breathe the light in through the top of your head, filling up your whole body and with each exhale, release the white light through your fingertips and toes. Inhale and exhale several times, circulating the light in, through, and out of your body.

6. Bring your attention back to the top of your head, to the ***seventh chakra*** located at the ***crown***. Slowly visualize the white light turning to a beautiful shade of ***purple***, breathe this beautiful shade of purple in and out of the top of your head, saturating it with this color. If you have a difficult time visualizing the color purple (or any color), visualize any object you own or may have seen that contains that color (e.g., a purple dress, flower or candle).

7. Then watch the light slowly move down to the ***sixth chakra between the eyebrows*** called the ***third eye***. As you continue to breathe into that chakra watch the light slowly turn into the color ***indigo***. Breathe the color indigo in and out of your eyes and ears.

8. As you continue to breathe, slowly watch the ball of light move downward into the ***fifth chakra*** located in the ***center of your throat***. Slowly it turns to the color ***sky blue***, filling up your mouth, throat and the back of your neck. Continue to breathe sky blue energy in and out of the areas several times.

9. Move your awareness down to the ***fourth chakra***, ***The Heart Center*** located in the ***center of your chest***. Slowly breathe the light down into the center of your chest watching the light turn to a beautiful shade of ***green***. Continue to breathe the green heart energy into your upper back, shoulders, down your arms and into your hands several times.

10. Continue to breathe the light downward into the ***third chakra***, ***The Solar Plexus*** located in the ***center of your ribs***, visualize the light turning into a beautiful shade of ***yellow***. With each breath imagine

yourself breathing yellow energy into your solar plexus, stomach, liver, gall bladder, large intestines and middle back. Continue to breathe yellow energy into these organs several times.

11. Move your awareness down to the **second chakra** located **two inches below the navel—The Social Center**. Slowly breathe the light in and out of your second center watching it turn into a beautiful shade of **orange**. Breathe the color orange into your small intestines, reproductive organs, spleen and your lower back. Allow the color to circulate and strengthen the energy from that center. Continue to breathe the color orange in and out of that chakra.

12. As you continue to breathe, slowly bring your awareness to your **first chakra** located at the **base of your spine—The Survival Center**. Take a deep breath and watch it turn into a beautiful shade of **red**. Breathe the red color in and out of the base of your spine, filling it with grounding red energy. As you breathe this color in and out, slowly let it circulate in and around your genitals, slowly filling up your legs, moving past your knees and ankles, through your feet and out your toes.

13. After you have finished breathing in the color red to your first chakra, slowly watch the color red in your legs and Survival Center turn back to a beautiful, glowing White Light. See the White Light filling up your legs, moving up to your Social Center, filling up your intestines and your lower back, continuing to move upward toward your Solar Plexus filling up your stomach, all your major organs and the middle of your back. Continue to breathe this beautiful White Light up into your Heart Chakra, filling up your chest, upper back, arms and hands. Allow your breath to continue to bring the White Light up into your throat and to the back of your neck circulating it in and through your mouth. With your next breath, move the White Light up into your Third Eye breathing it into your eyes and ears. Continue to breathe the White Light up into your head and circulate it in the Crown Chakra. Finally breathe the White Light up and out the top of your head, returning it to the safe resting place that is located six inches above the top of your head, where it will always watch over you and illuminate your path.

14. Take a deep breath in and slowly bring your attention back to your body, back to your room, and when you are ready you can open your eyes.

15. Make some notes. Take notice if any color seemed scarce, abundant or difficult to visualize. If so, go to your list on the chakras and read what various things each chakra oversees and is responsible for. Try to connect how those things are working or not working in your life. Decide if you need more or less of that color, then try to bring those colors into your energy field through the foods you eat and the colors you wear that day.

SIX

SOLUTIONS FOR DEALING WITH LIFE'S OBSTACLES

An old Chinese saying states that there are five main factors that will determine if you will have a good life: 1) fate or destiny, 2) luck, 3) Feng Shui, 4) accumulated good deeds, and 5) education.

What this proverb implies is that there are certain predestined things that affect our lives, such as fate or luck, that we do not have much control over. Other things that affect our lives—such as Feng Shui, accumulated good deeds, and education—we do have some control over. This means that our lives are made up of several different "systems," some more tangible than others, that interface with one another and collectively create a life that will either thrive, fail, or be mediocre. Although there are certain things in our lives we cannot change, I believe that we can ultimately make most situations better.

Our true power lies in our ability to understand what we can honestly bring to a situation and then in knowing how to access the rest through other means.

I believe **preparation plus opportunity equals success (P+O=S).**

This motivating equation means that in order for any success to occur, two very specific factors need to be present. The first is ***Preparation (P)***—this means that, first, you have to be prepared for the circumstances or the job that you are seeking and, second, there has to be an ***Opportunity (O)*** available for you to access and activate. The Preparation is the part of this equation that you become solely responsible for, but the Opportunity part of this equation is the part that is helped by other forces. It's the part where chance meetings, synchronicities, fate, destiny, and karma all converge to provide you with the Opportunity that allows you to apply all that you have been preparing to do. The way we prepare for things in our lives is not always in a typical or obvious manner such as going to school to become a doctor or training for years to go to the Olympics. Often our preparation is cultivated by just living our lives and showing up for the different lessons that we experience throughout our time here. **I believe the quintessential schoolroom in our lives is our lives.**

The Opportunity part of the equation is where **Feng Shui** comes in. It helps to clear away certain energy blocks, while opening up additional paths that lead us to or draw to us certain Opportunities. For example, if you go to college to study to be a lawyer *(P)* and you are having a hard time finding work, if you adjust, say, the Career and Helpful People corners in your home, the adjustments might help by lifting the obstacles and resulting in your finding a job *(O)*. Here's another example: You are looking for work and you feel that you don't have many skills because you never went to college, instead spent the last ten years raising three children and caring for a family. You decide to clear out junk from your Career section, hang a mirror in your Wealth corner, and after several weeks of interviewing for work, you finally land yourself a job managing a laundromat. Often these "overnight success" stories are marred by envious friends thinking *"How did she get that job?"* or *"His father must have known one of the owners."* But many times we are our own worst critics and unsupportive friends. Battling low self-esteem, the negative voices that reside in our head, we think quietly, "I don't deserve this job" or "I am going to be found out for the fraud that I really am." These are the very thoughts that sabotage our successes. Very rarely do we stop and think, "**Well** . . . *I did raise three kids, manage a household, pay the bills, organize five individuals' schedules, oversee twenty-one meals a week, etc., and I guess then, that makes me more than capable of running a laundromat.* **As a matter of fact,**

comparatively speaking, that laundromat job is starting to look more and more like a breeze."

We have been secretly preparing for most of the people, places, and things that come our way for a very long time. We rarely get anything we don't deserve, even though we may not be able to clearly connect the cause with the effect. *This is a very important concept to remember* because as you start working with Feng Shui, and especially when using transcendental solutions to your problems, you will be able to "own" more of the wonderful outcomes and not chalk everything up to just "magic" or "coincidence."

HELP COMES CLOAKED IN MANY DIFFERENT DISGUISES

As we go through life, expand on our sense of responsibility, and understand our choice of options, we become more empowered to consciously affect the outcome of our situations. If we choose to throw all caution to the wind, chalk up our lives totally to destiny and fate, then that's what our lives will amount to and be contingent on . . . *sheer luck and happenstance.* Fortunately, I do not believe that life is that simple, that we can hold our breath, cross our fingers, and relinquish all control. I do believe, however, that we were put here on this earth not only to fulfill our destiny and experience our karma, *but also to* create, transmute energy, and make personal contributions to the world. It is very difficult to do all these things voluntarily, if you don't consciously understand all the different levels on which we exist. That's why I believe that there are several different conscious and unconscious systems that are at work in our lives simultaneously providing backup systems for those of us who are not as connected with our life process. Some of these systems allow us much more opportunity to take control of the wheel, while other systems run on automatic pilot for those of us who would prefer to experience life with our homing instruments on "***cruise control***." Even without being totally aware of what our personal contribution to the world is or what all our feelings are, we are still able to do all these things, even without consciously knowing or having the awareness. It's very similar to how our breathing works; without thinking about it, we still automatically inhale and exhale twenty-four hours a day.

The universe has provided us with so many ways to deal with our problems and conflicts that all it takes is the willingness to change and an open mind to seek out some help. Our generation has been given choices which include twelve-step programs, self-help groups, twenty-four-hour hot lines, psychotherapy, Feng Shui, Oprah shows, even the *Psychic Friends Network!* Remember, help comes cloaked in many disguises. Choose the one that feels right to you and follow its lead.

How Do You Recognize Help?

There was once a man whose boat capsized in the middle of the ocean. After clinging to a plank of wood for hours, he started praying to God to save him from drowning. A few minutes later a helicopter appeared out of nowhere, and the pilot offered to throw down a ladder and haul him up; he waved his hands back and forth and sent the helicopter away. He continued to pray and trusted that the Lord would come to his rescue. Several minutes later, he noticed a small boat edging up next to him; the captain of the boat told him to hang on and that he would throw him a life preserver, but once again he shook his head and waved him away. Several hours later, dehydrated and very close to drowning, he managed to lift up his head and call out, ". . . God, I've followed you all my life and believed in your word that you would always be there for me; now I am drowning, how could you abandon me in my time of need?" Out of the sky came a loud, but surprised voice, ". . . My dear child, I would never abandon you. . . . I have sent you a helicopter and a boat. What else did you expect, for me to put on my Speedo, jump in, and save you myself?"

—Author Unknown

Often we don't recognize how help is sent to us because we are too busy being locked into a particular way that we envision it will come. This is very unfortunate because, many times, we unknowingly turn away the exact help that we are asking for. Take a moment and think about the different ways that you might turn away help. Make a list on a piece of paper of all the problems that you are currently seeking solutions to, then narrow the list down to your favorite three and carefully think about each one. Write down all the ways that come to mind that would serve as solutions to those problems. Then ask yourself if you are truly ready to challenge your limited thinking about how some of those situations might be resolved. If you are, then you have come to the right place because Feng Shui doesn't always adjust things by conventional means. Although it often brings about many changes that you might welcome, many times it might not be in the ways that you would expect. *This is important to remember* because if you are close minded to the different ways in which help might come, then it might also be hard for you to follow the synchronicities that will start to unfold in your life.

UNDERSTANDING TRANSCENDENTAL SOLUTIONS

The two main ways that we attempt to adjust the Feng Shui in our lives are through **mundane** and **transcendental cures**. As I explained in chapter 2, mundane cures are the type of solutions that are practical, reasonable, and deemed logical by most of the population. Transcendental cures are the solutions that are considered to be more mystical and spiritual in nature and don't necessarily follow any rules of logic or intellect. Both sets of solutions— and I cannot emphasize this enough—are equally important because they need to work in tandem to maximize their effectiveness. To give you a concrete example, let's say that your business is failing, you are having a hard time getting it back on track, and you have finally considered having a Feng Shui consultation. After a thorough assessment of the site of your business, several different solutions including mundane and transcendental cures might be suggested.

For example, distributing more advertisement flyers, having a red-tag sale, and purchasing a bigger sign for the front door would all be considered mundane solutions. These are the solutions that are practical, logical, and make intellectual sense. Then a Feng Shui consultant might suggest placing a wind chime in your Wealth area, hanging a red tassel in your Fame area, and placing nine rocks in a very specific location inside your store. These are examples of transcendental solutions. Technically these solutions make no rational or logical sense based on our intellectual understanding of how things should work. However, the *first* premise of transcendental solutions is believing that there are valid systems and realms of knowledge that exist in our world that we do not intellectually or fully understand.

The *second* premise is that these systems are valid and function on a higher order, enlisting the help and expertise of other spiritual forces.

The *third* and last premise is that you accept and understand that the process is part of a co-creative effort to work with all the invisible forces of nature collectively—to rebalance energy and to shift and heal the whole planet.

Although working with energy is an invisible and, at times, an intangible process, energy exists everywhere and has a profound effect on all our lives. And just because we are creating change through an invisible energy system doesn't make it any less valid or real.

The Chinese have been using the concept of working with energy as a way of medically treating people for centuries. Acupuncture, Chinese medicine, and Shiatsu massage are just a few examples of the many healing modalities that have made their way West and have become not only popular but also accepted as respectable alternatives to Western medicine. When a doctor or acupuncturist places a needle on a certain part of your body to open up or stimulate blocked ch'i, what s/he is really doing is placing the needle (or fingertips in shiatsu) on an energy pathway in the body that is referred to as a meridian. These meridians connect to different organs and regulate the flow of energy (ch'i) in a person's body. Blocked meridians mean blocked energy, which creates a reduced flow of the life force through certain areas of the body. These meridians all correspond to several different organs and systems in the body, affecting their health and well-being. These meridians are invisible. If you were to open up the body and look inside, you would never be able to see them as you would be able to see your heart or the way the "hip bone's connected to the thigh bone." The same invisible system of energy (ch'i) that governs these very reputable healing modalities also oversees the Feng Shui process. Feng Shui is like acupuncture for your home. The same life force of ch'i that lives invisibly in the body also lives invisibly outside of the body in your homes, offices, and outdoor environments. So when you place a crystal ball in your Wealth corner to stimulate the ch'i flow, you are actually using that particular adjustment item the same way acupuncturists use their needles and the same way shiatsu practitioners use their thumbs to move and unblock ch'i.

It has taken the Western world ***four thousand years*** to fully grasp these concepts. But now we are starting to open up our minds, tone down our arrogance, and welcome the concept that there are other ways to do things. If the idea of transcendental cures seems foolish to you, remember that research and science have always had a way of making the unexplainable acceptable. Imagine two hundred years ago trying to explain to someone about the Concorde Jet—or a basic airplane, for that matter! The idea would be inconceivable to most people and probably looked upon as a "wild fantasy" or just a "crazy idea." What about sending a man to the moon? Tapping into airwaves and creating television in your own home? **Today's modern technologies were yesterday's impossibilities!** We are the generation that has been chosen to consciously explore many "unexplainable" things and when we are through make them as "matter of fact" to the next millennium as booking a flight to Florida is to us now.

Transcendental cures, although mystical by nature, surprisingly come from the same realm of knowledge as all new ideas. This is true because at the core of who we are, we are basically spiritual beings living in human form during this incarnation; and the information that we receive, be it to develop the wheel or discover penicillin, is all derived from the same spiritual realm. When we fully grasp this concept, we will no longer need to separate out a certain type of knowledge from another. We will understand that many new ideas and ways to solve problems in our lives are only considered "new," "odd," or "unusual" because at one time they did not exist as part of our consciousness. Ironically, these solutions have actually always existed, just waiting for us to arrive at a particular need *and* time where we are able to grasp their concepts, usage, and value as means to further support and enrich our lives.

As discussed in chapter 5, we are basically units of "white light" that emit and receive energy through the seven energy centers in our bodies called the chakras. When our "receiving line of energy" connects with an "emitting line of energy" from another source or person, we are then able to draw on an idea or a solution to a particular problem. That is how all ideas, inventions, scientific theories, medical breakthroughs, and spiritual knowledge, etc., occur. Most of the time, these ideas and thoughts are "picked up" by many people at once, only to be publicly shared by the few individuals who, as part of their life's mission, bring that particular idea out to the people. For instance, how many times have you had an idea about something and no sooner had you realized it than someone else got the credit for it—or seen a gadget advertised on television and thought to yourself, I thought of making one of those years ago?

What about the scientists who fight over who discovered a particular cure first or the musician who claims he was the originator of a created tune? Our court system is filled with lawsuits and complaints about who stole whose idea. That is why we had to develop a system of copywriting and patenting our ideas. The significant point here is that when the time is right and the idea is ready to manifest itself in our world, many people, often at the same time, receive the same idea. The issue of timing, taking an action, and—if it is your personal karma—manifesting it, is what makes it your "original idea" or not. You may not be the only one to receive it from the universe, but it may be your calling to actually take the actions to make it real. That's why it is so important to stay open and clear throughout your life, especially during times of difficulty and transition. The more open you are, the more help and direction you will be able to receive. That is also another reason why it is important for you to stay focused and relaxed, meditate, take a walk on the beach, listen to your favorite music, feed the birds, pet the dog, and take some quiet time to think. Those are all the ways we communicate and connect with the guidance that is available to us. *It has been said that "prayer" is the format that gives us the opportunity to talk to our Higher Power, whatever name we give it, and "meditation" is the format that allows that Power to speak back to us.* I believe that transcendental solutions are one of the ways that we tap in and have access to the divine interventions from the other side that we so often pray for and call upon. Black Hat Sect Feng Shui, through its Buddhist teachings, draws on these solutions and makes them available to *all* people, to help them improve the quality of their lives.

YOUR HEALTH IS YOUR WEALTH

Those of you who are fortunate enough to possess good health are truly blessed with the greatest gift that no amount of money can ever buy. You have been born with the good karma that has provided you with physical ch'i that is strong and healthy. Others (and that includes most of us) have been side-tracked now and then with ailments ranging from broken bones and sprained ankles, to more serious, life-threatening illnesses. Many aspects such as genetics, diet, stress, allergies, and environment factor in to the overall quality and status of an individual's health. In Feng Shui, we acknowledge all these different components, but we also believe that the layout of your home, the positioning of your furniture, or the shape of your house can all contribute to either exacerbating, triggering, or causing certain physical and mental conditions. Your home is like a body with its own metabolism.* It mirrors your life as well as your health. A few simple things being out of place can disturb your physical body and your emotional outlook on life. Examining your floor plan as well as the placement of your furniture can help you diagnose problem areas and to make the correct changes needed to rebalance the ch'i and improve your health. Keep in mind that whenever a physical or an emotional problem arises, I will always encourage you to seek the proper medical advice, along with making the appropriate Feng Shui adjustments in your home. Feng Shui will greatly help solve the problem . . . *if the problem is Feng Shui related*, such as a poorly placed bed or an awkwardly shaped room. If it isn't directly related to the Feng Shui of your layout, then the Feng Shui process will help align you with someone who will be of help to you. Many times I recommend that my clients make certain changes in their home as a means of prevention, before the problem manifests itself physically. Often we don't know how an individual's health is going to unfold or which family member has a predisposition toward a particular illness. That's why two people can live in the same home that harbors very specific Feng Shui problems but the house layout may affect just one of them. All the other factors such as genetics and karma will determine if a particular individual will manifest a certain type of illness or life situation or not. The best way to shore up your own health and that of your family is by making all the adjustments you can (within reason) and keeping your home well maintained. Remember, using *both* the mundane solutions and the transcendental solutions is important and together they will strengthen and heighten the transformational benefits that each one has to offer.

One way to approach dealing with health-related problems is through the use of the Feng Shui Bagua map. Each one of the nine sections of the map is called a gua. Each gua oversees a different part of the body. Use the map to direct you to the particular area of the Bagua that coincides with the area of health that is of concern to you. For instance, let's say that you are having surgery done on your foot. Go to the Bagua map and locate the gua that oversees the ch'i of the foot. The ch'i of the foot is located in the FAMILY gua.

*Sarah Rossbach, *Interior Design with Feng Shui* (New York: E.P. Dutton, 1987).

THE BAGUA AND YOUR HEALTH

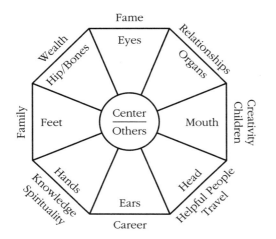

THE NINE AREAS OF THE BAGUA AND THEIR CORRESPONDING BODY AREAS

1. Fame - eyes
2. Relationships - organs
3. Children - mouth
4. Helpful people - head
5. Career - ears
6. Knowledge - hands
7. Family - feet
8. Wealth - hip/bones
9. Center - others

Then take out your floor plan and locate the area that oversees FAMILY on the overall floor plan of your house and locate the FAMILY section in each individual room. First check those areas for missing corners, clutter, or situations of concern. Check for leaks, accumulated newspapers, obstacles, dead space, things that you might trip over or might *trip you up*, etc. See if anything seems out of place or problematic. If it does, then clean it up and make the necessary changes. In addition, add one of the Nine Basic Cures and perform the three Secret Reinforcement (chapter 7), and visualize the operation being a success. This is one method you can use for all your health-related problems and concerns; just modify it to fit your particular situation. Remember, all parts or areas of the body that are not clearly listed in the eight surrounding guas are designated to be in the center area of the Bagua. This means that you would follow the same procedure as above, just locating instead, the center of your home and then the center areas of each individual room. The Three Secret Reinforcement is the spiritual backbone that reinforces and enhances this blessing process.

SPECIFIC HEALTH CONCERNS

Health problems can appear and be detected through several different methods while doing a Feng Shui assessment. Below are listed ten different physical and emotional problems that can be caused or exacerbated by common design errors or house-maintenance problems.

1. RESPIRATORY PROBLEMS: Check for dark or narrow entranceways to all rooms; especially check the front doorway for anything that may block the "mouth of the ch'i." Small entranceways that lead up to a house, small waiting areas, vestibules, and mud rooms should also be considered. REMEDY: Remove clutter, expand space with mirrors, use light-colored paints and bright lighting, and add a life force adjustment such as plants, fish, or birds to circulate the energy.

2. IMMUNE SYSTEM AND CIRCULATORY PROBLEMS: For any type of health problems that are related to the flow of the blood, the quality of the blood, or the lymphatic system, the occupants should check the electrical and water systems in the house. REMEDY: All frayed wires, electrical shorts, overloaded sockets, and the like should be repaired immediately. Dripping faucets and pipe and ceiling leaks should be fixed, while clogged sewers, drains, and cesspools should be cleared.

3. HEART DISEASE: Heart disease also falls under the above heading of circulatory illnesses, but because there are so many different types of interior problems related to heart disease, it required its own category. First and foremost, doors, hallways, and spiral staircases all directly affect the functioning of the heart. If the heart-related problem is focused around the ventricles' not working properly, check all the doors in the house. If the heart disease is due to blocked arteries, then check for clutter in hallways, entranceways, and behind doors. REMEDY: Clear all blocks from entranceways, hallways, and doors. Repair all electrical and plumbing problems as discussed in number

two, above. If you have a spiral staircase, add a light at the top and hang a faceted crystal ball on a nine-inch red string from the top of the ceiling. Check if you have three doors in a row at any one location in your house and hang two faceted crystals, each on a nine-inch red string, in between each archway.

4. EYE/SIGHT PROBLEMS: The eyes influence our ability to see the world and to figurally see our lives. When we develop eye-related problems, it's important that we take out the time to think about what we might be avoiding or choosing not to "see." When you are working with the Feng Shui process, try to remember that Feng Shui is rich with innuendos and metaphors. If you work with *all* the signals that it sends you, you will find yourself healing faster and changes happening more swiftly. In Feng Shui, the windows in the house and the Career guas are closely related to all aspects of the eyes. REMEDY: Replace all broken windows, mirrors, and window frames in the house. Keep the windows cleared and polish the glass often to retain clarity and insight. Check all areas of the house that oversee the Career guas and make adjustments accordingly. Watery eyes, due to allergies, can also be linked to water leaks and drainage problems.

5. HEADACHES: Headaches that are chronic and/or specific to certain locations, are a signal to check the front door and entranceways for blocks or problems. The entranceway areas oversee the head and if doors get stuck, don't close properly, or are not able to open all the way, the ch'i around the head can be suppressed and constricted, causing headaches and head-related problems. In addition, if you are finding that people in your life who should otherwise be helpful are starting to give you "big headaches," carefully check the Helpful People guas throughout your home, for they also oversee the head area of the body. REMEDY: Clear doorways, remove all heavy/tall pieces of furniture that are located over your head, and check for overhead beams. All beams that hang over your bed, desk, and stove should be augmented with two bamboo flutes, hung on an angle (see p. 49). Make sure all the Helpful People guas are uncluttered. Add one of the Nine Basic Cures to augment the ch'i and apply the Three Secret Reinforcement, visualizing all your headaches disappearing.

6. ARTHRITIS/JOINT DISEASES/T.M.J.: All problems or illnesses that have to do with the joints are directly related to the hinges, hardware, and locks on a door.

Doors that don't close correctly or squeak can create stiff wrists, knuckles, and knee joints. Cabinets, closets, dresser drawers, folding doors, and the like all should be checked, oiled frequently, and on track working smoothly. REMEDY: Fix and oil all hardware and doors, check all the Knowledge guas in the house, for they oversee all issues regarding the hands. Check for "bad bite" doors (see p. 52) and add mirrors to either side to offset any T.M.J. problems. Also, for any problems regarding the mouth, check the Children guas in the house. In addition, make sure all doorknobs are on properly. When doorknobs are loose or missing, the residents often have a hard time "getting a handle on things"!

7. LOW ENERGY: Having problems with low energy can be very subtle but pervasive in Feng Shui. First check the lighting in the house and make sure that all the bulbs are bright, working, and there are no empty sockets. Then check the positioning of the bed and the desk to be sure the occupants are facing the door and that there are no beds/mattresses on the floor. Check for good ventilation to circulate ch'i and for skylights that may be siphoning ch'i up and away from the main rooms in the house. Most important, check the house for dead batteries and broken appliances. Appliances that do not work, but are kept in the home anyway, drain the body of its natural ch'i flow. REMEDY: Fix all lighting, repair or discard all appliances that no longer work, and make sure that the main pieces of furniture are correctly positioned. In addition, hang a wind chime in the center of your bedroom and apply the Three Secret Reinforcement while visualizing your energy shifting and your ch'i getting stronger.

8. STOMACH/INTESTINAL PROBLEMS: These problems can manifest themselves in many different ways through the Feng Shui of your home. Stress related to relationships, finances, and family matters contributes to the makings of an ulcer or an overactive colon. So if you feel that your stomach problems are stress related, try to figure out the areas of concern, then go to those areas and make the adjustments accordingly. It is also very important that you check the center lines that run through the middle of your home and through the middle of each room. Those are the areas that oversee the stomach and the intestines. Try to avoid having your kitchen or bathroom over that central line; having them there will weaken your ch'i along that meridian. All running-type illnesses such as colds, bladder infections, and diarrhea stem from water or electrical imbalances and require checking the plumbing and wiring systems

thoroughly. Make sure the headboard on your bed isn't up against a wall shared with a bathroom or kitchen and that the bed itself doesn't cross with a bathroom door. REMEDIES: If the kitchen or the bathroom runs along the center line of the house, place mirrors on all four walls and hang a crystal ball on a nine-inch red string from the ceiling. Check all plumbing for leaks and rotted areas; replace all decayed areas. Locate all the Relationship guas in your home because these are the guas that oversee all the organs in the body, including the stomach. Use one of the Nine Basic Cures and bless your intention with the Three Secret Reinforcement, visualizing the condition healed.

9. ANXIETY: When certain layouts and conditions in a home are out of balance, they can trigger and exacerbate already-existing anxiety. Long hallways without any breaks or dividing objects can quickly accelerate the ch'i in one's house, causing unnerving and erratic energy. If the hallway is running perpendicularly to a bedroom entranceway or an area where the occupants spend a lot of time, the impact will be even greater on that individual's nervous system. Entranceways that connect directly to a window or open shaft will also create an energy push that forces the energy to move forward in a rapid fashion. Color also plays a very integral part in creating a space that is either soothing or anxiety producing. The color white, in China, is traditionally used as a color of mourning, as we use the color black in the West. When an apartment is completely painted in the color white, it can cause the ch'i to ricochet off the walls and ceiling, which brings about a lot of frenetic and unstable energy. Living in that type of energy pattern, seven days a week, three hundred sixty-five days a year can shape the pattern of your personal ch'i, causing lots of unnecessary anxiety. REMEDIES: Add energy dividers such as framed artwork and small throw rugs to long hallways, every five feet, to slow down and break up the energy patterns. In addition, you can add a heavy object such as a large vase or a concrete statue at the end of a hallway to slow down the energy. Another easy solution is to add some color to your home and break up the solid white walls. If you choose to keep the walls white, add color to the ceiling, doors, or trim in a room. Try to avoid having the walls, ceiling, and trim in a room all the same color, even if it's not white.

10. DEPRESSION: Another expression used to describe depression is "feeling low." It's important to check every room in the house and see if you notice any

heavy or large pieces of furniture that may be towering over your head in significant places such as in your bedroom, living room, or place of work when you feel depressed. These large pieces of furniture, including bookcases, tend to overpower and depress the ch'i in our body, causing the emotions to be thrown off balance. If the depression is chronic, check the overall Feng Shui of your house; you might find that your apartment needs a complete overhaul, requiring several adjustments. In particular, check the electrical wiring throughout the house; frayed wires and overloaded outlets also connect to an individual's nervous system and coping thresholds. Water also oversees the emotions; repairs that go unattended can directly affect the body's delicate chemistry. Poor lighting and dark colors and woods will also contribute to creating heavy, stagnant ch'i. Look for blank walls, particularly upon entering your space (brick-wall entranceways) or entering and exiting any of your main rooms. These bare walls tend to send out a depressing message of hopelessness and apathy. Another quick way to move stagnant and depressed energy is to clean out a closet or a drawer, or sort through and organize a stack of papers. Clutter, especially nonvisible clutter (closets and drawers), can accumulate and drain your energy unknowingly. The best immediate thing you can do for your depression is to clean up your space, throw things out, and get rid of the clutter. REMEDIES: Remove overhead objects that appear to be oppressive. Fix all leaks and repair all wires. Add brighter lighting to your rooms and introduce the color ORANGE into your choice of foods or clothing (second chakra). Clean out your junk drawers and closets! Add positive and uplifting pictures to blank walls and reduce the amount of dark colors in your home. Place crystals and/or wind chimes in the center of your rooms and bless them with the Three Secret Reinforcement.

ALL ILLNESS IS A THREEFOLD *DIS-EASE*

All illnesses have three main components that contribute to their manifestation in your body. In a combined process, the ch'i in your spiritual, emotional, and physical bodies comes together and develops a certain propensity toward a particular illness. This means that in order for an illness to be completely healed, all three aspects of that illness must be addressed. Feng Shui helps us with addressing those components, as it is mirrored and exists in our environment. The Feng Shui process acts similarly to a chiropractic adjustment, aligning you with the people who will be most helpful to you, the best possible treatment, understanding the emotional issues surrounding the illness, and the spiritual lessons that the illness is here to teach you. Because of this, it is very important that you pursue all the various mundane solutions, such as medical doctors, therapists, alternative treatment specialists, etc. If you only use the Feng Shui process to treat your particular ailment, then you are participating in just one part of the healing process.

BLACK HAT SECT TRANSCENDENTAL CURES

There are hundreds of transcendental cures that are available through *Black Hat Sect Feng Shui* for healing everything from pregnancy problems to career difficulties. These cures are seen as sacred information, highly respected and taken very seriously. They are not shared indiscriminately without justification or thought. The remedies that have been suggested in this book, particularly the Four Transcendental Cures below, were carefully selected and received approval to be shared with you by Professor Thomas Lin Yun, the head master and spiritual leader of the Black Hat Sect of Tantric Tibetan Buddhism School of Feng Shui. Whenever you share these cures, it's important that you adhere to Black Hat Sect Traditions and along with sharing the cures, that you participate in the exchange of the **Red Envelope Ritual**. By participating in this ritual you will not only protect yourself spiritually but keep the shared information sacred and not dissipate the powerful energy that surrounds the cures. The force that truly activates the power behind the cure is the act of transmitting the information orally to the person who is sincerely asking for the help.

Here are the four transcendental cures most requested.

1. TRANSCENDENTAL CURE FOR PROSPERITY JYÙ BAÙ PEŃG

Take a jar, bowl, piggy bank, or other container. On a red piece of paper write your full name and the words *JYÙ BAÙ PEŃG*. Tape or glue the paper to the container with the written words facing inward. Place it under your bed or in the Wealth corner of your bedroom.

THE RITUAL OF THE RED ENVELOPE

When transcendental cures are offered, the giver needs to request of the receiver one, three or nine new red envelopes, depending on how many cures were dispersed. Nine envelopes are usually given to the person with the cures when the receiver wants to express his/her greatest respect and thanks to the giver, but one or three are acceptable if only one or two cures are prescribed. These envelopes can be traditional Chinese red money envelopes (Hong Pao) or any generic red envelope from a local card shop. The important thing is that they were *never* used before and that after you complete the ritual they will be discarded and *never used again*. Inside **each** red envelope is a token monetary gift. The offering can be as little as 5¢ or 1¢ when it is being offered to a nonprofessional. When the envelopes are being presented to a Black Hat Sect Feng Shui expert or consultant, then the practitioner's fee goes inside the one, three or nine red envelopes. After the envelopes are received, before the individual/consultant can spend the money, she or he must sleep with it under his or her pillow or mattress for one night after blessing the envelopes, while reciting the ***Three Secret Reinforcement***. It is important to remember to follow the Red Envelope Ritual, no matter if you share the cures with friends, family, or clients. If you find that you are uncomfortable asking for the red envelopes or the person you are sharing these cures with doesn't want to follow through on providing them, then accept those signs as an indication that you are not ready to share these cures and most probably the other individual is not ready to receive the information just yet. Knowing when to help and when not to help is a very valuable and important skill to have. If you take this part of the Feng Shui process seriously, then be patient with yourself and the process—trust that you will know when it's the right time to share the information with others.

Choose a coin that you would like to work with: penny, nickel, dime, or quarter.

Every day, whenever that coin passes through your hand, *do not spend it.*

Instead, take it out and place it in a separate pocket. At the end of the day, put all the change collected into the "money jar" and recite the Three Secret Reinforcement (nine times) visualizing money coming to you and envision yourself depositing all of it in the bank, going on a vacation, or just spending it.

Do this every night for either 27, 99, or 108 days in a row.

At the end of the allotted time period, take the money out of the jar, count it, and write the amount on a piece of paper, then place the paper back in the jar. Take the money saved and deposit it into your checking or savings account.

While depositing the money recite the Three Secret Reinforcement *(nine times)*. *To strengthen this cure: Place a red cloth with a mirror under the jar and a mirror directly above the jar aligned with mirror below.*

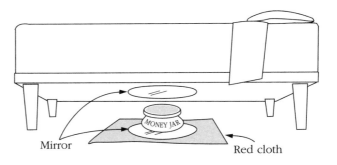

Mirror   Red cloth

2. TRANSCENDENTAL CURE FOR SECURING A GOOD MARRIAGE/RELATIONSHIP

Part I

Take 2 photographs, one of you and one of your partner. On the back of your photo, put your partner's name and the word *marriage* or *good relationship*, and on the back of your partner's photo, put your name and the word *marriage* or *good relationship*.

Under the moonlight, put both pictures face-to-face, and tie them together with a red string, wrapping the string around the photos ninety-nine times. Visualize that the two of you are perfect mates and reinforce that image with the Three Secret Reinforcement. Sleep with it under your mattress for nine nights, placing it under the Marriage gua of your bed. Then either toss the pictures into moving waters or bury them in the ground and put a beautiful, lush plant over them.

Reinforce this cure with the Three Secret Reinforcment, visualizing a happy, loving, successful relationship.

Part II

Make adjustments accordingly in regard to Relationship areas in the home. Hang a crystal ball, wind chimes, or a mirror in the Marriage gua in the bedroom. Reinforce with the Three Secret Reinforcement.

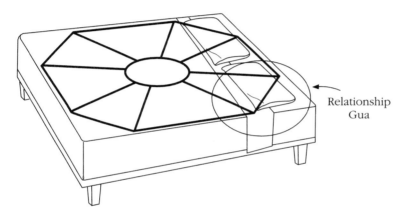

Relationship Gua

3. TRANSCENDENTAL CURE FOR PREGNANCY

Take your partner's dinner or lunch bowl and after he has eaten out of it, without rinsing it, fill it with clean but cold water (three-quarters full). Then add *nine raw lotus seeds, nine peanuts, nine dates and nine dry longans* (all can be purchased in a Chinese apothecary or herbal store). Bring the bowl to sunlight, visualize millions of "ling particles" (embryonic ch'i) coming to you, then place the bowl under the bed on the side that the woman sleeps on.

Perform the Three Secret Reinforcement, using the Ousting Mudra and the Six True Words Mantra (see chapter 7). Do this nine times. Every morning, take out the bowl and change the water, leaving the mixture in the bowl. Each morning, for nine days, repeat the Three Secret Reinforcement and visualize all the embryonic particles filling the bowl in the sunlight. After nine days, pour the water and the ingredients into the dirt of a plant and place that plant in the *main entranceway of the house.* Repeat the process for nine days and place the second plant in the *living room.* Repeat the process one more time for nine days and place that plant in the *bedroom. Do not* clean under your bed while trying to get pregnant.

4. TRANSCENDENTAL CURE FOR PROBLEMS THAT SEEM INSURMOUNTABLE: FOUR RED STRINGS CURE

Use this cure in your bedroom. Hang a *red string* from ceiling to floor in *all* four corners of the room.

This arrangement acts as a "Canopy of Heaven" holding up the problem, while linking together heaven and earth, while invoking the powers of heaven to intercede on your behalf and remove your difficulties.

On each string, in each corner, add a *nine-inch red string to the center of the hanging string.**

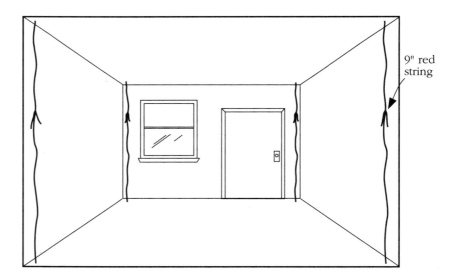

9" red string

* This smaller string represents the Chinese character for "human."

Apply the *Three Secret Reinforcement* (nine times). Visualize that you are the juncture between heaven and earth and that you will receive universal help to overcome your obstacles. Keep the strings up until the problem becomes resolved.

EMOTIONAL OBSTACLES THAT IMPEDE THE FENG SHUI PROCESS

Fear: As you begin to make your Feng Shui adjustments, you may start to notice many of your fears coming to the surface. This is a very common occurrence that you may encounter at several intervals during the Feng Shui process. The reason for this is that when we reposition furniture, add adjustment items, or employ transcendental cures we are moving and shifting around energy that has been gelled into a pattern that may have existed for decades. When we enter the energy patterns that have molded a certain condition or circumstance in your life, we are also entering all the emotional issues that are attached to that original set of circumstances.

We began the Feng Shui process with a wish list of three "life situations" to change or improve. Many of those situations you may have been trying to alter for years, long before entering the Feng Shui process, and since these situations have been important to you and close to your heart, it is easy to understand how changing them can create some anxiety. Those fears are also embedded in the energy patterns and contribute to the glue that holds the potential change at a standstill. When we break down and restructure the energy patterns through the mundane and transcendental solutions, we inadvertently cause the old energy pattern to come to the surface, bringing with it all the emotional baggage, including old fears. These fears are just flushing their way up and out of your vibrational system, but if you are not conscious of this part of the healing process, it is common to assume that things are feeling worse and not better. Remember, any major change, even a positive one, can be unbalancing at first. Keep in mind that your fears can be insidious and very convincing. Even if they are loud, frightening, or make you feel insecure, *go ahead, challenge them head-on, and do it anyway!*

Resistance: Many times as you attempt to begin the Feng Shui process you may find yourself stopping and starting until you are able to connect to the process and finally follow through. Sometimes the resistance emerges at the beginning of the process while you are reading or just after you have completed this book. You may find yourself eager at times to start your Feng Shui and, at other times, overwhelmed at the thought of beginning. You may begin to draw your floor plan or actually complete it, but not follow through on making any changes. I often hear from clients that they started to hang the wind chimes but never got around to hanging the mirrors, or they repaired the leaking plumbing but never repainted their all-white apartment. Even though you may truly want to change your life, you may not be ready to on a subconscious level. This type of block is more common than people think because it is the "nature of the beast" for human beings to want **situations** to change—*but not themselves*. In order for any changes to occur in our lives we have to be willing to meet them and embrace them on some level. Sometimes that may just mean to acknowledge them and be willing to change them. Otherwise, the changes that we are hoping for will be attributed to magical thinking, finger crossing, and polished genie bottles. In order for our lives to change, Feng Shui requires that we be willing to make the changes that are necessary on our end of the process. Sometimes that may mean moving our bed, other times that may mean just opening our minds and getting out of our own way. Most of the time the resistance we create surfaces in the form of setbacks and delays. Keep in mind that even though resistance has many faces, when it emerges it usually holds many important pieces of information. Deciphering its message will give you many valuable clues about the source of your resistance. If you perceive the obstacle of resistance as a necessary part of the transformation process, then you will embrace it and use it as a catalyst to help your process along.

For example, if you find that you were able to make certain adjustments but not others, check the neglected area. Go over your floor plan and then use your Bagua map to locate what that area oversees. Then give some thought to why you might be resistant to making a change in that area. Try to push past your resistance any way you can until you see your life unfold and the answers become more clear.

Expectations: Throughout this whole book I have been encouraging you to be as specific as you can with your wishes and to use "conscious intentions" at every opportunity; however, expectations are not necessarily the same thing as conscious intentions. One is a requested wish for wanting something and the other is a locked-in demand for a certain outcome. Often when we set our sights on a situation turning out one way or another, we fail to see any other outcome than the one we envisioned as fulfilling our wishes. When we work with Feng Shui, especially with the transcendental solutions, we are invoking a higher power to hear our request and help us place our energy in an alignment with the healing forces of nature. In doing so, we open ourselves to *other forms of guidance* such as our higher power, who may find our request not in our best interest or in the best interest of the bigger picture. This is often a difficult part of the process but one we need to make peace with in order for a true healing to occur. Many times our requests for certain things in our life stem from our limited understanding of the bigger picture and how those requests might factor into our lives further down the road. By including other types of help to screen out and manifest our wishes, we are graciously admitting that as human beings we are limited to a certain level of understanding and ***just maybe*** we do not have all the answers or always know what's best for us.

Having certain expectations of the outcome of Feng Shui also sets us up to feel as though the process may not be working if it doesn't turn out the way we envisioned. Comparing your process to a friend's or to another person's is also a common error we frequently make. Keep in mind that everyone's process varies and unfolds differently based on each person's karma, life experiences, preparation, and opportunities. Time is also very different in the spiritual and energy realms. We understand the concept of time from a linear perspective based on minutes, hours, days, and years. In the spiritual realm, however, time as we know it does not exist. Instead, everything is seen as part of an evolutionary flow, with each day being part of eternity. A lifetime to us is equivalent to a blink of an eye in the time concept on the spiritual realm. Often we set things in motion in Feng Shui (and in other areas of our lives) and get impatient and disillusioned when change doesn't occur fast enough, while in the spiritual realm circumstances are changing and transforming in perfect step and time. Be patient with your process and trust that the complex levels of energy are slowly being shifted, realigned, and transformed for your higher good and for the higher good of all.

Last year while grocery shopping I was tapped on the shoulder by a client for whom I did Feng Shui in her home. After exchanging greetings she said, "I guess it didn't work." I replied, "What didn't work?" "The Feng Shui. I'm still not married!" I politely responded, "Sometimes it requires patience and it takes a little time—but I'm sorry you feel that it didn't work." We said good-bye and parted. Several days later I came across her file in my office and checked the date of her Feng Shui consultation. *Only four months* had gone by! She *expected* to have met someone and gotten married immediately. If she had met a man who wasn't the best choice for her, but was willing to marry her immediately, she would have considered that a successful turn of events. My preference would be that the universe would send her a mate who would not only marry her but who would honor and love her as well, even if it took a longer amount of time.

Be patient with your process and wonderful things will unfold if you are willing to acknowledge all the synchronicities and coincidences in your life.

SUMMARY

A Writing, Meditation, and Transcendental-Cure Exercise: "Receiving Guidance from Higher Realms"

- Take out your Feng Shui notebook, a pen, and ***three red envelopes***. Any red envelope will do. If you can't find red envelopes, feel free to make them out of red construction paper. Just make sure the envelopes haven't been used before.
- Find a comfortable, quiet spot in your home where you will not be disturbed for twenty or thirty minutes.
- Think about a problem, decision, or choice that you are currently facing in your life right now. Write it down on a piece of paper from your notebook.
- Under the problem, make three columns. Label the first column "FEARS," the second, "RESISTANCE," and the third, "EXPECTATIONS."
- List all your fears, the ways you might sabotage or resist help, and all your expectations (good and bad) regarding the outcome of the decision or problem.
- When you are finished, make three identical copies of your lists.
- Fold the three papers and place each one in a separate red envelope.

- Place the red envelopes on your lap or in front of where you are seated.
- Get into a comfortable position either sitting or lying on the floor. Close your eyes, relax, and take several deep breaths.
- As you continue to breathe, visualize a beautiful white light circulating above the top of your head. Slowly breathe the beautiful light in through the top of your head, letting it fill your head, eyes, ears, and throat. Continue to breathe the light into your chest, arms, and out your hands. Take in another deep breath and send the light through your torso, through all your major organs, and down your back to the base of your spine. On your next inhalation, breathe the light down your legs, past your ankles, and out your feet. Take full breaths and with each inhalation fill up your whole body with light, then with each exhalation, breathe the light out through your fingertips and toes.
- In your mind's eye bring your attention to the center of your chest and focus your breathing on your heart chakra.
- Call on the light of your Higher Power. Discuss in detail your problem with him/her and then ask if there is any guidance or insight that he/she can provide for you regarding the situation. Listen carefully and accept any thoughts, images, or symbols that come to you.
- Now offer up to the Higher Power all your thoughts, fears, resistance, and expectations regarding the situation in question. Ask the power to pass his/her light through all your ideas and feelings that are keeping you limited and locked into a certain thought pattern. Send your own light to your thoughts, raising their vibration to a higher level.
- Combine your light with your Higher Power's and in your mind's eye surround the three red envelopes with this brilliant light.
- Ask to be released from your limited thinking and freed from the problem at hand.
- Ask the Higher Power if there is any type of Feng Shui adjustment you need to make in your home or office. Accept any information or thoughts that come to you. Make a mental note.
- Ask if there is anything else that you need to know regarding this situation. Stay open to receiving any guidance. Make a mental note of any information you receive.
- Thank your Higher Power and all the other guides that have assisted you in this meditation.

- Take in a deep breath and feel the light rise from the bottom of your feet, moving up and through your whole body, exiting out the top of your head, returning to its natural resting place six inches above your crown chakra (see chapter 5).
- Know that the light is always there, guiding you and illuminating your path.
- Take in another deep breath and slowly bring your attention back into your body, back into your room, and when you feel ready you can open your eyes and record any information that you were given.
- Take the three red envelopes and place the first one in the **Helpful People** corner of your **bedroom**. Place the second envelope in the **Helpful People** section of your **overall floor plan of your house**. Then place the third one in a **location** in your home **that you pass by daily**.
- Bless each of them with the **Three Secret Reinforcement** and visualize the situation resolved.
- Leave the envelopes in these locations for **twenty-seven days** or until the situation is resolved.

SEVEN

CREATING A SACRED SPACE

A sacred place is anywhere you can be alone with your thoughts. It doesn't matter if you are in a crowd of people, in church or in a room by yourself. I find the best time to be the five or ten minutes before I drift off to sleep, when I feel like I'm the only person in the world and I feel safe, secure and without any intrusions.

—SUSAN OLSEN

In your lifetime the most sacred space you will ever need to create is the space within yourself—the place deep within your soul where you go to find peace and serenity and to connect with your true self. It's the quiet place inside where you return over and over again that keeps your thoughts sacred, your heart protected, and your dreams alive. This is the quintessential sacred space, the one that you take with you wherever you go; the space you have total control over including who you let into it and whom you keep out.

Most of our lives, whether we are conscious of it or not, we strive toward making this inner space balanced, loving, and the safest place it can be. In order for our soul to grow, we need to be able to make this internal space into a place that is safe to go into, to hear our inner voice, the part of ourself through which our Higher Power speaks to us. This is where we make our decisions, contemplate life, and feel connected to our lives. When our sacred space has been wounded, gets too confusing to enter, or hasn't been given the attention it deserves and requires, it shuts down and turns off its internal lights. This creates a distance within, keeping us separated from ourself and the ways we need to commune with our soul.

When we disconnect from our soul we create confusion, indecision, and tend to "lose our way." Life becomes muddled and our goals and desires such as relationships, finances, and careers become unclear. Often you'll find that little things in life such as daily stresses, lack of time, and our many responsibilities contribute to our cutting ourselves off from our sacred place inside. Difficult childhoods, abusive pasts, or painful memories also keep us at a distance from our center, for it is there that we carefully store our most precious memories—the good as well as the bad. If we are removed from our sacred place or we are too fearful to enter it, we often create distractions or obstacles that will not only keep us from the space but also help us forget that it is there.

Our mission, and one good reason for using Feng Shui, is to find ways that are safe and comforting to allow us to reconnect with our inner self so we are always able to go there to receive higher guidance and solace. By understanding how to create sacred spaces outside of ourselves, we are then able to design areas that will "mirror back" to us our "vision of inner sacredness." By turning our home into a sacred space, we create very special places that help us reshape and reopen to our sacred place inside.

WHAT IS A SACRED PLACE?

When you think about a sacred place, what sort of places usually come to mind? Churches? Houses of worship? Stonehenge? Rain forests? Mountaintops? Machu Picchu? What makes some of these places so special that people from all over the world travel thousands of miles to bask in their healing energies? Most of the people I've spoken to say that these places are special because of the way they make them *feel*—that there is "something special" imbued in their energy that feels magical, transformative, and speaks as if only to them. These are the places that we usually retreat to after a long period of work or an emotional crisis of some sort. These places emit a special energy force, and just being around them for a short period of time helps us center ourselves, clear our minds, and feel at peace. These are the places that you instinctively know are special, holy, and somehow have been touched by God. These places are some of the most special places that exist in our world—not because of where they are located but because of how they make us feel. Being able to sit in them, walk through them, or spend time near them creates a sense of safety that connects us with our true inner self and our spirit. Making that connection, even if ever so briefly, brings us back to our self and closer to our Higher Power. It re-creates a body, soul, and spirit memory that is so primal, it takes us back to our childhood and the safety of our first sacred space, the womb. As children, we intrinsically knew how to create places that were sacred and special. We made forts out of bedsheets, castles out of sand, and clubhouses in large trees. Before we learned to think like "critical, rational adults," we trusted our intuition, created imaginary friends, and assumed that the world and the people in it were safe. For most of us, reality set in around the age of five or six when we started to realize the concept of "cause and effect," becoming aware that life was not all benign and not always fair. To most of us, that caused a major jolt to our sense of reality and prematurely catapulted us into the beginning stages of "early adulthood."

At whatever age that process started to occur in your life, either through a particular crisis or life event, that was the moment in time when you started doubting the safety of the world around you. The event or situation didn't necessarily have to be a horrible or negative thing, either—just a particular set of events that shifted your energy and the way that you continued to perceive the world. The event could have been seeing your parents fighting, falling down and skinning your knee, or being traumatized in some abusive way. Left unresolved, these experiences stay with us and calcify in our ch'i, affecting the way that we see life. If these life events happen to have occurred in your homes or in regard to your families, then they will also affect how you will feel about your home. After the womb, the next sacred place that we came in contact with was our childhood home. All the events, good and bad, that occurred there shaped and colored how we feel about our homes today. Many of us, for that exact reason, have a difficult time dealing with the current places that we live in as adults. Decorating them, getting them organized, or just keeping them clean can become an awesome task for many of us who have gotten stuck while trying to push past old memories or events of the past. For those of us who have had difficult childhoods it is particularly important to especially create a home that is a sacred, loving, and fun place to be.

As you have witnessed throughout this book, the Feng Shui of your home acts like a mirror to your life and its circumstances. The ch'i that exists in your life, in your home, and in your body is an accumulation of all your life's events. That includes the experiences from childhood on up through the present moment. To face the joy and the sometimes rocky road of life, we all need a stable, safe, and loving place to return to, a place that provides us with a feeling of connectiveness and belonging. We need to give thought to how to create such a place and, then, how to draw on that wisdom to create a sacred place wherever we go.

Back in August of 1995, I was traveling home on a flight from Seattle, Washington, to New York City. I was in the middle of writing chapter 5 of this book and was looking forward to having five hours of quiet time to do some editing. When I got on the plane I quickly realized that I had somehow been reassigned to another seat and was not going to get the window seat that was issued to me on my original ticket. When I sat down, to the left of me were two children, a boy and a girl. My first thought was that it probably wouldn't be such a good spot to work in and that as soon as the seat belt sign went off I would move to another seat. As I sat down, my two neighbors, Will and Coleen, introduced themselves, told me that they were brother and sister (nine and seven and a half years old), and were flying alone to New York City to visit their grandmother. As these kids started to talk to me, I quickly realized that there was something very special about them. They were bright, alert, and wonderfully inquisitive. Two hours into the flight, I found myself losing badly at gin rummy, putting puzzles together, and discussing religion, family, and my life as a writer. Three hours into the flight, I found myself ordering their food, taking them to the bathroom, and showing them the clouds outside the porthole window of the plane. These children were not only endearing but they provided me with a much-needed break from my writing. They provided the *child within me* an opportunity to play and to take some time off, time I would have never given to myself otherwise. Together we created a safe, nurturing environment that was not only sacred but fun for all to be in. Although we were high up in the air, surrounded by two hundred people, with no candles or Buddha statues, we still created a sacred place.

Children intrinsically know how to turn any space into something special and fun. They know how to go to the core of their needs and create, imagine, and manifest their wants. They do this simply by bringing their innocence, open hearts, and a few toys with them.

That flight became very important to me. It reminded me how important and rewarding it is to take some time away from work and play a bit. Those children became my muse and, through their innocence, inspired parts of this chapter. Till this day we still remain pen pals, keeping each other in touch with our very different lives. That sacred space and time has bonded us in ways that still continue to touch my heart today. Look around, take notice, and you will find those sacred places too. Once you understand the simplicity behind what is needed to create a sacred space, then you will be able to create one wherever you may go. You can create a sacred space at the beach, in your car, or in a hotel room. *Wherever you are, there it will be.*

A SIMPLE RECIPE FOR A SACRED SPACE

After you have made all the necessary furniture changes and completed most of the Feng Shui adjustments, you will be ready to take your Feng Shui process to the next level—working toward transforming your home into a sacred place. Each step of your process, beginning with the drawing of your floor plan to the understanding of the transcendental cures, was designed to bring you precisely to this part of your journey. In this chapter you will explore the many different ways in which you can turn your home into a sacred space that is personal, supportive, and reflective of who you are. Technically, ***all space is sacred space*** because every place that exists in the world is built on the soil of **Mother Earth**. Over the centuries, our society has forgotten that basic truth and has destroyed much of the sacredness that was a natural part of the universe's gift to us. By acknowledging and re-creating sacred places in our home, we in essence are restoring the sacredness to the earth one house at a time. Like any good recipe, there are certain ingredients that contribute to the success of its final outcome. When you begin to create a sacred space for yourself, it is important to remember the four major components that will help you design a space that will honor your wishes, clarify your thinking, and enhance and nurture your soul. The four major components that will help you create a sacred space are: **1) claiming the space, 2) conscious intentions, 3) creating an altar for making offerings, and 4) blessing the space.**

1. CLAIMING THE SPACE

Take a look around your house, walk through each room, and think about the areas in your house where you feel most comfortable. Look for a place that is open and available for you to create a sacred space. It may be in a corner of your living room or a lounge chair in your bedroom. It can be the top of a dresser, a small table in the corner, or a windowsill in your kitchen. It doesn't have to be very large, just big enough for you to be able to claim it as sacred. Once you find an area(s) clear out all objects from that space, dust it, clean it, and in your mind's eye draw the boundaries around where that space begins and ends. Creating a visual boundary helps you "claim your space," define its parameters, and acknowledge its sacredness. If the area isn't first cleared it becomes harder for your thoughts and intentions to manifest themselves in this newly appointed sacred space. By clearing the space, you make room for the "new energy" that you are creating to enter. By clearing the space out, we honor it and welcome in the new. Think about how good you feel when your house is cleaned or when you throw out old junk and clutter. The next step is clearing out any stagnant, heavy, or negative energy from in and around the space. Energy, even the most positive and uplifting kind, over time will tend to stagnate. It can accrue in areas that aren't frequented regularly or in areas that tend to have a lot of traffic. Sometimes certain places in your home will attract and absorb the ch'i not only from the environment but also from the people who go there and the events that take place there. Even though we can't see it, the energy force exists all around us and when it gets heavy, it stops the ch'i from flowing properly and connecting you with the things and people that you need and want. The best way to clear out stagnant energy from a space is by burning the herb white sage or by using a smudge stick. Both methods are frequently a part of Native American rituals and are used to clear a space, commence a ceremony, and to call on spiritual help from other realms. By lighting an herb, walking through your home, and letting the smoke it emits pass over every area in your house and in your sacred space, you can create a ritual that purifies and releases all energies that are no longer needed. (Make sure that you have a dish under it, to catch all the ashes.) As you walk through your home and around your sacred place, visualize all the non-serving energy lifted (see Blessing Ceremonies, page 177). In a pinch, you can use any other incense that you prefer, but white sage and smudge sticks are really the most powerful things to burn.

2. CONSCIOUS INTENTIONS

When you are creating a sacred space in your home, your thoughts regarding how and why you are creating that space become very important, for they set up the framework from which the energy accumulates and gathers its focus. As previously discussed, your thoughts are very powerful; you need to visualize in your mind what you want to create, and hold the objectives of that space within your thoughts. Remember, everything that exists in the world today is the direct outcome of one individual's or group of individual's thoughts. Take a moment out at this juncture and think about why you want to create a sacred space in your home. What will that space do for you? How will it affect you and make you feel? Will you use it to be still and shut out the world? To connect with your higher self? Meditate? Contemplate? Release the stresses of the day? Give some thought to its purpose and let your conscious intentions shape its energy. Keep in mind that you can use this space for many different things, changing its objective by renaming your intention. As you change, your needs will also change. Think about the people that you would feel comfortable with entering your space. Sometimes, especially when we have little privacy in our homes or a few children around, it's hard to create a space that is not frequented often. Give some thought to how private or personal you want this space to be. Make conscious decisions about who will be allowed to enter the space once it has been created. You might choose to have no one enter and make it off limits or have your partner and your family go there. This is a decision only you can make based on the amount of privacy you need, the amount of room in your house, and the location of your space. For instance, if your sacred space is around your tub in your bathroom, unless it's a private bathroom, you would have to accept that other people will come in contact with it. If it is in the corner of your bedroom, you probably will have more control over who comes and goes and whom you would really want to share its sacredness with. The important thing is that you be clear in your mind so at no time will you feel violated that someone entered your space without your permission. This boundary is particularly important for those of you who have been physically, emotionally, or sexually abused. Being able to control who we "let in" becomes a very empowering exercise that allows us to take back our personal space and our lives.

3. CREATING AN ALTAR

Within your sacred space it is always very important to create an altar of some kind. An altar doesn't necessarily have to be "spiritual" in nature, just an area that you put aside to place things that are important to you and have special meaning. There are two types of altars you can create, one that is spiritual and one that is nonspiritual. It could be on a windowsill, a shelf, the mantel of a fireplace, an area on the floor, or the edge around your bathtub. Wherever you have been drawn to to create it is probably the exact place it needs to be. Once you have "claimed your space," you'll know within that space where it will be. Keep in mind what your conscious intentions are; if one of them is to meditate, then make sure you have enough space around the altar. If one of the "conscious intentions" is to use it for relaxing and thinking, make sure you can sit by it. All your efforts to make this a consciously planned place will activate the ch'i energy around the altar and throughout your home.

Once you determine where your altar is going to be (you can have several), then the next step is making offerings and placing the objects on that altar. Below is a partial list of items you can use to create an altar. Feel free to add anything else that will help you personalize your altar and have it reflect you and your intentions. Remember that wherever you place your altar, you will enhance that area's Feng Shui. Your altar, in addition, will become a powerful adjustment for that gua.

Altar Objects

- Candles
- Bells, cymbals
- Incense
- Statues, deities, Buddha cards
- Rocks, seashells, driftwood
- Prayer, inspirational books
- Feathers
- Photographs
- Affirmations, personal writings
- Music, chants
- Water, fountains, vessels
- Food, teas
- Crystals, gemstones
- Aromatherapy oils
- Other special objects

Candles: When you place candles on the altar (or anywhere else) their light and warmth bring in the Fire element energy, raising the vibration of the altar space and all that occurs there. The flame itself burns away all negative energies that are in the area where the candle is lit.

Bells, Cymbals: These items invoke "sacred sound." Each tone represents different energy vibrations depending on how high or low the pitch is. Higher tones and softer frequencies resonate to energies in the spirit world; low tones and dense frequencies resonate to energies of this world. Ringing the bells can open and close a meditation, ritual, or ceremony. Bells also "freeze" the energy of the moment or the intention with sound.

Incense: The smoke rising from burning incense is considered to represent "visual prayer." It stands for the wind character in the term Feng (wind) Shui (water). The smoke takes your intentions and wishes and carries them through the air to different etheric levels to be heard and granted. Smudge sticks or white sage have additional healing properties that are able to clear away blocked, stagnant, or negative energy from rooms, homes, and from around people's aura.

Statues, Deities, Buddha Cards: All these items help "name your altar" and bring in the spiritual guidance of the particular deities to whom you choose to pray. You can place several on one altar or set up different altars for each deity.

Rocks, Seashells, Driftwood: These items are what I call the "collectible items." They are the things that you "accidentally" come across in your travels that call out to you and summon you to pick them up. You might come across just one or wind up collecting a whole set. They somehow remind you of a memorable vacation, a particular time in your life, or a special place that you visited. Feel free to design your altar with these items, especially if you want to re-create the energy around the memories they hold. Rocks bring in the energy of the earth element. Seashells bring in the water element and the energy of the sea. Driftwood brings in the elements of wood and water. Other special things can be placed on top of your altar also.

Prayer, Inspirational Books: These books can be spiritual or nonspiritual in nature, but they should reflect literature that you find inspiring and uplifting. Having them on or near your altar will help you develop a routine that will guide you to the altar area every time you feel the need to center yourself.

Having the books in one area also sets up a "quiet zone" that will condition and shape your ch'i, giving out a constant message of peace and serenity.

Feathers: Feathers, especially in the Native American culture, are considered very special healing "medicine." Although all animals are honored and considered sacred, the feathers from birds are thought to be very special. This is because birds are said to be able to share a part of their very powerful medicine with us, without ever having to give up their lives. Each species has a different medicine and a different message to teach us. The eagle teaches us about our connection to the divine. The hummingbird teaches us about joy. The hawk teaches us to be observant and to seek out the truth.

Photographs: Pictures of places and people that we love and admire are wonderful additions to any altar space. All these photographs hold a certain energy and memory vibration. Our muses, mentors, and teachers all reflect back to us aspects of ourselves or ways that we are striving to be. By keeping their energy in a sacred place on our altar, we not only amplify their gifts to us but we also pay homage to them by having their image watch over us.

Affirmations, Personal Writings: Positive sayings, fortune cookies, and clichés that you come across that touch you are very important mementos to add to your altar. They also carry energy and remind us of things that we need to remember. These "words of wisdom" help shape the way we see ourselves and our lives. Sometimes the most profound writings are the poems and thoughts we write ourselves. These include excerpts from our journals that speak of our true feelings and record our life experiences, and especially the writings that reflect memories of painful relationships or our childhood traumas. By placing those thoughts and feelings on the altar, we are actually offering them up to higher powers and asking for assistance in helping us heal and transform those memories.

Music, Chants, Drumming: Bringing sound to the area near your altar is a very powerful way to raise the vibration of the altar and all objects on it. Meditation music is great for guiding you through creative visualizations, while the different sounds of the ocean are soothing and relaxing to the psyche. Playing music that involves chanting or drumming of any kind also sets up a higher vibrational pattern that can accelerate personal healing on all levels. Using sound is also one of the Feng Shui cures. So decide which guas you would want activated more, then consciously place your stereo speakers, drums, and music there.

Water, Fountains, Vessels: The element of water is one of the major characters in the term Feng Shui, so naturally it is considered a very vital element in regard to our survival, for without water we cannot live. Water represents purity and is used in all the cleansing rituals in our life. Our bodies are made up of 85 percent water and by placing a small vessel of water on the altar, in essence, we are offering a part of ourself to be healed and purified. Make sure to empty the vessel daily and replace it with fresh water. The most powerful form of water energy that you can add to your altar or to your home is "moving water." By placing an indoor fountain on your altar or creating an altar around one, you can successfully enhance everything ranging from your wealth ch'i to your health.

Food, Teas: Many religions, especially Buddhism, pay homage to their gods by making food offerings to statues on the altar where they sit. It is a very beautiful way to show thanks for the food and sustenance that we have been given. Food offerings acknowledge the importance of food and all the blessings that come from being well fed and nourished. My clients from Thailand show thanks by making these offerings first thing in the morning and just before each meal. To represent the meals that they are not home for, they leave small bowls of fruit or something sweet to represent the drawing in of the "sweet things in life."

Crystals, Gemstones: When used in combination with conscious intentions, crystals and gemstones can amplify your thoughts, raise the vibrational levels of your ch'i, and enhance the Feng Shui of your home. All crystals and gemstones have piezoelectric properties and are able to vibrate at a certain frequency that can resonate to the different areas of your life, the different chakras in your body, and various health conditions. When used on an altar, in a car, in different parts of your home, or carried on your person, they will work toward healing imbalances and shoring up weaker areas of energy. Natural crystals also bring in the element of earth to wherever they are placed because they are thousands of years old and mined from the earth. Make sure to clear their energy fields before you activate them for your personal use (see Crystal Chart p. 166–168).

CRYSTAL AND GEMSTONE PROPERTIES

CRYSTAL/GEMSTONE	PROPERTIES	CHAKRA ACTIVATED
Agate	Encourages acceptance, grounding, emotional and physical balance. Raises consciousness, helps digestion.	First chakra survival center
Moss agate	Encourages acceptance, self-confidence, and security. Relieves hypoglycemia and depression.	First chakra survival center
Botswana agate	Relieves depression, helps in quitting smoking.	First chakra survival center
Amethyst	Assists spiritual, psychic opening in a grounded way. Encourages creativity, sobriety, courage, intuition, self-esteem.	Seventh chakra crown center
Aquamarine	Calming, improves mental clarity, spiritual inspiration, enhances self-expression.	Fifth chakra throat center
Aventurine (green quartz)	Encourages joy, mental clarity. Promotes calming, positive attitude.	Fourth chakra heart center
Carnelian	Strengthens body and mind, promotes creativity, relieves lower-back problems, strengthens reproductive organs.	Second chakra social center
Citrine	Breaks up energy blocks in body, strengthens will, vision, balance, self-confidence. Helps in letting go of addictions.	Second chakra social center
Clear quartz	Powerful transmitter. Amplifies and directs thought-form. Healing energy balancer, promotes clarity, attunes one to higher self.	Overall
Emerald	Improves relationships, meditation. Relaxant, heart balancer. Strengthens clairvoyance and psychic abilities, aids in combating mental illness.	Fourth chakra heart center
Fluorite	Relieves arthritis. Strengthens ability to perceive higher levels of reality. Clears air of psychic clutter.	First and seventh centers together
Garnet	Improves circulation, especially in lungs, skin, and intestines. Promotes heat, energy, and vitality. Stimulates imagination, self-esteem, and willpower. Calms anger.	First chakra survival center
Hematite	Improves blood disorders. Increases self-esteem, aids in astral projection. Protection.	Third chakra solar-plexus center

CRYSTAL/GEMSTONE	PROPERTIES	CHAKRA ACTIVATED
Jade	Blood cleanser. Strengthens immune system and kidneys. Generates Divine Love. Encourages altruistic nature and expression of feelings. Protects from injuries and accidents.	Fourth chakra heart center
Lapis lazuli	Increases psychic abilities, opens third eye. Worn on throat—increases expression. Cleansing. Aligns etheric, mental, spiritual bodies. Thought amplifier.	Sixth chakra third-eye center
Malachite	Balances right/left brain. Strengthens body and mind during mental illness and overtoxification. Protects against radiation. Promotes tissue regeneration. Inspires giving of self, self-expression. Assists vision on all levels.	Third chakra solar-plexus center
Pyrite	Digestive aid, good for red corpuscles. Eases anxiety, frustration, depression. Good for circulation. Money magnet.	Third chakra solar-plexus center
Rhodochrosite	Cleanses subconscious. Strengthens self-identity. Combines the healing properties of the heart chakra with the strengthening power of white light.	Fourth chakra heart center
Rose quartz	Increases confidence, personal expression, and creativity. Emotional balance—self-love. For "heartbreak"—opening to universal love. Comfort.	Fourth chakra heart center
Rutilated quartz	Breaks old patterns, childhood blockages. Tissue regeneration, builds immune system. Eases depression.	Second chakra social center
Smokey quartz	Increases fertility, creativity, joy. Balances emotional energy, grounding. Strengthens adrenals, aids protein assimilation.	Second chakra social center
Sodalite	Encourages harmony, balance, courage, communication. Strengthens lymphatic system, alleviates subconscious fear and guilt.	Third chakra solar-plexus center
Black tourmaline	Eases arthritis, strengthens adrenals. Protects against negativity.	First chakra survival center
Green tourmaline	Strengthens immune system, balancer.	Fourth chakra heart center
Blue tourmaline	Encourages communication. Strengthens lungs.	Fifth chakra throat center

CRYSTAL AND GEMSTONE PROPERTIES (*continued*)

CRYSTAL/GEMSTONE	PROPERTIES	CHAKRA ACTIVATED
Watermelon tourmaline	Stimulates other tourmalines, strengthens their effect. Balancer, strengthens heart and endocrine glands.	Fourth chakra heart center
Pink (rubellite) tourmaline	Heart balancer. Increases depth of insight and perception. Creativity, fertility. Balances passivity/aggression.	Fourth and sixth chakras heart/third-eye centers
Tourmaline in quartz	Attunement to higher self, increases spiritual understanding, promotes peace.	Seventh chakra crown center

Crystals and gemstones have sensitive energy fields that can easily pick up energy from humans and other sources. These stones, at one time or another, have all been handled by other admirers. To remove any imprinted energy, clearing the object immediately after purchase is recommended.

To Clear the Energy Field of All Crystals

1) Submerge your crystal or gemstone in a solution of salt water. Mix a teaspoon of *sea salt* to a quart of water (spring water is preferable but not essential) for approximately three to seven days. Rinse.
2) Pass the crystal or jewelry piece through the rising smoke of a piece of burning sage or smudge stick twenty-seven times.

The second method is recommended for any "power object" or piece of jewelry that has been soldered, glued, or drilled in any way. Certain crystals that have a metal base—such as hematite, pyrite, or amber (which is a resin) should *not* be cleansed in a sea salt and water solution. It will harm their finish.

Sources: Gurudas, *Gem Elixers & Vibrational Healing*, Boulder, CO: Cassandra Press; Julia Lorusso and Joel Glick, *Healing Stoned*; Nancy SantoPietro, *Three of Cups*, Woodstock, NY; crystal shop.

Aromatherapy Oils: Another way to activate an altar and change the energy of a space is through the use of aromatherapy oils. These oils are derived from flowers and plants and are used for beautifying and healing the body, as well as for rituals and religious ceremonies. Aromatherapy oils work on the physical, emotional, and spiritual levels allowing the body to absorb their scents and shift its energy. These oils can be used in a bath, during a massage, or in a pump called a diffuser which distributes the oils into the air so they can be inhaled by the individual. The diffuser method activates the Western astrology element of AIR (see Aromatherapy chart pp. 169–172).

Aromatherapy Oils and Their Properties

OIL	HEALING PROPERTIES	MIND/EMOTIONS/PSYCHE
Bergamot	Essence from fruit. Astringent, helps clear acne and eczema, antiseptic. Relieves cystitis, urinary tract infections, and digestive problems. Reduces fevers. *Note:* may promote sunburn	Uplifting sedative, relieves anxiety, depression, and nervous tension. Cools off anger and frustration. *When used in a diffuser:* will have above effects as well as promoting peace, happiness, and restful sleep.
Eucalyptus	Essence from leaves. Relieves common cold, respiratory disorders, bronchitis, and urinary tract problems. Cleans lymph nodes, antiseptic, reduces fever, analgesic—helps heal wounds and sprains. *Note:* keep away from eyes. Powerful oil—use in small dosage, avoid if you have high blood pressure or epilepsy.	Cooling effect on emotions, aids concentration, strengthens nervous sytem. *When used in a diffuser:* will have above effects as well as promoting healing and purifying room of negative energy.
Geranium	Essence from herb. Promotes circulation, reduces inflammation, diuretic, astringent, anticancer, relieves and reduces herpes and PMS. Relieves eczema and sore throats, balances hormones and nervous system. *Note:* may cause irritation to sensitive skin. Best used in combination with other oils. Do not use during pregnancy.	Uplifts the spirits, dissolves sluggishness, depression, anxiety, and stress. Puts mind into balance. *When used in a diffuser:* will have above effects as well as promoting happiness and protection. Builds up defenses against unwarranted negative energy.
Jasmine	Essence from flowers. Aphrodisiac, used in perfumes for its exotic scent and effect. Promotes soft, glowing complexion and relieves skin problems of young people. Relieves PMS, uterine difficulties, and aids with childbirth. Eases anxiety and coughs, used as nerve sedative. Helps sleep. One of the most expensive oils. *Note:* Not to be used in pregnancy until about to give birth—will help to ease labor.	Remedy for severe depression. Produces optimism, confidence and inspiration. An aphrodisiac. *When used in a diffuser:* will have above effects as well as promoting love, peace, spirituality.

OIL	HEALING PROPERTIES	MIND/EMOTIONS/PSYCHE
Juniper	Essence from fruit (berries). Relieves headaches, indigestion, colic, and flatulence. Detoxifies body, antiseptic, strengthens nerves during states of stress and anxiety. Helps sleep during worries and tension. Stimulates circulation and blood purifier. *Note:* avoid in cases of severe kidney disease or other inflammatory conditions and pregnancy.	Clears, stimulates, and strengthens the nerves, relieves anxiety. Supports spirits in challenging situation. Dispels apathy and paranoia. *When used in a diffuser:* will have above effects as well as purifying room (ward off negativity and danger). Healing.
Lavender	Essence from flowers. Mint. Calming, familiar scent. Relieves burns and sunstroke, reduces inflammation and spasms, aids in healing of wounds and infections. Decongester, relieves headache, urinary problems, insomnia, poor digestion. Sedative action on the heart (hysteria, palpitations). *Note:* people with low blood pressure may feel a bit drowsy.	Warms the heart. Calms the emotions, steadies the nerves, lifts mental depression and nervous exhaustion. Calms uncontrolled emotions. Relieves anger. *When used in a diffuser:* will have above effects as well as enhancing health, love, and peace.
Orange	Essence from peel of fruit. Uplifting, antiseptic qualities and lovely scent create a popular face oil. Improves fatigue due to emotional stress, warming uplifter, calming action on stomach, aids absorption of vitamin C.	Uplifting. Spreads light on gloomy thoughts, gives positive outlook. *When used in a diffuser:* will have above effects as well as used for purification, promoting joy, physical energy, and magical energy.
Peppermint	Essence from herb. Healing scent. Stimulant, relieves stomachache, nausea, sinus decongester, clears lymph nodes. Reduces fevers, relieves asthma, colds, and coughs. Uplifting. Relieves headaches and migraines due to digestive problems. Sipping on a cup of water mixed with five drops of peppermint relieves sore throat.	Memory, rouse the conscious mind, remove negative thinking, cooling nature relieves anger, hysteria, and nervous trembling. Excellent for mental fatigue and depression.

	Note: can disturb sleep, dangerous to eyes, can irritate the skin, best used in small dose with other mixture, or diffuser.	*When used in a diffuser:* will have above effects as well as used in self-purification rituals, purify from negativity.
Rosemary	Essence from leaves. Circulatory stimulant, detoxifies, rids of inflammation, reduces fibrous tissue and cellulite. Stimulates the scalp, relieves general fatigue headaches and muscular pain. ***Note:*** toxic in large doses. Do not use in cases of epilepsy, high blood pressure, and pregnancy.	Enlivens brain cells, clears head and aids memory. Combats dullness, lethargy, strengthens nerves. *When used in a diffuser:* will have above effects as well as promoting longevity, procuring clear sight.
Sandalwood	Essence from wood. Aphrodisiac. Exotic scent. Popular for its spiritual effects. General sedative, cooling, softens skin and reduces acne, relieves itching and inflammation of the skin. General relaxer. ***Note:*** because of high sedative quality perhaps best to avoid in chronic states of depression—may lower mood further.	Calming, soothes nerves during tension and anxiety. Aids in dealing with obsession, cutting ties with past. Induces spirituality, aphrodisiac. *When used in a diffuser:* will have above effects as well as creating mood for meditation and healing.
Tangerine	Essence from fruit. Happy scent. Antiseptic, refreshing, soothing, makes uplifting face oil, reduces acne, improves breast muscles, relieves stomach problems and PMS, gentle, warm uplifter; easy on children and during pregnancy.	Helps stress, soothing, uplifting. Good oil to use at gatherings, promotes party atmosphere. *When used in a diffuser:* will have above effects as well as promoting joy and returning to inner child.
Ylang ylang	Essence from flowers. Aphrodisiac. Popular youth and beauty oil. Used in perfumes and face oils because of soothing and antiseptic effect on the skin and beautiful scent. Decongester, uplifter, antidepressant, sedative,	Calming anger especially due to frustration, and all negative emotional states, comforting, aphrodisiac.

OIL	HEALING PROPERTIES	MIND/EMOTIONS/PSYCHE
	relieves hypertension and insomnia, heart regulator, euphoric. ***Note:*** too much may cause headache or nausea.	*When used in a diffuser:* will have above effects as well as promoting peace, love, and joy.

Chart researched and developed by Greer Jonas, Aromatherapist/Licensed Massage Therapist, NYC. Sources included: Robert Tisserand, *The Art of Aromatherapy*, Rochester, VT: Destiny Books, 1977; Wanda Seller, *The Directory of Essential Oils*, Essex, England: C. W. Daniel Company, Limited, 1992; Ann Berwick, *Holistic Aromatherapy*, St. Paul, MN: Llewellyn Publications, Inc., 1994.; and Scott Cunningham, *Magical Aromatherapy*, St. Paul, MN: Llewellyn Publications, Inc., 1989.

Please Note: Essential oils are powerful and should be mixed with a vegetable oil base if used externally. When used in a diffuser, make sure the essential oil is used in its pure form and *not* mixed in any oil base.

Others: Flowers, prayer beads, runes, medicine cards, tarot cards, and any other item that you feel you would like to include on your altar space will all be a welcome addition and help personalize your space. Don't be afraid of being imaginative or avant-garde. *Let the altar reflect you, even if you march to the beat of a different drummer.* Don't worry about conforming. I recently performed a Blessing Ceremony for a client who wanted to bring a relationship into her life. I instructed her to gather certain items that reminded her or connected her to relationships for the altar. Aside from a ring and several other objects, she brought ***nine condoms***! Those items, although not *traditionally* offered, were her unique contribution to her own cause. It reflected her creativity and her individuality. I was proud to be able to bless those condoms, which she chose as an offering for her wishes. *Go for it and be different; you have my blessings!*

Different Types of Spiritual and Nonspiritual Altars

To strengthen the effects and the energy around any altar, use a *mirror* as a base for your objects and water vessels or place a mirror behind the altar to duplicate its image. If your altar is in a precarious place or if you are concerned about having lit candles around, try using electric candles that plug in or are battery operated. Remember to ***NEVER leave candles unattended***. Even the safest candles can drip haphazardly or tip over to one side causing an unexpected fire. When you use the white sage or smudge sticks, keep a watchful eye on the ashes; they have a tendency to flake off. Keep a metal dish under the incense at all times.

In many cultures people place the altars in the highest place in the house at a significant distance over their heads. They feel that this is the most honoring and respectful thing to do. I personally do not feel that is necessary, but if that type of thinking rings true for you, then go ahead and creatively set up your altar that way. *Try to think of your altar as the special place you go to— to meet with your higher self over a hot cup of tea.* Let it reflect that thought and you will always have a place to go where you can contemplate your life, regroup, and get back on track.

Empty Space Altar: This type of altar is created around the "Zen Concept" that "emptiness is an illusion." Take a room or a section of a room and clear it out and create an "empty space." Within that space, make a "conscious intention" of what that space will be used for. Your offering to the universe is the sacredness of the empty space itself. You can use this space to meditate in, sit zazen, do yoga, dance, paint, write, contemplate life, or watch cartoons. You keep this place sacred by only doing in this space what the space was created for. The emptiness of the space is what "holds the energy" for you to create within. Place a circle of candles around the space and burn incense if you want to raise the energy and its vibration.

Water Vessel Altar: These altars are designed on or around an indoor fountain or water vessel. They bring the energy of moving waters into your home, circulating the ch'i that activates your wealth. You can add plants, seashells, crystals, or other objects. The trickling sound that the moving waters make is not only soothing to your psyche but calming to your whole being. Where you place the fountain or water vessel will further activate the ch'i of that gua. If you want to activate your wealth, place the water vessel in your entranceway to your home or in the Wealth area of your living room, bedroom or office.

Buddha Altar: These altars can be created two different ways. One type of Buddha altar is specifically geared to worship of one deity for a specific purpose or intention. You can create these altars when you are in need of a certain type of help or guidance. For instance, if you are suffering from an illness and you want to create an altar to call on the help of Medicine Buddha or St. Anthony, you would then create your altar, with all its offerings, around a statue or picture of one of them. You can also create this type of altar with several deities or saints on it. Keep in mind that there is no wrong way to create an altar. If you use animal spirits as guides or work with angels or goddesses, feel free to substitute for the concept of Buddha any other entity or higher power you worship.

5 Element Altars: These altars are created with the objective of paying homage to the importance of the five main elements in our life: fire, earth, metal, water and wood. By having these five elements represented on your altar, you symbolically and figuratively bring those elements into your environment with the intention of restoring their balance to your home and life. Having an imbalance of one or more of these elements can adversely affect your finances, health, relationships, and overall well-being. When designing this altar make sure you place offerings of equal amounts of each element. For instance, two candles (fire), two small vessels of water (water), two crystals (earth), two coins (metal), and two small tree twigs (wood). You can also add other objects to this altarpiece, if you choose to do so. Make sure you change the water every day and use sage regularly to clear the energy around the crystals and other objects.

Outdoor Altar: This kind of altar can be located in your garden, backyard, front lawn, or near your driveway. It should have a main centerpiece that the eye can focus on such as a Buddha statue, a birdbath, or an outdoor water fountain. Around it you can plant flowers, create rock gardens, and design shrubbery. Add whatever items will help you develop an outdoor altar with items that you consider to be sacred. One of my associates, Pamela Laurence, is an award-winning sculptor who places her works of art on her front lawn and in specific locations around her home. Each of her sculptures is a beautiful piece of sacred art which she uses as an altar to make offerings to the birds, trees, and land around her home. Be creative and don't be afraid to show the world who you really are.

Traveling Altar: If you travel a lot or go on vacation, keep in mind that you can set up a small altar anywhere. It doesn't have to be as elaborate or evolved as the one you have at home. It just needs to have one or two items that are familiar to you, to re-create the peaceful and serene feeling that it invokes at home. These items are affectionately called "transitional objects." They are the objects we take with us to connect with safe, secure and loving feelings when we are away from home. Linus had his blanket in the Snoopy comic strip, children take their favorite toys with them on trips, and adults carry pictures of our loved ones and anything else our pocketbooks can carry! So pick out a few items that are small, nonbreakable, and don't weigh too much to re-create your altar wherever you may go. When I travel, I always have a small candle and candleholder, a few pieces of white sage (to clear the energy), a picture of Buddha, and a prayer card with Professor Lin Yun's photograph on it. These items occupy little space in my suitcase but bring me so much comfort and serenity. They allow me to create an altar anywhere I go. I also have a portable altar I take to all my Blessing Ceremonies and workshops I teach. Take what's important and you will re-create the original intentions begun in your home.

Blessing the Space

After you have made your Feng Shui adjustments and found a home for your altar, you will be ready to proceed with the most important part of the Feng Shui process for your home—the Blessing Ceremony. The Blessing Ceremony is the final stage in your process, for it takes all the work you have done and raises it to a higher energy level where, along with your conscious intentions, it is offered to the goodness of a higher power for guidance and manifestation.

There are as many ways to bless a space as there are spaces to bless. Most blessing ceremonies are rituals that are put together by individuals or religious groups and then passed down over the years. These various rituals are used to acknowledge a certain "right of passage" and honor that individual with a celebration. Weddings, Bar Mitzvahs, baptisms, First Holy Communions are a few such ceremonies. *The Blessing Ceremony is a housewarming party that acknowledges the space as officially a "sacred ground."* It signifies that you are committed to creating a home that is nurturing, loving, and safe where you can live happily and "raise your soul." It also acknowledges your connection with your higher power's existence in your life and in your home. It symbolizes your desire to join the energy in your home with the energy that connects you to the natural flow and healing forces of nature.

You Have the Power to Bless Yourself and Your Home

Discussing the issue of "power" is an uncomfortable topic for many people. So often in life, we have come in contact with individuals who are in a position of authority and we watch them abuse their power and take advantage of whoever is within their reach. Those types of experiences have left many of us with a "bad taste in our mouth," feeling like power is something that is used against people, to control or to oppress individuals in some way. Unfortunately, the image that power holds in our minds acts as a deterrent, stopping us from accessing our own power comfortably. This is really unfortunate because having a continual flow of "healthy power" in our lives is our birthright. It was given to us by the same universal force that supported our birth process and our incarnation here on earth. Healthy power is generated from above and is a force that works toward the good of all humankind. ***The biggest abuse of power is not owning it.*** We have a responsibility to take "correct action" with all the wonderful gifts that we are given, and power— with all its healing abilities—is no exception to that rule.

There are many among us who interpret power, especially spiritual power, as a force that only belongs to a selected few. Priests, rabbis, priestesses, Yogis, gurus, and other spiritual leaders are thought of as the ones that have been "chosen" or received the "calling" to spiritually serve, and many of us believe only these chosen leaders have the power to bless our homes. Although it is a great honor to provide that type of service and guidance, there are also many unsung heros among us who possess the same type of ability, who serve quietly and often unknowingly. As we become more comfortable with our own sense of spirituality and our ability to access its power, we will then be more apt to focus its energy and use it to strengthen and change our life. Each time you acknowledge your spiritual connection with the universe, you raise your vibration and your level of energy. As your light strengthens, you become a clearer conduit, able to bring in and generate more light through your aura. Having the ability to bless something or someone only means that you have the ability to bring more light to that person, place, or particular situation. Being able to put a situation "in the light" or just provide that extra light for yourself or someone else is what allows most things to transform, heal, and evolve. When we search our hearts and our souls we often realize that the things we have in common far outweigh our differences. If we value life and see the god in all living things, then I believe we will repeatedly stumble across that simple message over and over again.

This past year I had the honor of being called in to do a Feng Shui consultation and a Blessing Ceremony for a wonderful couple who lived in a nearby state. The husband was a rabbi, and both he and his wife were very special people. Over the years in my practice, I have performed numerous consultations and Blessing Ceremonies for many clients but the one that I did at their home was particularly special to me. As I was nearing the end of the Blessing Ceremony it occurred to me that I was blessing "a man of the cloth" who served other people in the same capacity that I was now serving him. What a great honor and experience it was for me, as a woman, spiritualist, and Buddhist, to be conducting this ceremony for him and his wife in their home. It reminded me of how powerful we can be in unity, when we open up our hearts and put our differences aside for the higher good of all. It was a special day for me, for them, and for the message we stood for.

BLESSING CEREMONIES

1. HOUSE CLEARING

Even though you have cleared out the clutter from your house or apartment and made all your Feng Shui adjustments, often the energy that was attached to those discarded items and to the old patterns lingers long after you made the changes. There are several methods that you can use to clear the stagnant energy from your home and lift the vibration of its ch'i.

Clearing the Energy with Sage

Purchase a bag of **white sage for burning** or a **smudge stick** from an herbal or crystal shop. A smudge stick is a stick of herbs such as sage and cedar or lavender that is tied together and then lit at one end. The smoke that rises from the herbs acts as a clearing agent that lifts the ch'i and removes all stagnant, negative energy from a space. When using this method, make sure you keep a dish or plate of some kind under the herbs. While it's burning, the ashes have a tendency to flake off and scatter; the dish will catch all the ashes and prevent any fires from occurring. Take a few leaves of the sage or the whole smudge stick and, before lighting it, think about the things in your home that you would want to clear and the energy patterns that you would like to shift. Then light the end of the sage and blow out the flame and allow the smoke to rise upward. Move the smoke around the outside of the frame of your body, passing it under your turned-down palms, under the soles of your feet, and around the top of your head. The smoke from the sage will help clear your aura and the different energy fields around your body. You should do this clearing process first before you clear the rest of your home and then again after you have completed the process. Take your burning sage leaves and walk through your house. Starting with the room farthest from the front door, light a sage leaf and pass its smoke around the parameters of the room, over all the furniture, through each section of the Bagua, and then around the frames of all the windows and doors in the room. Continue this smudging ritual throughout each room of your home, and if you have access to your outside hallway or the grounds around your house smudge there also. Work your way backwards toward your front door as if you were not only clearing the energy in the house but also symbolically walking all the negative energy out the front door. Remember, as you are smudging your home, think about all the things that you would like to let go of and transform. Give thought to how you would like the energy to feel in your home after you have cleared it. Lighter? Expansive? Nurturing? Then program those thoughts and wishes into the clearing process. Make sure you clear your own energy field once more before you reenter your home. You can do this clearing process as often as you like or whenever the energy feels backed up or stagnant. On an average, once every three to four weeks should keep the energy fields clear.

Clearing Your Home with Orange Peels

To clear all stale and negative energy from a home/office or to clear the energy field from a newly purchased/rented home, you can employ Professor Lin Yun's cure for clearing the energy of a space. First purchase a fresh, new orange. While sitting in a peaceful, quiet spot in your home, start to peel ***nine round sections*** of the rind off your orange. As you peel the orange rinds, think about the energy that you would like to clear out from your home and all the things from which you would like to be released. Then place the nine round orange peels in a small bowl of water and, starting at the front door of your home, walk through each room of the house and sprinkle the water with your hand in an *"ousting mudra" position* (see page 181). Apply the ***Three Secret Reinforcement nine times*** (see page 180) to ensure a successful clearing process. Make sure to visualize the energy in the house clearing and all negativity being removed.

2. PURIFYING A HOME DURING DIFFICULT TIMES

Sometimes in life we run into a stretch of bad luck and it seems whatever we do turns out not the way we planned. The loss of a job, ending of a relationship, or the passing on of someone dear to us can take its toll on our energy and the energy in our homes. During difficult times or after a specific event, it is very helpful to realign the energy of your home. ***Tracing the Nine Stars*** is a transcendental cure, from Professor Lin Yun, used by the Black Hat Sect School of Feng Shui. Its objective is to change a negative energy trend in a home and transform it into a flow of positive energy.

Take out your overall floor plan and trace the nine different Bagua points as illustrated starting with *1, the Family* section, continuing to point *2, the Wealth* section, then point *3, the Center* section, move on to point *4, Helpful People* section, then on to point *5, Children* section, continuing on to point *6, the Knowledge* section, then on to point *7, the Fame* section, then on to point *8, the Career* section, and finally to the last point, *9, the Marriage* section.

TRACING THE NINE STARS

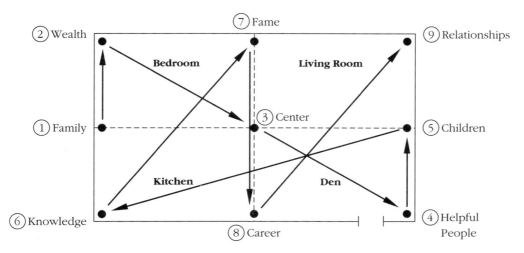

Then walk over to the first point, the Family section of your house, and call on the light of Buddha (or whomever you worship) and ask Buddha to add his energy to yours and join you in purifying your home. Then recite the *"Heart Sutra" nine times—GATE GATE, BORO GATE, BORO SUN GATE, BODHI SO PO HE* (Gate is pronounced Gatay). Starting with the Family section, walk to each Bagua point and send your energy to each gua by either touching the point or discussing the area that it is connected to. Follow this format all the way through until you reach the ninth point, the Marriage section. Send your energy, along with Buddha's blessing, to each point.

THE THREE SECRET REINFORCEMENT

The Three Secret Reinforcement is one of the most important teachings in the Black Hat Sect School of Feng Shui, for it combines three very important concepts: **THE BODY SECRET, THE SPEECH SECRET, AND THE MIND SECRET**, which when performed together can raise the effectiveness of any transcendental blessing or cure. After you have completed making your Feng Shui adjustments, moving your furniture around, and hanging your plants, crystals, and wind chimes up, go back and bless all the changes by using the Three Secret Reinforcement Method. In addition, use the Three Secret Reinforcement on all red envelopes that you receive for shared cures and remedies.

1. THE BODY SECRET

This "secret" is in the form of a "hand mudra, or body gesture." A mudra is a hand or body gesture that relies on the body to convey an unspoken message. It is the use of the body to express a particular thought or objective. Actually in our everyday life, we are not strangers to the use of hand mudras. We use different mudras all the time to convey a variety of messages. The most common ones are our greeting handshake, placing a finger to our lips to convey silence, or the wink of an eye to signal agreement. Throughout the ages we have used these gestures over and over again. In the Black Hat Sect School, we use a variety of these "mudras" to convey a specific spiritual objective. Each mudra is used to emphasize a different intention.

Mind-Calming Mudra

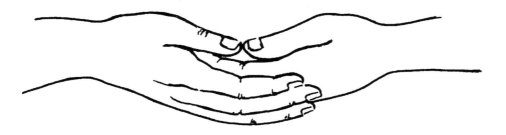

This mudra is usually accompanied by the "Speech Secret Mantra," The Heart Sutra, and is used to calm the mind and the heart, bringing serenity and balance back to a situation fast. Left hand over right. Thumbs together.

Ousting Mudra

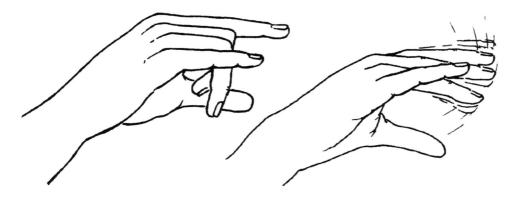

This mudra is usually accompanied by the "Speech Secret Mantra," The Six True Words, and is used to rid oneself or one's home of unwanted issues, bad luck or obstacles. Use thumbs to "flick out" the two middle fingers. Women should use right hand. Men use left hand.

2. THE SPEECH SECRET

The second element of the Three Secret Reinforcement is the Speech Secret. The Speech Secret is the reciting of a group of words that convey a certain intention or request. These phrases, when said repeatedly through the power of the Speech Secret, are called mantras. Just like the Body Secret, the secret of speech is something that we are also very familiar with in our daily lives. For example, using provoking cuss words can easily get you into a fight, while yelling out the word *fire* is usually a signal for someone needing help. Words are very powerful, for they invoke feelings, convey messages, and resonate to various tones that imply a certain attitude. Each mantra that is used in Black Hat Feng Shui emphasizes a different intention or objective. There are many different mantras used in Feng Shui, but the two most common are listed below. These mantras are used in conjunction with the mudras listed above. All these mantras are usually repeated nine times each or in multiples of nine such as eighteen, twenty-seven, or thirty-six.

The Heart Sutra: Mind-Calming Mantra

GATÈ GATÈ BORO GATÈ BORO SUN GATÈ BODHI SO PO HE
(*Gatè* is pronounced Gatay)
This mantra is usually accompanied by the Mind-Calming Mudra (Body Secret). Loosely translated it means—for our prayers, wishes, or intentions to be heard and granted quickly.

The Six True Words Mantra

OM MA NI PAD ME HUM
This mantra is the most commonly cited and can be used with the Ousting Mudra (Body Secret). Loosely translated it means, "I bow to the jewel in the lotus blossom" or "I see the God within you and I acknowledge and bow to that light."

3. THE MIND SECRET

This secret is in the form of how we think and use the power of conscious intentions. It is the part of the Three Secret Reinforcement where you visualize the outcome of your prayers, requests, and wishes. As you position your hands in a mudra position and recite a mantra nine times, you should also *visualize, in nine steps* the positive results you desire to achieve. If you wanted to change your job, for instance, you could first visualize:

1. looking in the want ads
2. making the calls to certain companies
3. getting the interview
4. meeting the interviewer, shaking hands
5. being told you got the job
6. saying good-bye to your boss at your old job
7. happily toasting to your new job with your friends
8. showing up at your new office, smiling and happy
9. receiving your first paycheck, thrilled and very content.

There is really no "right way" to do this part of the visualization. Just trust your instincts and visually create nine segments of what you want to establish. Some of you may find that at the beginning it is very hard to do all Three Secrets at once, so feel free to take your time. Do the mudra (Body Secret) and mantra (Speech Secret) together nine times, then while your hands are still in a mudra, do the nine-part creative visualization (Mind Secret). After a while, with experience and practice you will be able to do them all at once. Either way, both methods will work. The more often you do the mudras and mantras, the stronger your ch'i will become and the more spiritual power you will have to help others and yourself make changes. *Professor Lin always says, "What is most important is your sincerity."* I also believe that if you combine your sincerity along with your willingness to change, things will manifest themselves quickly and appropriately.

SUMMARY

Below is a meditation that will help you create a sacred space inside your heart that will serve as your meditation/contemplation space: a special place that you can go to and release the stresses of the day, gather your thoughts, and ask for guidance.

CREATING A HEART ROOM: YOUR SACRED SPACE WITHIN

Find a comfortable, quiet space where you can either sit or lie down. If you like you can play some soft meditation music, light some candles, or burn some incense. Close your eyes and take a deep breath. Focus on the inhaling and exhaling of your breath—slowly allowing yourself to relax and release the stresses of the day with each exhalation, while breathing in new, fresh energy. Bring your attention to the top of your head. About six inches above the top of your head is a very beautiful white light; with each breath that you take in the light becomes brighter and brighter. Allow your breath to inhale the light into the top of your head, slowly breathing the light into and throughout your whole body. Continue to breathe the light in and out of your body, then slowly bring the light and your attention to the center of your heart. Visualize that you are walking down a long hallway and at the end of the hallway there is a door; walk toward the door and, as you open it up, know that you are walking into your "Heart Room." As you go inside, look around and see how it is furnished. Take notice of the colors, the lighting, and the overall feeling that the room gives you. Is it comfortable? Too small? Too empty? Too dark? Ask yourself as many questions as you'd like. Then feel free to walk around and make all the necessary changes that you desire. Add furniture. Repaint it. Clear it out. Add lighting. Hang wind chimes, crystals, or mirrors to areas that you feel need adjustments. Walk around the space and find a spot that feels most comfortable to sit in and call on your Higher Powers to ask for their higher guidance with a specific problem, situation, or dilemma that you have. Talk to them about this situation in detail and ask for their advice. If no problem is pressing, then ask them to add their light to yours to raise the energy level of your vibration. Afterwards, when you are ready to complete your Heart Room visit, thank the Higher Power that assisted you and slowly get up and walk toward the door. Exit into the long hallway that will lead you back to the center of your heart. Continue to breathe the white light into your heart and then slowly breathe the light up and out of the top of your head, back to its safe, natural resting place six inches above the top of your head. Take in a deep breath and slowly bring your attention back into your body, another deep breath in and bring your attention back into your room and, when you feel ready, open your eyes and record your findings.

Your Heart Room can be redecorated each time you enter it or you can keep the decor the same each time. It is common that one's Heart Room changes over time. Very similarly to the Feng Shui in your home, it will require revamping as your home and/or your life changes.

SACRED SPACE

Sacred space
Nurturing and safe
My heart reveals
Its vulnerable beauty.
Spirit at peace
Transforming fears
Into limitless passion.

Compassionate mirror
Reflecting inner strength.
Womb of wisdom
Honoring my truth.

Candles melting
to savor the silence.
The power within
Caressing my soul.
Rose quartz illuminating
Clary sage burning
In a sacred
Most sacred space.
—ROBIN SPIEGEL

EIGHT

CHANGING YOUR LIFE:
ONE ROOM AT A TIME

When you begin to do your Feng Shui process of your home, you might find it hard to connect with the bigger picture of what's happening in your process and your life. Without having a Feng Shui specialist at your side, guiding you every step of the way, it can be difficult to be objective about your own space, thoughts, and resistance to various aspects of your project. In the past six years, I have done numerous consultations and Blessing Ceremonies for homes, businesses, and offices that were in need of my Feng Shui services. In this chapter, I have compiled five different client stories to help you see the Feng Shui through a professional's eyes. I hope that through the experiences of my clients you will be able to identify with some of their life situations, ambivalence, and frequent procrastination. Their stories were specifically chosen to help you see the diversity in problems, and in the different solutions used. Although my clients' names have been changed to assure anonymity, these stories were written in their own words from their hearts. I am grateful to them for contributing their experiences to my book and opening their lives, so that you can learn from them.

CLIENT STORY #1: MELISSA

Melissa is a single woman in her thirties who works as a manager in a very prestigious design firm in New York City. She is also a very talented screenwriter specializing in comedies written about gay women and their lives. At the time I had known her for about three years and knew that she was struggling to make certain changes in her life regarding her career, her love life, and her finances. Although she always made a respectable salary, she was in need of finding investors to finance her new film. After several months of her inquiring about the benefits of Feng Shui, she decided to set up an appointment and have me come to her home. The first thing I noticed about her apartment was that all the rooms were painted white and it was sparsely furnished, barren in a way that gave the impression that she had just moved in. She had felt a lot of ambivalence for many years about furnishing her apartment. I quickly realized that if Melissa was to move forward in her life and attract the things that she wanted, she would first have to move into her apartment—which is acting as a metaphor for her life. Our Feng Shui work had to focus on her fixing up her home and analyzing how she was creating obstacles in her life, through the emptiness she'd subconsciously created in her environment.

MELISSA'S STORY

Spring 1994. I am in a rut. Bored with my "day job," not writing, alone, in debt from medical bills. I have a rather large apartment by New York standards but it's furnished with a TV, stereo, bed, and a few lamps. I've never felt comfortable here; it's too much space. People would kill to live here but I think I'll move any minute, so what's the point of lugging furniture up a five-story walk-up? For me, owning furniture means I will have my parents' life. Domestic entrapment and terror.

My good friend Nancy travels to people's homes and offices, rearranges their furniture (I think) and somehow their lives turn around, fall into place, work. Uh huh. She talks to me for months about this, but I'm too busy enjoying my rut to really hear her. What makes me change my mind? I'm not sure—desperation, maybe.

Summer 1994. Nancy comes to my apartment for our first meeting. I'd previously sent her a drawing of my apartment (that's the first step); she tells me it's a little "off." She's seen my peculiar handwriting, why would my drawing be any different?

I'm feeling defensive. Is this the way it's going to be?

We talk a long time, she mostly explaining what I need to do, what I need to move, to buy. I feel OK—what she's telling me and asking me to do is not too overwhelming; I don't have to buy that much and it's within my budget. I notice Nancy's being very careful, very delicate with me. Strangely the process is very moving, it's like therapy. Something is opening up for me, I'm thinking and talking about what I truly desire in my life. Things I've denied myself my entire life.

I'm supposed to do everything within two months. It takes me nine. I used to see myself as a quick study but I don't anymore. I reread *The Tortoise and the Hare*. Slow and steady wins the race, it takes the time it takes. It's more emotional than I thought. But I find myself wanting to do much more than Nancy asked me to do. More than we'd planned. I use my Christmas bonus to buy a couch, mirrors, rugs, plants, tables, pictures. I set up an office to write my screenplays. I paint my kitchen cabinets. Each thing I do, every purchase I make, every picture I frame and hang makes me increasingly excited. I'm creating a home. I've never done this, it's odd. I walk around feeling safe, nourished, peaceful. I like it here, maybe I don't have to move so fast, this is a great space.

I love the experience, who am I anyway?

Fall 1994. My apartment is broken into. My roommate and I are both, thankfully, out. It's 10:00 A.M. on a Saturday. Broad daylight. A heroin addict jumps from the fire escape to a very thin ledge, jimmies the window, and climbs in. I find out later he's nicknamed "Spiderman." No kidding. A neighbor watches him, calls the police, they meet him right outside my apartment door, loot in hand. He's arrested and gets seven years in prison. I send flowers to my neighbor and tell the story that evening at a party. I'm entertaining, it's a good story. I meet someone I'm interested in, it's been awhile, it's fun. It turns out to be a serious relationship and I'm learning a lot about myself.

I start to write a new sitcom, go back and rework an old script. I love my office.

Winter 1995. Nancy comes to do my "blessing ceremony," which is essentially closure for the work I've done and a blessing for my space. It's exhilarating. I have a "painting party" and we paint my bathroom, hallway, and bedroom doors.

Today, the present. Well, I'm no longer in a rut. I just started a new job that doubled my salary and increased my visibility. I've paid off my medical bills. My relationship has its ups and downs but I am learning so much from it and feel it's preparing me for a long-term commitment. I'm finishing up a new screenplay, having a reading of a completed screenplay, and have a new lawyer and producer representing me.

I've never felt closer to having the life I've always desired. A life of passion, commitment, spirituality, love, creativity. Was it because I created a home? I believe so.

I only know my life looks and feels completely different than what it was a year ago. There's no turning back now.

HOW WE ADJUSTED THE FENG SHUI IN MELISSA'S APARTMENT

After speaking with Melissa and hearing her concerns about her work and her personal relationships, I decided to start our Feng Shui work in the three back guas in her apartment which oversee her Wealth, Fame, and Relationships. My biggest concern was her guest bedroom. This room was sitting right in the middle of her Relationship area, and as we sat in that room she began to tell me that the guest room was the room her ex-lover used when she was still involved with her. She hadn't changed anything around since her lover left. The most interesting thing that I discovered was that her lover still had some of her clothes that she had left behind hanging in the closet! All the old energy from the past relationship was still hanging around, unresolved. This would have been crucial enough if her ex's clothes were in the house at all but having those clothes in the Relationship area made this block even more intense. With all the rooms that this apartment had, Melissa still didn't have her own office to work in. My first suggestion was for her to clear out the guest room, remove the clothes, and turn that room into her "new office space." We used the top of the dresser and made it into an altar, she purchased a new desk, and we hung two crystals, one on the inside and one on the outside of her "slanted" door to offset any negative consequences from the skewed wall and entranceway. Then we went to work in her bedroom, which was all white including the bedspread and had relatively few things on the walls. I attempted to negotiate with her to get her to add some color in the room by way of painting it. She agreed to think about it but we settled on agreeing that she was going to replace the shades with ones that had some soft but vibrant color. Among other suggestions, I recommended that she place a copy of her screenplay in the Wealth area of her bedroom and hang a wind chime above it. In the next set of adjustments we targeted several of the Fame areas in her home to enhance the ch'i around her becoming well known as a screenwriter. We added a mirror between her windows, in the Fame area in her bedroom; we added another mirror on the wall at the end of her hallway (which is in her Fame area); we placed artwork on the Fame wall in her living room and positioned her desk in the Fame area of her office with a decorative mirror above it. Several months later Melissa got into a relationship and a few months after that she was in a wonderful job that *doubled her salary!* The most interesting thing about doing her Feng Shui was that in opening up the Fame energy and doing a transcendental cure in her bedroom regarding Career, *she was contacted* by a headhunter and was offered two different positions. Althought she didn't outwardly seek new employment, the energy shift still drew to her these two job offers, even though her original "intention" was to find the right contacts to finance her film.

From a Feng Shui perspective, I was thrilled that Melissa was able to draw a job to her that doubled her salary. I see money from an energy perspective and I believe that what happened was that Melissa's "money vibration" needed to be raised to a "higher level" in order for her to attract the six-figure financing that she needed to produce her film. Her old salary, although respectable, reflected her energy's money vibration, which differed significantly from the amount she needed to pull in. The jobs offered indicated to me that we had accomplished the first step to our goal in that we had raised her vibrational level and the probability of her attracting the money she needed for the film was raised significantly also. By aligning her energy with the ch'i in her environment, we set off a ripple effect that will continue to unfold each and every day of her life.

Before

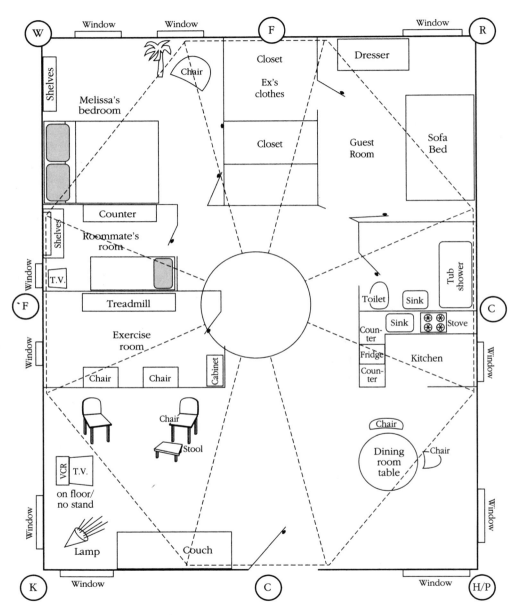

FENG SHUI: HARMONY BY DESIGN

After

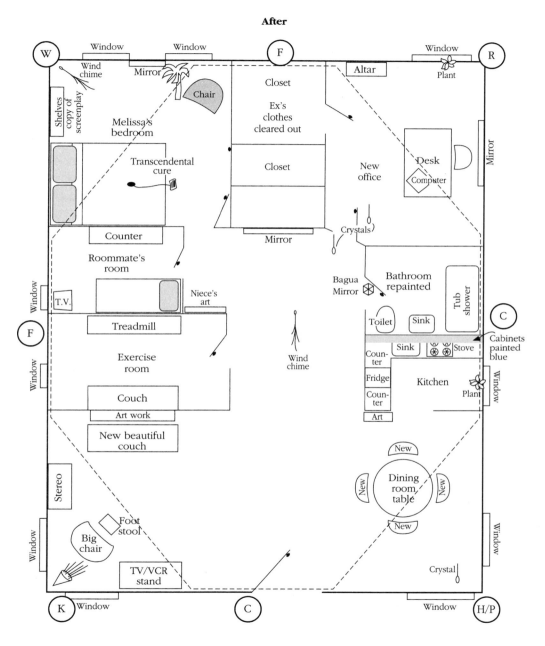

I was called to do the Feng Shui for Basha and Woody's apartment by Basha, who was a former client of mine when I was a psychotherapist in private practice. I had the advantage of knowing Basha's history and her past emotional patterns. This was a new relationship for Basha, and she wanted it to start off on the right foot and to create a home that was not only functional but nurturing and loving too. She and Woody had just met a few months earlier, he was recently divorced, and Basha had ended her marriage just a few years ago. Woody had an eleven-year-old son, Harry, from a previous marriage who would be spending a lot of time with them. His son was promised his own room in this one-bedroom apartment that Woody had just purchased. They both wanted to do many things with the space and make the space serve many functions. Woody was a trial lawyer, who in his spare time wrote books and plays. Basha was a writer also, having gone back to graduate school that fall to receive her Master's in Social Work. Both needed a work space, office space, and some private space for Harry. I was originally called in to help them with the layout of the apartment and to figure out ways to make the space more homey in the midst of a busy, noisy, high-traffic area in New York City.

BASHA AND WOODY'S STORY

Nancy SantoPietro was my psychotherapist for five years. When Nancy said she was doing Feng Shui, I became curious. During our five years of work together we touched on so many alternative forms of healing that the assessment of my physical living space seemed like a natural progression of our work together. It was during that time that I had my first experience with Feng Shui. I was living with my now-ex-husband in the Queens section of New York, the neighborhood I grew up in, and I drew Nancy a sketchy floor plan of my apartment. I was shocked when we implemented her suggestions and found ourselves packing and moving a month later. For twenty-six years my feet had been glued to the pavement of my childhood, and now I was stepping out of that neighborhood as if I were emerging from a Rip Van Winkle sleep. I moved to Manhattan, divorced a few years later, and when I found myself living in a yoga ashram in Massachusetts, Nancy came for a visit and assessed my tiny living space. Again the Feng Shui was a catalyst in my movement. I experienced an outpouring of tremendous grief, and the completion of my grief two months later signaled my departure from the ashram.

I was hesitant to call Nancy when I was deciding to move in with my new boyfriend, Woody, last July. For me, Feng Shui was starting to be synonymous with collecting boxes from the supermarket and packing up again. This time I thought I would head off the energy and do the Feng Shui consultation before I moved in. I was tired of renting U-Hauls and notifying the post office of address changes.

My other hesitancy about calling Nancy was my boyfriend, Woody. Somehow I didn't think that an ex-communist and playwright turned personal-injury lawyer would be open to having his New York apartment assessed according to a Chinese philosophy of energy movement. But since Woody and I recognized many potential problems of our proposed living arrangement, and our relationship was already something of an anomaly, he agreed, thinking it couldn't hurt.

At times the energy in the apartment felt draining, exacerbated by the two rectangular rooms that sat side by side like two cold boxes. The building is located on Fourteenth Street, which is a busy city street, not quaint in any way. The apartment is on the sixth floor facing an ugly, grungy, ailing building. I don't just hear the constant traffic, it's like living in a high-action movie with Sensurround: so loud and lifelike at times that when I get out of bed in the morning I feel like looking both ways.

This was not a choice location for me, but Woody had purchased this apartment prior to our decision to live together. The size and the location were also convenient for him and his eleven-year-old son, Harry, who lived with him part-time. Even though we would be moving in at the same time and fixing it up together, it still felt to me like I was moving into Woody and Harry's space.

It is a one-bedroom apartment and Harry does not have his own room at his mother's house, so Woody had decided prior to my decision to move in that Harry would have the bedroom and Woody would sleep on the futon in the living room. This meant that Harry, who is there only one night a week and on every other weekend, would occupy 187 square feet by himself, while Woody and I would use the larger room of 252 square feet for our bedroom as well as the living room and dining room. This would give Woody and me no privacy and no distinction between our bedroom area and the rest of the living space. Some other problems for both Woody and me were the apartment's aesthetic coldness and lack of office space. Woody is writing a book, and I would be starting graduate school in the fall so it was paramount that we have a comfortable, functional office space. In fact, there were not too many positive points about developing a fairly new relationship in this inadequate place.

The Feng Shui consultation was an amazing intervention. It operated on so many levels simultaneously that after it was over Woody and I felt as if we had been in some kind of therapeutic workshop. It used physical space and moved us on emotional, psychological, and energetic levels. During the consultation the hidden ambivalence both Woody and I had about living together and our fears about greater intimacy came to light. Nancy showed us that how we were intending to set up the apartment reflected a desire to tiptoe around each other rather than engage with each other in a direct and concrete way. I was trying to move in invisibly and anonymously. I was reluctant to claim any stake in the apartment because that luxury implied responsibility. I was nervous about invading the relationship between Woody and Harry, especially because Woody's second marriage had ended a year earlier and he often talked about the uneasiness of the relationship between his son and second wife. It also showed us that the lack of distinctiveness in the different proposed living areas would end up diluting some of our personal goals and intentions. But we agreed to follow Nancy's suggestions.

Initially we were trying to implement every adjustment as if we were participating in a relay race. I saw that with each few things we did, I seemed to need some time to get used to the changes. Woody would want to forge ahead, and I would sit back for integration. But basically what we have accomplished has transformed this apartment into something beyond either of our expectations, and we did it without spending a lot of money.

The aesthetic coldness of the apartment has been warmed up with beautiful shades of pastel paints. We have divided our bedroom/living-room/dining area from the foyer by painting the former a light peach and the latter a sea-foam green. Woody and I joked for the first few weeks that it felt as if we were living in the Caribbean, not New York City. But what was most striking and almost eerie was the day we started moving our things in, painters started painting the ugly dreary building across the street that we viewed from our windows. That building is now a velvety cream color with playful turquoise columns. We have made ourselves a cozy little bedroom in the rear half of the larger room and have sectioned it off with four panels of light-colored curtains which we can close for some privacy or tie separately for a soft romantic look. I have also placed lots of plants in the bedroom since according to the Feng Shui consultation both Woody and I are missing the earth element in our Chinese astrological charts and Nancy suggested that having potted plants in the apartment would help balance that out. We have divided Harry's room and are using the rear half as an office. We set up a bookcase as a divider to give the illusion that there are two distinct parts to the room. He still has plenty of space for playing and we all have an office space. We are not sure yet if we will divide it more concretely. But what has been nice about these adjustments is we can take them as far as we feel comfortable, and try different things out.

Some of the things that I have procrastinated about are hanging the wind chimes and painting Harry's room and the office, so the walls in there are still stark white. I have noticed how much calmer it feels in the painted area of the house.

It is hard to pinpoint what kinds of changes are specifically taking place with the exception of that building across the street that was painted. Woody hated the view of that building more than anything else about the apartment. But we have noticed that separately and together we seem to be moving through things very quickly. There is a deepening happening on a lot of levels. We are feeling more comfortable in our home than we thought was possible, and I can actually find warmth and quiet in what initially felt like a cold and noisy place. The overall apartment feels both more functional in the traditional sense, and more pleasing and friendly. This doesn't mean that Woody, Harry, and I don't have our struggles and difficulties in living together, or that the space meets all our needs. But it certainly feels as if we're making the most of what we have, and giving ourselves the best chance that we can.

HOW WE ADJUSTED THE FENG SHUI IN BASHA AND WOODY'S APARTMENT

When I was first called in to do this apartment, Basha and Woody were thinking about putting up a solid wall in the living room to divide the room for privacy. The other thought Woody had was to create an opening from the original bedroom to the dining-room area of the apartment for more space. I agreed that they needed to divide up the space, but instead I suggested a bookcase as a wall divider in the bedroom area and full-length curtains as a divider wall in the former living-room area. Both dividers would allow some light to pass through into the new office and dining room. Both rooms did not have any windows or natural light. That combination could easily depress and stagnate the ch'i. In addition, the curtain in their bedroom could be pulled back for more space and openness during the week and on the weekends when Woody's son is not visiting. Placing the son's bedroom and the office in the section of the house that had the only interior door allowed for further privacy and quiet for his son to sleep at night or for work to be done. The desk was placed facing the doorway on an angle, with a faceted crystal over it to stimulate the thinking ch'i and improve work habits. Wind chimes were placed on the door to circulate the ch'i in a small area where it can easily get trapped. I suggested that they paint the office/bedroom a light blue color. The color blue activates the fifth chakra—the Throat Center. The Throat Center is the center that oversees IDENTITY and CREATIVITY helping both writers to write more and support Harry as he begins to develop his identity and his sense of self as he enters early adolescence. All four columns that jut out were sending cutting ch'i through different areas of both beds. To remedy the problem I suggested that each column point be covered with a plant with leaves that cascade down the angle of the point. The plants were also chosen as adjustment items because Basha, Woody, and Harry were all missing the EARTH element in their

Before

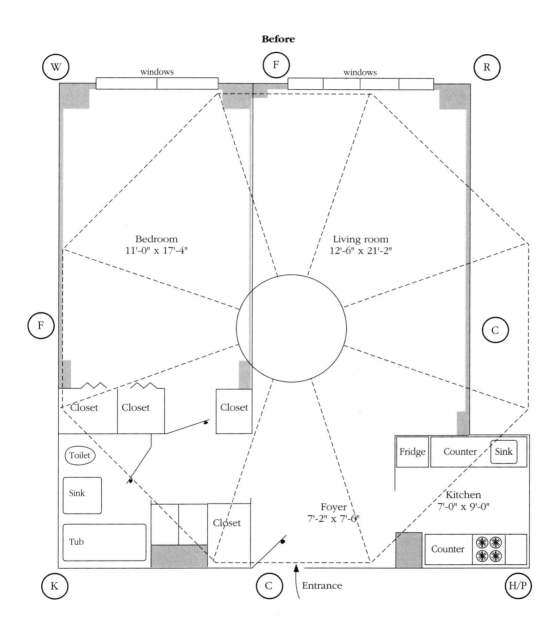

W

windows

F

R

windows

Bedroom
11'-0" x 17'-4"

Living room
12'-6" x 21'-2"

F

C

Closet

Closet

Closet

Fridge

Counter

Sink

Toilet

Sink

Kitchen
7'-0" x 9'-0"

Tub

Closet

Foyer
7'-2" x 7'-6"

Counter

K

C

Entrance

H/P

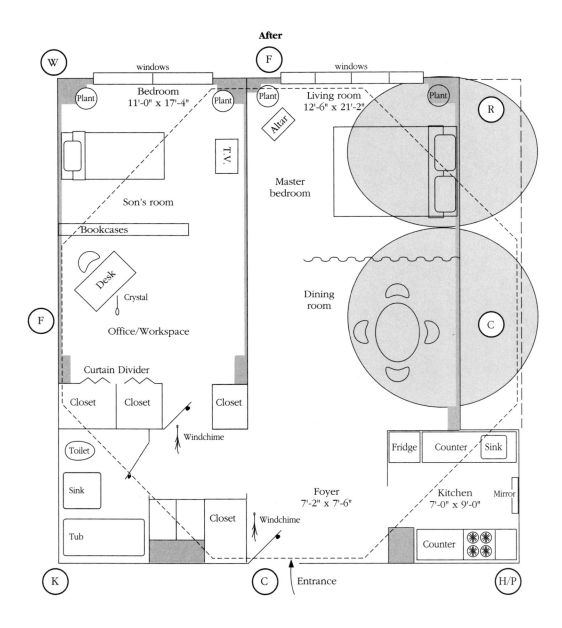

After

W

F

windows

windows

F

R

Plant

Bedroom
11'-0" x 17'-4"

Plant

Plant

Living room
12'-6" x 21'-2"

Plant

Son's room

T.V.

Altar

Master
bedroom

Bookcases

Desk

Crystal

Dining
room

C

Office/Workspace

F

Curtain Divider

Closet

Closet

Closet

Windchime

Toilet

Sink

Fridge

Counter

Sink

Tub

Closet

Windchime

Foyer
7'-2" x 7'-6"

Kitchen
7'-0" x 9'-0"

Mirror

Counter

K

C

Entrance

H/P

Chinese Astrology Chart which I prepared. The home's altar was placed in the WEALTH corner to help increase their income as writers, and the plant above it was stimulating the wealth ch'i as well as preventing the energy from the front door from exiting out the window. The apartment had a very "cool" feel to it with every wall painted white. Chimes were placed in the entranceway to enhance the energy of the space, and the color GREEN was added to the foyer wall and kitchen, and PEACH to the larger bedroom/dining room to create a warmer, softer energy feeling. Mirrors were placed to the right of the entranceway to enhance CAREER opportunities, and another mirror was placed in the relationship corner of the master bedroom to help Woody and Basha smoothly grow together and build their new relationship.

CLIENT STORY #3: JOAN

I received a phone call from Joan, who was interested in having me do the Feng Shui of her home. She told me that it has been on the market for some time and although she lowered the price, she still wasn't able to sell it. She told me that she had two buyers but both deals fell through. After several unsuccessful attempts at setting up an appointment, I finally decided to do the Feng Shui with her over the phone. I instructed her to send me her floor plans and pictures of her home and to relay to me a brief history of the house and her inability to sell it. We discussed the family history of her house and all the different memories attached to it over the years. Joan explained to me that all her children had been raised in that house and that in part it was hard for her to let go of it. I felt that energetically her ambivalence was getting in the way of her selling the house. After she spoke about some of her feelings regarding the sale, I felt that some of the energy had already started to shift.

JOAN'S STORY

In November 1990, my husband and I purchased a condo in Naples, Florida, as an investment. Sometimes when we least expect it, life presents us with surprises: my husband fell in love with Naples and decided to retire. We decided to sell our home of thirty years in Tallman, New

York, and relocate to Naples. In January of 1994 we spoke to a realtor and listed the house. Within three months we had a buyer, but at the last minute something went wrong with the house they were selling and the deal ended.

In Naples, a metaphysical bookstore that I frequently go to was having a class on Feng Shui. After taking the course, I returned to New York and made the adjustments in my home that were suggested in class. We had another buyer and another setback. This time the mortgage rates went down and the couple purchased a larger home. I was looking for a Feng Shui consultant in the New York area, and Nancy SantoPietro was recommended. Because of our conflicting schedules, we could not make an appointment for her to come over. Nancy realized how desperate I was becoming and suggested she do the Feng Shui consultation through photographs and via the phone.

Pictures were taken of the inside and outside of the house and then mailed to Nancy along with a floor plan. Nancy asked me to call her at nine A.M. Saturday morning. For three hours, going from room to room, she explained the adjustments that should be made.

We started at the front doors. There were two red doors, and the adjustment was to change the color of the flowers in the wreath. The house was a split-level with doors along the back upstairs and downstairs. We hung a colorful wind sock outside under the deck. It was visible as you entered the front of the house. Upstairs on the outside wind chimes were hung under the soffit. The side of the house was anchored by placing large rocks by the driveway, garage, and side door. Under the rocks I placed red circles with affirmation on them. The red circles were also placed under plants throughout the house. The house had dark paneling downstairs in the family room. Mirrors and pictures along with flowers were used to lighten the heaviness of the paneling. On the upper level two bamboo flutes were used on the beams in the living room. Crystals were hung at various places throughout the house. At twelve P.M., following Nancy's instructions, I began the next adjustment. I started by removing something from the stove area, placing it in a red envelope, and putting it in a body of moving water. Specific blessings were done along with the cure.

In April of 1995, we got two bidders on the house and closed June 14, 1995. The buyers not only purchased the house but most of the furniture outside and in. The best part was they purchased all the contents in the garage. They were from the city and needed tools, lawnmower, snowblower, etc., along with our car that we no longer wanted!

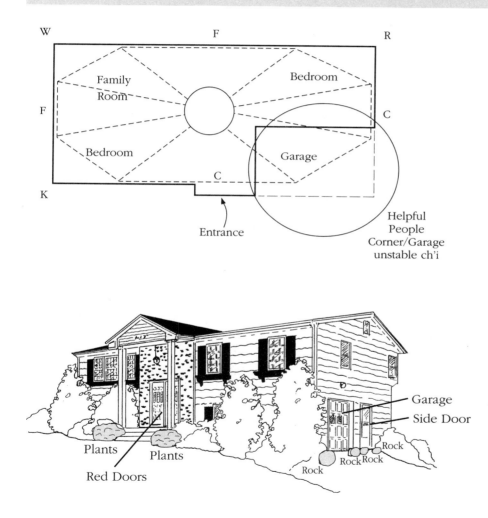

HOW WE ADJUSTED THIS HOUSE'S FENG SHUI

Joan's situation was very frustrating but also very common. I decided to work on the Feng Shui of her house from an anchoring perspective. From the information that she gave me regarding the cycles of her house's selling then not selling, she provided me with very valuable information about what might be some of the Feng Shui problems in her home. The thing that stuck with me the most was that her home *was* attracting buyers but not able to hold on to them, for one reason or another. This indicated to me that some of the problem had to do with the energy of the home not being stable. When I reviewed her floor plans further, I noticed that the HELPFUL PEOPLE section of her house is where her garage was. This was important because the energy in and around the garage area is usually unstable due to the back-and-forth movement the ch'i makes with the cars pulling in and out all the time. The "future owners," which would be Helpful People to her if they bought the house, were not able to stabilize and follow through. One of the first things I recommended was for her to strategically place several large rocks by her driveway, garage, and back door. This adjustment I felt would "hold down the ch'i" and help the energy, especially in the Helpful People area, stabilize more. I also worked with several transcendental cures that included using specific affirmations written on red pieces of paper, which we placed under several rocks around her house. In addition, I performed a series of blessings from my office that would enable her home to be sold without any delays or setbacks. We used a wind sock as an adjustment, which I had her place under the back deck because I felt that was another area where the ch'i was getting stuck. I also suggested that she add another color to her "very red" front door. Although red is usually a very auspicious color, I felt that it might be too intense and not conveying a very welcoming message. Outside her front door she placed beautiful yellow mums and hung a wind chime in her entranceway—making that area much easier to access and stay in. We also made a host of internal adjustments ranging from hanging crystals to increased lighting. Within a short period of time she found a buyer and was able to fully move on to her new home in Naples, Florida.

Client Story #4: John

John was divorced, fifty years old, and a very talented photographer whom I met when he signed up to take one of my Feng Shui classes. John had a big interest in Feng Shui, had read several books on its principles, and had applied some of the cures to his home prior to taking my classes. When he first invited me to do the Feng Shui for his home, John was in the process of healing from a very traumatic divorce and getting his life back on track again. His career and financial situation were improving and although he lacked a relationship, he sounded resigned to the fact that he had no interest in gettting into one anytime before his children went off to college. His children, who lived with him half the time, were his main priority and concern. The issue that jumped out and concerned me the most was the sleeping arrangement he and his kids had. Because of lack of space in his apartment, the three of them, although in separate beds, were sleeping in the same area. We both agreed that this was an issue that we needed to work on and look at a little more closely. In addition, John's apartment also lacked color, something that I felt very strongly would need changing if John wanted to enhance the positive things that were already at work in his life and shift the energy that oversaw the other aspects of his life.

John's Story

My life came apart at age forty-six when a thirty-one-year relationship (twenty-four-year marriage) ended suddenly and unexpectedly. My wife had been actively changing the focus, friendships, and direction of her life for several years. She felt that the long history and habits of our marriage had become a wall that her new self could neither remain behind nor climb over. It was the wall from which I fell Humpty Dumpty-like, and it felt like all the king's horses and men would not be able to put it together again.

I moved into the top floor of a small brownstone in Park Slope. It was essentially one long white room with a bathroom and dressing room tucked into one side. I had lived in a 2,700-square-foot loft in Tribeca for twelve years and the new place felt like a sweater shrunk in a dryer. I am an art photographer and college teacher, which is to say I was broke. My closest friend had died a year earlier. At the time, my fourteen-year-old son and eleven-year-old daughter were the only continuing threads in my life. They were living with me half the week. I do not know how to describe my initial romantic ventures. I was last unattached at age fifteen. To call my attempts awkward would be charitable; hilarious and humbling would be more accurate. Overall my energy was manic, my impulses ambivalent, my trust nowhere to be found. Several years later entered Black Hat Feng Shui.

I had heard of Feng Shui during a class in the I Ching. Both of these seemed to involve the mystery between the sensual and the ethereal, something and nothing; action on one plane affecting energy on another. Feng Shui was especially appealing to me as a photographer in its joining of the aesthetic to the spiritual, the visible with the invisible, sight with insight. Its remedies and cures give meaning, even prayerfulness to a simple gesture: lighting a candle, painting a wall, or even, like Wallace Stevens, placing a jar in Tennessee. To change our home is to change our life. The world becomes poetic, metaphorical; our finances may be going down the drain, our relationships may need to come out of the closet, our self-knowledge could use some light.

My apartment has wonderful light with the sun coming in windows at one end in the morning and the other end in the afternoon. It also has problems. The entry door is on a diagonal wall. There is a small piece missing in Career. The Family and Children/Creativity areas are pinched in proportion to Fame and Career. The entrance to the bathroom is through a small anteroom kind of space with shelves on one side. The room in Helpful People is too small for a bed or a desk. Three of us had to sleep in what was one long space. I was sleeping on a futon daybed when my kids were with me, and on either of their two beds in the end space when I was alone. No room for a bed of my own. Worse yet, my kids were sleeping in my Relationship area, and my adolescent daughter had no privacy in a living arrangement with an older brother and her father. I was still using the darkroom in my old loft but had not been able to adjust to photographing in my apartment as I had in the loft.

I took Nancy's introductory Feng Shui class and soon after hired her to assess and adjust my apartment.

In preparation she asked me to collect nine objects of (or made from) the earth and to put them in a bowl. I was to write down what I sought in each of nine areas of my life corresponding to the Bagua and place each message in a separate red envelope and put all of them under my bed for nine days. I gave her my birthdate and those of my children. Nancy made determinations for our animal signs and elements. I am a wood Monkey with three metals and a water; my son is a fire Dragon with metal, wood, and water; my daughter is an earth Sheep with fire, metal, and wood.

Nancy came nine days later. She walked the space in silence, stopping occasionally, like a dog listening to what we can't hear. After some questions, she began to make suggestions. Some were about placing mirrors to expand certain spaces, other suggestions were to hang crystals and wind chimes in strategic areas around the house. The adjustments ranged based on the situation and the need.

We then cleared space on the floor and Nancy arranged a mandala of candles, a bowl with objects from the earth, and eighteen red envelopes. We sat on opposite sides of the circle. I read aloud each of my wishes and each time we spoke the Six True Syllables Mantra together. In conclusion she asked that things be granted as well as other blessings. I asked a blessing for her. We finished by leaving blessed rice throughout the apartment and repeated one last mantra. In the time since, my life has changed. I have managed to pay my share of private college costs for my son, publish a book, and had shows in New York, San Francisco, and Atlanta. I am in the second year of a good relationship. My children are doing well in school and in life. Things are not perfect; they are in flux, and I am with them.

The listing of problems and cures may make this seem clinical, categorical, formulaic, but this is far from how it felt. Nancy has a deep intuitive sense and a strong spiritual presence that raised activity into ceremony and wishes into prayers. The adjustments were not decorative touches; they were moves made in concert with soul, in recognition of pain, in hope with our heart.

Feng Shui continues to be a force in my life. Everywhere I see, sit, stand, or sleep, I find myself within a specific aspect of my life with an opportunity to reflect on it, to reimagine it, to enliven it; as John Cage once said, "to thicken the plot." Feng Shui gives honor to the things of the world, paralleling the Native American saying "Every object has a breath." And every space, nook, and cranny . . . a soul.

Before

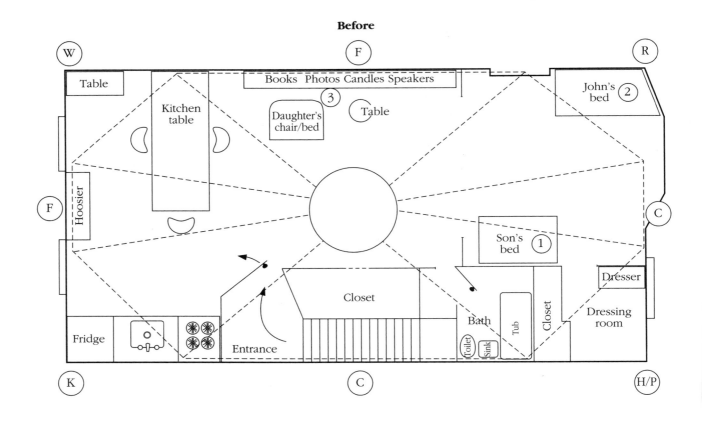

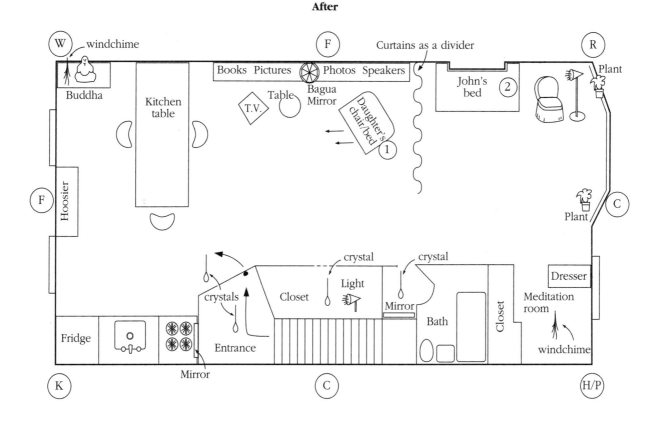

After

How We Adjusted John's Apartment's Feng Shui

The first major recommendation I made was for John to set up a curtain or bookcase, or add some doors to divide up the living/sleeping space for privacy for himself and his adolescent daughter. To further create a sense of division, we turned the chair bed around and moved it to the newly erected "wall," so that even the energy flow where his daughter would be sleeping would be moving in a separate direction. John's bed was moved out of an incredibly tight space in the corner of the room to an area that was more open and freer. I felt that the cramped space, in combination with his resistance about getting into a relationship, was limiting his ch'i and shutting out any possibilities if a relationship came his way. His son was eighteen by then and heading off to college so we were able to remove one bed from his home. We opened up the Wealth corner of his bedroom by adding a plant, a rocking chair, and a lamp for reading—trying to create an area that would lend itself to having John in it more often, in a comfortable and relaxed way. I felt that was the type of "energy feel" I wanted to create for John regarding his finances. In addition, we shored up the Wealth gua of his overall apartment by hanging a wind chime over a statue of Buddha in the corner of his kitchen and we placed a mirror on the side of the stove to double his burners, thus symbolically doubling his wealth. His Career and Fame area, which faced one another, was enhanced by adding a crystal on a nine-inch red string and a light to the closet that corresponded with his Career gua. Across the room was a set of shelves that had some pictures and photos on it. To that we added a Bagua mirror to symbolically open up and expand his Fame.

We also "opened up" a very small and oppressive area that led to the bathroom by placing a full-length mirror on the wall that he faced upon entering the bathroom. Part of that section also fell into the Career area and the small darkened nook appeared to be trapping and stagnating valuable ch'i. The dressing room was being underused because of its minute size. Instead, I suggested that he turn that space into a meditation room with an overhead wind chime, candles, and a low altar for prayer and contemplation. The space itself was sitting directly in the Helpful People corner of the overall apartment, which would make for wonderful energy to draw on. Our last significant adjustment was made to his front door, which was built on an angle due to a slanted interior wall. A Feng Shui crystal on a nine-inch red string was placed on either side of the doorway to offset any negative repercussions that can occur due to having a door, especially a front door, on a slanted wall.

After much initial resistance about getting involved in any serious relationship, several months after my visit, John, who is one of the nicest people around, got into a relationship with another very terrific person. Last check: it was two years young as they continue to find love and happiness with each other.

CLIENT STORY #5: HELENA

Helena is a single woman in her late thirties. She is a former fashion model who was born in Korea, traveled throughout the world, and lived in several countries including Belgium, Spain, Italy, and the United States. When I first met her approximately one year ago she was not dating and hadn't been involved with anyone for several years. After three marriages and a fifteen-year-old son, she made a conscious decision to be alone to learn more about herself and the things that she wanted in a relationship. Strikingly beautiful and incredibly modest, Helena was searching for a direction, path, or sign that would point her toward her life's work. After many years of hearing about Feng Shui and feeling very ambivalent about it, she decided to take one of my introductory courses, as a last-ditch effort. Following the class, she hired me to do the Feng Shui of her apartment and to assist her in realigning the energy forces in her life.

HELENA'S STORY

For me, what Feng Shui did was to make me define my life—who I am, what I want, where I've been, and where I want to go—so I can release the past patterns to create something truly new for my life.

Years ago, when I first started to learn about Feng Shui, it made a lot of sense to me that we are affected by our environments. But I am now just beginning to understand how much and how big it is. Winston Churchill once said, "First we shape our dwelling, then—our dwelling shapes us."

The first time that I had met Nancy was at one of her introductory workshops called "Feng Shui Made Simple." Prior to that class, I had read a couple of books on the subject and while in Asia, saw some architectural examples of Feng Shui at work. But it seemed to me that the businesses that were using Feng Shui were misusing it. I was very confused about how to apply it to myself, so by the time I got to Nancy's class I was just about ready to give up on it and her class was my last stab at trying to understand it. As the class unfolded, my confusion cleared and my lost interest was reignited.

That evening when I returned to my home, I decided to have Nancy come over and do an on-site consultation. Two weeks later she came by and, after she had reviewed my floor plan and asked me a host of questions regarding my life, she started making recommendations for my apartment ranging from hanging mirrors up in "missing corners" to repainting a particular wall. As I was writing down her suggestions, I specifically remember thinking "piece of cake, two weeks tops." Well, that's not exactly how it went. The consultation was over seven months ago and although the end is in sight, I am still working on it. Initially I was quite surprised at how long it seemed to take. Nancy would say to me over and over, "It's a process, it's a process." She was right. I needed to go through each stage and be ready to have that particular change happen, because change it will!

One of my major concerns was the lack of relationships in my life. Nancy noticed that the Relationship area in my bedroom and living room had a missing corner! She recommended that I should put a mirror up on the one in the bedroom, so that I would fill in the missing corner and start to "see" myself in a relationship. To my surprise, within three months, I had more dinner dates than I knew what to do with. My social life got very busy, but I still wasn't drawing to me anybody that I would want to date more frequently or spend the rest of my life with. After my three divorces, I was being very selective, not wanting to ever repeat my old mistakes again.

I continued to take courses with Nancy and at one of her meditation classes on "past lives," I saw myself in a very happy relationship and then a couple of months after that I had a wonderful dream of myself in a relationship, unlike any relationship that I had ever been in. It was completely real and he felt like he was a "soul mate" of mine.

Shortly after that dream I took Nancy's course titled "Feng Shui, The Chakras and Relationships." It was at that class that I received more information about my past patterns of relationships and clarity on the ways that I wanted them to change. That class was given on a Sunday, the next day I left for a previously planned trip to Miami, Florida. Three days into the trip, I went out to dinner with some friends and afterwards went out to a bar with them. This in itself was odd for me because I don't like bars nor do I drink. That night in the bar I met this wonderful guy, who turns out to be a surgeon. We connected immediately and I have been spending a lot of time with him, getting to know him. If this guy is not my soul mate, he comes very close. The relationship is very new so only time will tell, but I do know that I care about this person a great deal and that we have a very special connection.

This is just one of many examples of the many changes that have gone on in my life since working with the principles of Feng Shui.

For years after raising my son, I had been searching to find my life's work. With no clear direction or clue I went about my business and slowly got involved in exercising and bodybuilding. After working with Feng Shui for several months, I was surprised with a job offer in Miami to manage a gym in a condominium complex. The job itself didn't turn out to be what I wanted, but it put me on the right track, finally, about my work. I never before considered doing for work the things that I loved doing naturally such as bodybuilding and rock climbing. In addition, that trip to Miami was where I had the good fortune to meet my new lover.

As I look back on the past seven months, it seems like things have been moving so fast, it seems like my whole life has turned on a dime, as I have Feng Shui'd myself into another whole life.

I have been working toward this for years in therapy, but until I started working with Feng Shui, I did not see it as a reality. Almost instantly it seemed that as soon as I made an adjustment, put my personal will and focus on a particular area in my life, a change happened. To me, Feng Shui is a catalyst that propels you into the space you want to be in because it makes you focus on how you want your life to be. When you place your intentions, will, and focus behind the changes you want, it becomes an incredible moving force.

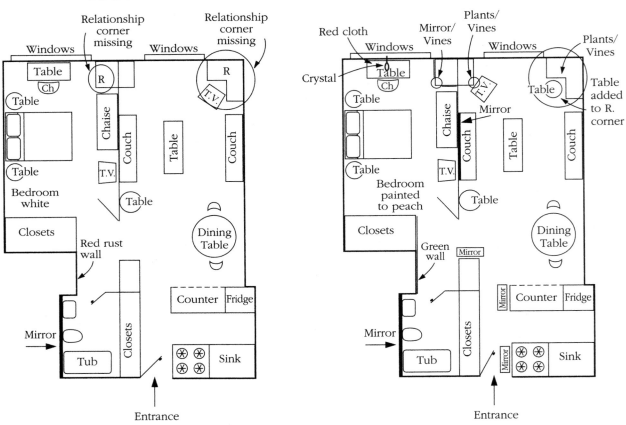

Before

Windows · Windows

Relationship corner missing

Relationship corner missing

Table
Ch
R
R
T.V.
Table
Table
Chaise
Couch
Table
Couch
Bedroom white
T.V.
Table
Closets
Dining Table
Red rust wall
Mirror
Tub
Closets
Counter · Fridge
Sink

Entrance

After

Red cloth · Windows · Windows

Mirror/ Vines
Plants/ Vines
Plants/ Vines

Crystal
Table
Ch
T.V.
Table
Table added to R. corner
Table
Mirror
Chaise
Couch
Table
Couch
Bedroom painted to peach
T.V.
Table
Closets
Dining Table
Green wall
Mirror
Mirror
Mirror
Counter · Fridge
Mirror
Sink
Tub
Closets

Entrance

How We Adjusted Helena's Apartment's Feng Shui

Helena's apartment was designed very nicely. Although the living room and the bedroom were relatively large rooms, her foyer was a bit smaller and dark. To open up the entranceway, I suggested that she add mirrors to the two walls in her foyer on her right-hand side, along with hanging a faceted crystal on a nine-inch red string. Besides the bathroom mirror, Helena had no other mirrors in her house. She is a very beautiful and attractive woman who never comfortably integrated her beauty and how others have responded to it. During our consultation she shared that she has been in conflict about all the attention she has received over the years. The lack of mirrors in her home reflected her inability to "look at herself," her beauty, and the many different aspects of her life. To assist her in facing these issues, I tried to incorporate as many mirrors as possible into her adjustments without having them seem excessive. Shortly after our consultation, she said that she made peace with the uncomfortability that had been plaguing her for years, and it became a non-issue. To bring in more prosperity, I suggested placing a large mirror over her couch on the left-hand wall of her living room, to reflect into the room the water view that was just outside her windows. The Relationship (upper right) and the Wealth corners of the room (upper left) both had sections missing. Helena added plants to those areas and creatively shaped green artificial vines to offset the points on the structural columns. Her bedroom, although the bed was properly positioned, was also lacking a piece of the Relationship corner. I suggested that she add some mirrors to the missing corner along with a faceted crystal on a nine-inch string to the middle window. She also added wooden twig vines with beautiful roses cascading down the point of the structural column to soften the cutting ch'i that was passing through her bed. She also painted her off-white bedroom a soothing shade of peach, added two pink lamps and a red tablecloth to her dressing table, thereby creating a warmer and more nurturing room. Outside of her bedroom, I had her repaint a wall that was a brick red color to a more open color, green. This wall was in the missing Family section of her apartment, and I felt that the color green would help open her heart again. Her Eastern element chart showed that she was missing the element wood. The corresponding color of wood is the color green. We tried to incorporate both color and element into as many adjustments as possible to help her absorb the element that she was intrinsically lacking. Several months and a few classes later, Helena was back on track. She had decided to build and manage a "rock-climbing gym" and was back open to dating and exploring all the ups and downs that relationships bring.

CONCLUSION

MAKING THE CHANGES THAT WILL CHANGE YOUR LIFE

As you come to the end of your Feng Shui process remember to congratulate and thank yourself for creating a wonderful place that will every day welcome your spirit and celebrate your life. Your Feng Shui process is a physical, emotional, spiritual, psychological, and aesthetic journey that will profoundly change your life in many ways for the better. So the more you are able to strengthen these various connections, the more energy you will have to access the things you desire and illuminate the path that you choose to walk. Knowledge is power. We all have the power to draw on guidance and direction from higher sources. Feng Shui makes that evident to all who choose to participate in its process. Most individuals do not understand that a spiritual connection to a higher power is not just a luxury available to a certain few but a birthright available to everyone. Not being taught this basic right early in our lives has forced many of us, in attempting to feed our energy needs, to go outside of ourself to connect with the source of power. When we go outside of ourself to connect for energy, we are actually borrowing from an energy supply that basically belongs to other people, places, and things and not ourself. When we draw on energy from the universal source, we are absorbing energy that is always in abundance and specially designed just for you. Working with Feng Shui makes this personal energy source available to you. As a society, we need to realize that we are merely participants in a co-creative process in life with nature, the elements, animals, other human beings, the universe, and God. And as is true of any other system that relies on teamwork, everyone on the team needs to be considered in order for the best decision or outcome to be made. When we ignore those other factors and don't include them at least in our thinking, then we stand the chance of making decisions and changes that are narrow and limited, serving only us and not the bigger picture. As you start working with these principles, you will come to see that Feng Shui is not only a system of design based on energy but a system of mindfulness that eventually becomes a way of life. In many respects, Feng Shui really doesn't have a beginning, middle, or end. It is really more of a lifelong process that changes and moves with your own life cycles, reflecting back your life and all that it consists of during a certain period of time. ***And as your life changes, the Feng Shui of your space should change too***. This means viewing your Feng Shui experience as an ongoing process that will require regular checkups, periodic adjustments, and, on occasion, complete overhauls. These changes will be contingent on different life events, times of stagnation, or spiritual transformations. Try to stay fluid with the process and trust your intuition to guide you when the time is right to hang another wind chime or add another adjustment. As you learn to trust yourself and your spiritual connection, you will become witness to your whole life unfolding and manifesting around you. You have the power to change your life and to access the loving and nurturing support of the universal forces. When we consciously open ourself up to accepting help through other means, we become open to receiving more assistance elsewhere than what we were able to give ourself alone.

Be an active participant in your own life's story—make it wonderful, make it count, and always remember . . .

When you feel that you need a change, become the alchemist, when you feel that you're in deep waters, become the diver, and when you feel that you need a little "magic" in your life, become the magician!

Nancy SantoPietro is a full-time Feng Shui specialist who teaches introductory and advanced classes on the practical and spiritual use of Feng Shui principles. She has taught at The Omega Institute for Wholistic Studies in Rhinebeck, New York, and The New York Open Center, and her cutting-edge workshops incorporate Feng Shui with color theory, the Chakra Energy System, and meditation techniques. Recently appointed ***Chairperson of the Feng Shui Studies Department of The Metropolitan Institute of Interior Design in Plainview, New York,*** she has coordinated the country's first full-year Feng Shui training program to be offered as a curriculum in an accredited school. Her company—***Nancy SantoPietro & Associates***—has offices located in Brooklyn; Huntington, New York; and Seattle, Washington, which provide consultation and educational services for homes and businesses throughout the country.

Ms. SantoPietro has the continuing honor of studying Feng Shui under the tutelage of ***Professor Thomas Lin Yun, world-renowned Feng Shui Master and Spiritual Leader of the Black Hat Sect of Tibetan Tantric Buddhism.***

Prior to consulting on Feng Shui, Ms. SantoPietro was a psychotherapist in private practice for ten years, specializing in the psycho-spiritual healing process. As one of the few female Feng Shui experts in the country, she uniquely combines her skills as a former therapist with the principles of Feng Shui design—helping individuals as well as businesses create environments that can enhance relationships, health, prosperity, and healing.

Nancy can be reached at her Brooklyn, New York, office.

FENG SHUI SERVICES AND INFORMATION

Ms. SantoPietro is available to lecture, teach workshops, and provide Feng Shui consultations for homes and businesses throughout the country. She and her associates also provide Feng Shui consultations via mail/fax/phone for clients who are out of state or at inconvenient locations.

Her *MAIL-ORDER* business, *"Gone with the Wind . . . Chimes,"* offers a wide array of Feng Shui products and services including:

Feng Shui Bagua Mirrors	Quartz crystals and gemstones
Feng Shui Crystals	Buddha statues
Wind chimes	Bamboo flutes
Audiotapes and videotapes	Red envelopes
Meditation music	Indoor water fountains
Chakra meditation tapes	Copper altar plates
Aromatherapy oils and diffusers	Altar offerings
Numerology readings	Chinese astrology charts

To request a mail-order catalogue from *"Gone with the Wind . . . Chimes,"* please call or write:

Gone with the Wind . . . Chimes
1957 86th Street
Brooklyn, NY 11214
Suite #108
(718) 256-8773

For information regarding consultations, workshops, or lecture presentations, contact:

Nancy SantoPietro & Associates   Nancy SantoPietro & Associates
1684 80th Street   or   7418 32nd Ave. NW
Brooklyn, NY 11214   Seattle, WA 98177
(718) 256-2640   (206) 784-9840

For information regarding training programs for Feng Shui consultants, contact:

The Metropolitan Institute of Interior Design
13 Newtown Road
Plainview, NY 11803
(516) 845-4033

For additional information regarding Black Hat Sect Tibetan Tantric Buddhism and Master Lin Yun, contact:

The Yun Lin Temple   The Lin Yun Monastery of New York
2959 Russell Street   or   920 Middleneck RD
Berkeley, CA 94705   Great Neck, NY 11024
(510) 841-2347   (516) 466-2125